YEATS, SLIGO AND IRELAND

IRISH LITERARY STUDIES

YEATS, SLIGO AND IRELAND

Essays to mark the 21st Yeats International
Summer School

edited by
A. Norman Jeffares

Irish Literary Studies 6

BARNES & NOBLE BOOKS
Totowa, New Jersey

First published in the U.S.A. 1980 by Barnes & Noble Books,
81 Adams Drive, Totowa, New Jersey, 07511

Library of Congress Cataloging in Publication Data

Yeats, Sligo and Ireland.
– (Irish literary studies; 6   ISSN 0140–895X)
1. Yeats, William Butler – Criticism
and interpretation
I. Jeffares, Alexander Norman
II. Series
821′.8   PR5907

ISBN 0–389–20095–6

Printed in Great Britain

Contents

Acknowledgements

The Publisher thanks Michael B. Yeats and Anne Yeats, Macmillan Publishers Ltd., London and Basingstoke, and Macmillan Publishing Co. Inc., New York, for permission to quote from W. B. Yeats's writings, Curtis Brown Ltd. and Faber & Faber Ltd. for permission to quote a passage from *The Faith Healer*, by and copyright by Brian Friel, and Faber & Faber Ltd. and Farrar, Straus & Giroux Inc., for permission to publish passages from Robert Lowell's 'Epilogue' which appeared in his *Day by Day*, and from 'Dolphin' which was published in *The Dolphin*.

INTRODUCTION

A. NORMAN JEFFARES

This book of essays celebrates the twenty-first year of the Yeats International Summer School. Some of the essays were originally delivered as lectures at Sligo, where the Summer School is held for two crowded weeks each August. It began in Sligo in 1960; visitors were coming there in increasing numbers to visit the countryside with which the Yeats family had been associated, since the time when the Reverend John Butler Yeats was rector of Drumcliffe. The rector's grandson, John Butler Yeats, the artist and conversationalist, married a local girl, Susan Pollexfen, and their two sons, the poet and the artist, both found inspiration in the place and in its people.

The Summer School came into being largely through the inspiration of three people, now no longer with us. They were Frank Wynne, who sought to establish a memorial to the memory of W. B. Yeats and to create a permanent venue for Yeats studies in Sligo, Sheelah Kirby, whose drawings in *The Yeats Country* (1962) are delicate reminders of the beauty of the area, who suggested that the group of people in Sligo interested in Yeats should approach Dr T. R. Henn, Fellow of St Catharine's College in Cambridge, to seek his advice on how to set up a Summer School. Tom Henn -- a Henn of Paradise, Co Clare - realised what could be done, in a unique way, in the west of Ireland. He rightly stressed the need to keep the Summer School independent of official educational bodies, to involve the Yeats Society of Sligo, to make it a school which should 'cater for a wide cross-section of scholarship, abilities and tastes'. He later became the longest serving, most influential Director of the School.

From the launching of the school in 1960 it was obvious that the audience was of as wide and as international a scope as could have been imagined. Indeed, the Irish part of it was one perhaps more catholic than Yeats had had in his lifetime: dignitaries of church and state, scholars from distant lands, local people, teachers, students and tourists. And from the beginning it has worked wonderfully. There have been two lectures from distinguished scholars in the mornings; in the afternoons seminars encouraging discussion, arranged to suit students' varying interests and abilities; and in the evenings entertainment of all kinds: music recitals, dancing, poetry-readings, art-exhibitions, lectures, films and plays. And always, everywhere, the talk and the hospitality for which Sligo is famous. There is a lively social centre. There are so many places to see: in Sligo itself the Garavogue river laps the quays where the Pollexfen ships arrived; there is the Metal Man, the village of Rosses Point, the waterfall at Glencar, Sleuth Wood, the cleft that's christened Allt, the houses, the trout streams, Knocknarea and Ben Bulben, and Drumcliffe Churchyard with its gravestone and commanding message. And beyond the pre-historic sites of Sligo students visit farther afield: Lough Key, where Yeats would have established his Castle of the Heroes, Boyle Abbey, Clonalis House, and south to Dooras House, Kinvara, Tulira Castle, and, of course, to Coole and Ballylee, Yeats's tower, now well preserved, and the rebuilt foundations of Coole Park. All of this makes clear much of the visual loading of a word or phrase, keys to the genius of a place of beauty hidden beyond the Curlew mountains:

I am thinking of a child's vow sworn in vain
Never to leave that valley his fathers called their home

The audience in the Summer School is perhaps most difficult and most rewarding for a lecturer. There are about two hundred who are enrolled as students; they come from far and near, some whose life work is Yeatsian studies, other dropping in *en passant,* led by the fame of the poet or merely by curiosity. It is an audience part of which is very erudite and part of which may have little or no knowledge of literature, just an admirable desire to know about Yeats and his contemporaries. For Yeats reshaped Ireland's literature and also influenced her future as a state; he spurned Anglo-Irish Literature as a young man and came to claim it as an inheritance when he was a senator, 'a sixty year old smiling public man'; he read the history of Gaelic Literature avidly in translation and adapted it to his purposes in, say, *The Wanderings of Oisin;* he knew the oral traditions which were a natural part of his growing up in Sligo and made him ever conscious of the supernatural.

So there in the front rows are the lecturer's peers, scholars who have coughed in ink, and the would-be doctors of philosophy, pens poised to impale some new truth within a thesis or to query some critical theory with all the sharpness of the competitive young specialist. It is indeed a challenging audience, and, as a result, it gets the best from its lecturers, who must constantly be aware of the need to make their scholarship, their interpretations, both academically significant *and* generally interesting. Two things aid them: the place itself, of course, with all its rich associations, its reminders that poetry arises out of life not abstraction: and the people of Sligo themselves. The School is probably unique in its shared functions. The Director is responsible for choosing the lecturers and tutors, and for all the academic aspects of the school. The Yeats Society provides the evening events which complement the academic work of the morning and afternoon sessions. These evening programmes give an extra or practical dimension to the school and provide its social focus.

The Directors and the Yeats Society have thus catered for a wide range of interest, since too narrow a concentration on the work of Yeats could be limiting.

In addition to general and specialised lectures and seminars on the work of Yeats students have also had a programme ever varying over the years which has covered other germane figures in Irish literature, has dealt with the Irish political, social and economic background, with the history of art and music, of drama and dancing in Ireland. And there has been a notable growth in the material available for study in Sligo, in the Sligo museum in the imaginative charge of Miss Nora Niland, and in the collection of books, tapes and pictures held by the Society, which has been handsomely housed, though the generosity of Allied Irish Banks Limited, in the former Royal Bank Branch on Hyde Bridge. The Society's acquisition of a building was a dream of Frank Wynne's come to life in 1973, with Tom Henn there suitably to unveil the plaque announcing the buildings new purpose.

Many other activities have been undertaken by the Society; these include organising a poetry competition, sponsored by the *Irish Times,* – the provision of courses in English for foreign students, a winter programme of lectures, and scholarships for students attending the Summer School. Two members of the Society's Council, John Keohane and James P. McGarry, have put us in their debt, the one for the admirable service given to

ix

scholars and students by his bookshop in Sligo, the other for his excellent guide to *Place Names in the Writings of William Butler Yeats* (1976). The future of the Society continues in the good hands of its President, Thomas Mullaney, its Secretary, Mrs Kathleen Moran, and its Treasurer, Mrs Georgie Wynne, while its Patron is the poet's son, Michael Butler Yeats.

The Yeats International Summer School, then, packs a great deal into these two weeks in August. It has become an event. Former lecturers and students frequently drop in; it is, in effect, a club, where friendships develop and multiply, bearing out one of Yeats's own desires: 'Always we'd have the new friend meet the old'. Sligo is a beautiful and memorable backdrop against which all this intellectual and social life takes place. There is much to celebrate in the way of learning extended and understanding achieved in Sligo over twenty-one years, and much to look forward to in the future.

Stirling, 1980

A MATTER OF CHARACTER: RED HANRAHAN AND CRAZY JANE

LESTER I. CONNER

We think of Yeats as primarily a lyric poet – and correctly so. That Yeats has also a great dramatic gift, that he was, in fact, an excellent creator of characters – dramatis personae – both in poem and story, has been much less generally acknowledged. When we think of the characters – drawn from real life, from the imagination, or from legend – we must admire the skill with which he makes them apparent to us and with which he makes them his own creation, regardless of their original sources. I see the basis of this commanding gift in two of his life-long aspirations as an artist: his desire to be a maker of myth or legend and his desire to project various, even contrary, aspects of himself.

Yeats wrote, 'A poet writes always of his personal life, in his finest work out of its tragedy, whatever it be, remorse, lost love, or mere loneliness; he never speaks directly as to someone at the breakfast table, there is always a phantasmagoria.'[1] By phantasmagoria is meant those 'imaginary figures, as seen in a dream or as called up by the imagination, or as created by literary description' (OED). Though his figures are not always the product of his dream or his imagination, they are treated imaginatively, raised to the level of myth or legend, and they are fashioned by very careful literary description.

The presence of his friends, embodied in his work, is well known. He fashions them into 'beautiful lofty things.' Those that come to Coole Park

> . . . came like swallows and like swallows went,
> And yet a woman's powerful character
> Could keep a swallow to its first intent . . .

Thus Lady Gregory. 'And here's John Synge himself, that rooted man.'

1

In this poem 'Beautiful Lofty Things' the traits that Yeats gives his friends are carefully selected epiphanies that emphasise wit and courage and beauty. Yeats is singing the lords and ladies gay. He will also sing the peasantry and randy porter drinkers' laughter as well.

Observe, too, how he uses in one poem, 'September 1913', men of Ireland who were already long a part of the legends and mythology of a nation:

> Was it for this the wild geese spread
> The grey wing upon every tide:
> For this that all that blood was shed,
> For this Edward Fitzgerald died,
> And Robert Emmet and Wolfe Tone,
> All that delirium of the brave?
> Romantic Ireland's dead and gone,
> It's with O'Leary in the grave.

And in another, 'Easter 1916', he swings from the old heroic myth to the figures that he knew would be transformed by the events of the Rising into the new heroic myth. And his lines to them would help to fashion the myth and be a part of its permanence:

> I write it out in a verse –
> MacDonagh and MacBride
> And Connolly and Pearse
> Now and in time to be,
> Wherever green is worn,
> Are changed, changed utterly:
> A terrible beauty is born.

But Yeats's skill at making myth and legend is nowhere seen better than in those characters he fashioned in his own imagination. Two of them – Red Hanrahan and Crazy Jane – will serve well as examples.

Yeats presents Red Hanrahan to us principally in a series of stories that bear his name. Though these stories were given several versions and orders, the story that now opens the series – entitled simply 'Red Hanrahan' – is a good beginning from which to illustrate the Yeatsian process of creating character into myth or legend.

A Matter of Character: Red Hanrahan and Crazy Jane

The story opens: 'Hanrahan, the hedge schoolmaster, a tall strong, red-haired young man –'[2] Elsewhere, Yeats had described him as 'a man with a great mass of red hair and a pale vehement face' and as 'fierce and passionate.'[3] The name Hanrahan itself, Yeats said, came from a shop-front in Galway.[4] But Hanrahan was not Yeats's first choice for the name of his hero. Initially, Yeats had called him O'Sullivan the Red after an actual eighteenth century bard. The stories, in their early versions, all used the O'Sullivan name, and the name was used as well in the titles of a number of poems in the volume *The Wind Among the Reeds*. Yeats changed the name to Red Hanrahan in later editions of the stories and poems, finally removing the name entirely from the group of poems. Professor Michael Sidnell has advanced the idea that, in the stories

Perhaps the name of the actual eighteenth-century Gaelic poet was eliminated . . . to avoid confusion, for the titles of songs traditionally attributed to O'Sullivan are given in the texts, but the poems of which the words are given belong, of course, not to O'Sullivan or to tradition but to Yeats. 'And I myself created Hanrahan,' he says in 'The Tower,' and no doubt the declaration is a reminder to the self of the poem, as well as to the reader. Hanrahan was not the product of another's imagination (as, in 'An Acre of Grass,' Timon and Lear were of Shakespeare's and Blake was of Blake's). O'Sullivan's name and nature belong to O'Sullivan, Hanrahan is not a figure Yeats has made himself *into,* but one he has made.[5]

In other words, allusion, which serves so many writers effectively, Yeats among them frequently enough, was not sufficient for Yeats in his development of the character of the hedge schoolmaster. He moved from the allusion to O'Sullivan the Red to original creation – 'And I myself created Hanrahan.'

But even in this very original creation he was helped along the way by what he had learned of the history of hedge schoolmasters, particularly what he had learned on the subject from the works of William Carleton, whose tales, including the story entitled 'The Hedge School,' Yeats had collected and produced with an Introduction in 1889, the volume called *Stories from Carleton*.

The terms 'hedge school' and 'hedge schoolmaster' were literal. One account of the origins of the hedge school is as follows:

3

The beginnings of the Hedge School date back to the 17th century. The 'Popish School Masters' mentioned in the Cromwellian Records who taught 'the Irish youth, trayning them up in Supersticion, Idolatry, and the Evil Customs of the Nacion' were probably the first hedge schoolmasters.

But it was in the early part of the 18th century, when the continued rigorous enforcement of the laws against education rendered teaching a dangerous calling, that the Hedge School really took root. It was then, no doubt, that the term 'Hedge School' was first used.

Because the law forbade the scoolmaster to teach, he was compelled to give instruction secretly: because the householder was penalised for harbouring the schoolmaster, he had perforce to teach, and that only when the weather permitted, out of doors. He, therefore, selected, in some remote spot, the sunny side of a hedge or bank which effectively hid him and his pupils from the eye of the chance passer-by, and there he sat upon a stone as he taught his little school, while his scholars lay stretched upon the green sward about him. One pupil was usually placed at a point of vantage to give warning of the approach of strangers, and if the latter were suspected of being law-officers or informers, the class was quickly disbanded for the day – only to meet again on the morrow in some place still more sheltered and remote.⁶

It was certainly to that tradition that Yeats wished to attach his Red Hanrahan. And certainly Carleton makes it simpler for Yeats to form the character of Hanrahan when Carleton, with rich comic irony, describes the typical 18th century schoolmaster:

The opinion, I know, which has been long entertained of Hedge schoolmasters, was, and still is, unfavorable, but the character of these worthy and eccentric persons has been misunderstood, for the stigma attached to their want of knowledge should have rather been applied to their want of morals, because on this latter point only were they indefensible. The fact is, that Hedge schoolmasters were a class of men, from whom morality was not expected by the peasantry, for, strange to say, one of their strongest recommendations to the good opinion of the people, as far as their literary talents and qualifications were concerned, was an inordinate love of

4

whiskey, and if to this could be added a slight touch of derangement, the character was complete.[7]

Yeats, of course, gives Hanrahan these very characteristics, but also, in the series of stories, he endows Hanrahan with mythic characteristics as well that parallel some of those of Cuchulain himself. The first story, 'Red Hanrahan,' sets forth the passion of a woman of the Sidhe for the man, not unlike Fand's passion for Cuchulain. But Hanrahan fares less well than the Ulster hero in his many affairs with women. In his escapade with the women of the Sidhe Echtge, he not only rejects her and his chance for immortal life, but in the delay he loses Mary Lavelle, his mortal girl friend. And in 'The Twisting of the Rope' he loses Oona, the daughter of the household whom he holds in thrall, when her mother gets him to help to twist the hay into rope, for which he must keep moving backward with the strands, until, in the process, he backs out the door which is then slammed upon him by the determined mother.

In the third story, 'Hanrahan and Cathleen, the Daughter of Houlihan,' Red is doing well enough for a man no longer young, living with two women, Margaret Rooney and Mary Gillis, and entertaining them and all their friends with his songs and stories. But when the two women fear, because of his sudden sadness, that he plans to leave them, they learn it is a third woman, Cathleen, time-honoured symbol of Ireland, who is in his sad thoughts. He is not thinking of going away.

'but of Ireland and the weight of grief that is on her.' And he leaned his head against his hand, and began to sing these words, and the sound of his voice was like the wind in a lonely place.

The old brown thorn-trees break in two high over Cummen
    Strand,
Under a bitter black wind that blows from the left hand;
Our courage breaks like an old tree in a black wind and dies,
But we have hidden in our hearts the flame out of the eyes
Of Cathleen, the daughter of Houlihan.

The wind has bundled up the clouds high over Knocknarea,

And thrown the thunder on the stones for all that Maeve can
  say.
Angers that are like noisy clouds have set our hearts abeat,
But we have all bent low and low and kissed the quiet feet
Of Cathleen, the daughter of Houlihan.

The yellow pool has overflowed high up on Clooth-na-Bare,
For the wet winds are blowing out of the clinging air,
Like heavy flooded waters our bodies and our blood,
But purer than a tall candle before the Holy Rood
Is Cathleen, the daughter of Houlihan.

While he was singing, his voice began to break, and tears
came rolling down his cheeks, and Margaret Rooney put down
her face into her hands and began to cry along with him. Then
a blind beggar by the fire shook his rags with a sob, and after
that there was not one of them all but cried tears down.[8]

Thus Yeats associates Hanrahan with national sorrows and
ideals and with the Irish soil itself. He associates him too, in
the story's title and in this poem which, in the *Collected Poems,*
is called 'Red Hanrahan's Song About Ireland' with a true figure
of Irish legend, Cathleen ni Houlihan.

The fourth story in the series, 'Hanrahan's Curse,' deals only
indirectly with women: to help young Nora who, against her
wishes, is being married off to an old man, Hanrahan agrees to
put a curse on him and on all old men, forgetting that he himself
is old. The curse succeeds only in bringing the old men in rage
to burn down Hanrahan's humble shack, forcing him to take
once again to the road and to the hope that there will be women
who will help him yet. Yeats leaves him praying to the Blessed
Queen of Heaven.

'Hanrahan's Vision' relates him to all the great women of the
Irish love legends, among them Blanaid, Deirdre, and Grania,
who parade past him in his vision. But the vision also brings
before him, and she is the only one who speaks to him, the
historical-legendary figure of Dervorgilla whose sin had brought
the Normans into Ireland, the beginning of centuries of occupation of Ireland by foreign powers. This situation Yeats was later
to dramatise in the play called 'The Dreaming of the Bones.'

The final story in the series, again somewhat a parallel to

6

Yeats's treatment of Cuchulain, is 'the Death of Hanrahan.' Hanrahan, in his last hours, is being cared for by the old beggar-hag, Winny of the Cross-Roads, to whose mud hut he had staggered as though by the force of fate. But as Winny stands over him, it is not her voice that he hears but the voice of Echtge, daughter of the Silver Hand, the woman of the Sidhe whom he had rejected in the first story, and she tells him now in a whisper, even as her lovely white arms seem to emerge from Winny's mud-stiffened rags:

'You will go looking for me no more upon the breasts of women.'

'Who are you?' he said then.

'I am one of the lasting people, of the lasting unwearied Voices, that make my dwelling in the broken and the dying, and those that have lost their wits, and I came looking for you, and you are mine until the whole world is burned out like a candle that is spent. And look up now,' she said, 'for the wisps that are for our wedding are lighted.'

He saw then that the house was crowded with pale shadowy hands, and that every hand was holding what was sometimes like a tall white candle for the dead.

When the sun rose on the morning of the morrow Winny of the Cross-Roads rose up from where she was sitting beside the body, and began her begging from townland to townland, singing the same song as she walked: 'I am beautiful, I am beautiful. The birds in the air, the moths under the leaves, the flies over the water look upon me, perishing woods, for my body will be shining like the white waters when you have been hurried away. You and the whole race of men, and the race of beasts, and the race of fish, and the winged race, are dropping like a candle that is nearly burned out. But I laugh aloud, because I am in my youth.'

She did not come back that night or any night to the cabin, and it was not till the end of two days that the turf-cutters going to the bog found the body of Red Own Hanrahan, and gathered men to wake him and women to keen him, and gave him a burying worthy of so great a poet.⁹

The total effect of Hanrahan is all but overwhelming. Yeats had managed to give his character the force of one who actually has lived or seems to have lived (as Shakespeare does with Hamlet) or who has been a figure in the mouths of the people through all remembered time. Yeats himself had, as he wrote in a letter to Lady Gregory, 'A notion that the Red Hanrahan Tales will be about the most popular thing I have done in prose.'[10] And to add just a little insurance that the character would seem to have come from folk legend, as if more were needed, Yeats persuaded Douglas Hyde to do a Gaelic dramatisation of 'The Twisting of the Rope' and to keep in it Yeats's Red Hanrahan. Yeats writes about it in his *Autobiographies*:

> Lady Gregory and I wanted a Gaelic drama, and I made a scenario for a one-act play founded upon an episode in my *Stories of Red Hanrahan,* I had some hope that my invention, if Hyde would but accept it, might pass into legend as though he were a historical character.[11]

Hyde, as we know, did consent to use Red Hanrahan in the Irish play that he made from Yeats's scenario, and Lady Gregory, of course, kept Hanrahan there when she translated Hyde's Irish into English, no one better since she had also helped Yeats, in the final versions of the stories, to give his words the real feel of peasant speech.[12] It is only a small digression here to point to this great interchange of help that marked the early years of the Celtic Renaissance, and it is true to say that this interchange of help made possible much that remains the best work of the period. Here we see how important collaboration was in assuring Yeats the great success of Hanrahan, now more legend than literary creation. Augustine Martin puts it extremely well when he writes:

> So in Hanrahan we can see one of the larger tributaries to that complex unity of being towards which the poet was striving, larger because Hanrahan embodied far greater complexity – historic, aesthetic, esoteric, religious – even than (Michael) Robartes. This is probably why he is so powerfully realized, so vivid and credible as a character in fiction.[13]

But Yeats was to have yet another triumph, perhaps his greatest, in creating a character with all the force of mythology, folk legend, history and literary allusion, a triumph of charac-

8

terisation. This, of course, was Crazy Jane, central figure in a series of poems that appeared in 1933. However, she and her lover began to take form in Yeats's mind around 1903 when he was working on his play *The Pot of Broth*. In it he includes a song that goes:

> There's broth in the pot for you, old man,
> There's broth in the pot for you, old man,
>   There's cabbage for me
>   And broth for you,
> And beef for Jack the journeyman.
>
> I wish you were dead, my gay old man,
> I wish you were dead, my gay old man,
>   I wish you were dead
>   And a stone at your head,
> So as I'd marry poor Jack the journeyman.[14]

In a note to the play, Yeats wrote that 'The words and air of "There's broth in the pot" were taken down from an old woman known as Cracked Mary, who wanders about the plain of Aidhne and who sometimes sees unearthly riders on white horses coming through stony fields to her hovel door in the night time.'[15]

Later, as Richard Ellmann points out, Yeats 'returned to Cracked Mary, combining her apparently with another old woman who lived near Lady Gregory . . . He changed the name from Cracked Mary to Crazy Jane because of possible invidious religious implications.'[16] Yeats, in a letter of 1931, wrote that

> Crazy Jane is more or less founded upon an old woman who lives in a little cottage near Gort. She loves her flower-garden – she has just sent Lady Gregory some flowers in spite of the season – and (has) an amazing power of audacious speech. One of her great performances is a description of how the meanness of a Gort shopkeeper's wife over the price of a glass of porter made her so despair of the human race that she got drunk. The incidents of that drunkenness are of an epic magnificence. She is the local satirist and a really terrible one.[17]

Very likely there were other reasons for changing the name, both politic and literary. Relatives of Cracked Mary were extent and could have proved embarrassing. But Yeats may have changed it to avoid any association of the name with Queen Mary of England. But about the same time, King George the Fifth opened the new wing of the Tate Gallery in London, where the controversial pictures of Hugh Lane were housed, rather than in Dublin where Yeats and Lady Gregory so strongly felt the pictures belonged, and Yeats wrote a poem called 'Cracked Mary's Vision.' However, he never published it, and this suggests he did not wish there to be any implied association of the names.[18]

Of the things which we may say contributed to forming the character of Crazy Jane, a great many may be found in literary sources and in his dreams; Yeats himself wrote of the kind of woman Crazy Jane represents, saying:

> Last night I saw in a dream strange ragged excited people singing in a crowd. The most visible were a man and woman who were I think dancing. The man was swinging around his head a weight in the end of a rope or leather thong – I knew that he did not know whether he would strike her dead or not, and both had their eyes fixed on each other, and both sang their love for one-another. I suppose it was Blake's old thought 'sexual love is founded on spiritual hate' . . .[19]

There is in the ancient Irish poem 'The old Woman of Bare' alluded to by Yeats in the Hanrahan poem, a fierce old woman who had known great love, an early poem of reference for the evolution of Crazy Jane. Another possible contribution is to be found in a translation of Francois Villon's 'An Old Woman's Lamentations,' made by John Synge, in which occur the lines:

> The man I had a love for – a great rascal would kick me in the gutter – is dead thirty years and over it, and it is I am left behind, grey and aged. When I do be minding the good days I had, minding what I was one time, and what it is I'm come to, and when I do look on my own self, poor and dry, and pinched together, it wouldn't be much would set me raging in the streets.[20]

Yet another possibility is a poem that Yeats would have been aware of, a poem actually called 'Crazy Jane,' the work of the

highly regarded 19th century writer, M. G. 'Monk' Lewis. It is
not the kind of poem Yeats would ever have written, and one
wonders how he would have reacted to it. But for the record,
here is Monk Lewis's Crazy Jane:

> Stay, fair maid! On every feature,
>   Why are marks of dread imprest?
> Can a wretched, helpless creature
>   Raise such terrors in your breast?
> Do my frantic looks alarm you?
>   Trust me, sweet, your fears are vain:
> Not for kingdoms would I harm you –
>   Shun not then poor Crazy Jane.
>
> Dost thou weep to see my anguish?
>   Mark me, and escape my woe:
> When men flatter, sigh, and languish,
>   Think them false – I found them so!
> For I loved, Oh! so sincerely,
>   None will ever love again,
> Yet the man I prized most dearly
>   Broke the heart of Crazy Jane.
>
> Gladly that young heart received him,
>   Which has never loved but one,
> He seemed true, and I believed him –
>   *He was false,* and I undone!
> Since that hour has reason never
>   Held her empire o'er my brain.
> Henry fled! -- with him, for ever,
>   Fled the wits of Crazy Jane.
>
> Now forlorn and broken-hearted,
>   Still with frenzied thoughts beset,
> Near the spot where last we parted,
>   Near the spot where first we met,
> Thus I chant my lovelorn ditty,
>   While I sadly pace the plain,
> And each passer by, in pity,
>   Cries 'God help thee, Crazy Jane!' '[21]

A much more likely indebtedness is to Robert Burns's 'The Jolly Beggars,' for example in the song beginning 'I once was a maid, tho' I cannot tell when,/and still my delight is in proper young men.' Or again in 'There's not a lad in a' the lan'/Was match for my John Highlandman.'

One does hear echoes of these possible sources in the Crazy Jane poems. Take for example, 'Crazy Jane and the Bishop':

> Bring me to the blasted oak
> That I, midnight upon the stroke,
> *(All find safety in the tomb.)*
> May call down curses on his head
> Because of my dear Jack that's dead.
> Coxcomb was the least he said:
> *The solid man and the coxcomb.*
>
> Nor was the Bishop when his ban
> Banished Jack the Journeyman,
> *(All find safety in the tomb.)*
> Nor so much as parish priest,
> Yet, he, an old book in his fist,
> Cried that we lived like beast and beast:
> *The solid man and the coxcomb.*
>
> The Bishop has a skin, God knows,
> Wrinkled like the foot of a goose,
> *(All find safety in the tomb.)*
> Nor can he hide in holy black
> The heron's hunch upon his back,
> But a birch-tree stood my Jack:
> *The solid man and the coxcomb.*
>
> Jack had my virginity,
> And bids me to the oak, for he
> *(All find safety in the tomb.)*
> Wanders out into the night
> And there is shelter under it,
> But should that other come, I spit:
> *The solid man and the coxcomb.*

But what do we learn in the poem of Jane herself? We learn that she practices occult methods for cursing her enemies, as did Red Hanrahan. Her beloved was Jack the Journeyman, now dead, but years before the clergyman had banished her lover because of their open relationship. Yeats's description of the Bishop, incidentally, is very like descriptions of contemporary churchmen found in Swift's writings.[22] Yeats would also have known of the Bishop O'Dea whom the artist Augustus John refers to as the 'author of the celebrated phrase, "the degrading passions of Love." '[23] Yeats establishes Crazy Jane among those who see Love quite differently. The banishment, as well as the attitude toward love, echoes the fate of Red Hanrahan's friends Margaret Rooney – 'The priest routed her out of the place at last'[24] – and her friend Mary Gill. We also learn that Crazy Jane meets the spirit of her lover, still wandering in the night, as so many spirits do in Yeats's works, spirits who have not completed their mortal relationships.

In 'Crazy Jane Talks with the Bishop' Jane is admonished by the Bishop to 'Live in a heavenly mansion,/Not in some foul sty,' and her reply, bearing echoes of *Macbeth,* of Swift, of Blake, is on eof Yeats's strongest statements on love, on the inseparable nature of body and spirit, pride and humility:

> 'Fair and foul are near of kin,
> And fair needs foul,' I cried.
> 'My friends are gone, but that's a truth
> Nor grave nor bed denied,
> Learned in bodily lowliness
> And in the heart's pride.
>
> 'A woman can be proud and stiff
> When on love intent,
> But Love has pitched his mansion in
> The place of excrement;
> For nothing can be sole or whole
> That has not been rent.'

Through Jane, then, Yeats announces a great theme that will dominate the late poems of his career, bringing Crazy Jane to the very forefront of his dramatis personae – her point of view, her tone, her frank and open sensuality will appear again and again in the poems, sometimes in the personna of the wild old wicked man, sometimes in Yeats's voice, sometimes in the voice of the man behind the Mask, sometimes as the Delphic Oracle giving us the news that 'nymphs and satyrs/Copulate in the foam.'

For Crazy Jane was not easy for Yeats to shake off, as he admits in a letter to Olivia Shakespear.[25] And in yet another letter he wrote, 'I want to exorcise that slut, Crazy Jane, whose language has become unendurable.'[26] But he never does rid himself of Crazy Jane or her language. He revives her specifically in 'Crazy Jane on the Mountains' in *Last Poems*, but her toughness, her randy laughter, her indomitable Irishry are everywhere apparent in Yeats's late work. And she remains one of his most formidable creations, a character who will be mentioned whenever, and as long, as Yeats's work is mentioned. She has entered the mythology of art.

T. S. Eliot, in an article famous in criticism, writes of the use of myth:

> It is simply a way of controlling, of ordering, or giving shape and a significance to the immense panorama of futillity and anarchy which is contemporary history. It is a method already adumbrated by Mr. Yeats, and of the need for which I believe Mr Yeats to have been the first contemporary to be conscious.[27]

Yeats mastered the method not simply by drawing upon the world's wealth of myth and legend for ordering and giving shape to his work but by raising his own characters – real people and the imaginary ones – to the same mythic level as, say, Cuchulain or Helen of Troy. By making Red Hanrahan seem a figure out of the oral tradition, by making Crazy Jane (like Winny of the Cross-Roads in her mud-caked rags singing, 'I am beautiful, I am beautiful,' by making Crazy Jane 'one of the lasting people, of the lasting unwearied Voices'[28] Yeats finally makes them 'All the Olympians, a thing never known again.

NOTES

1 W. B. Yeats. 'A General Introduction For My Work.' *Essays and Introductions*. Macmillan. London. 1961. p. 509.

2 W. B. Yeats. 'Red Hanrahan.' *Stories of Red Hanrahan*, reprinted in *Mythologies*. Macmillan, London. 1959, p. 213.

3 See various descriptions in Michael J. Sidnell. 'Versions of the Stories of Red Hanrahan,' *Yeats Studies No. 1* (Bealtaine. 1971). eds. Robert O'Driscoll and Lorna Reynolds (Printed at Shannon. Ireland, by the Irish University Press for University College. Galway, and St. Michael's College. University of Toronto). *passim.*

4 Allan Wade, *A Bibliography of the Writings of W. B. Yeats*, rev. and ed. Russell K. Alspach. Hart-Davis. London. 1968. p. 74, also cited in Sidnell.

5 Sidnell. p. 122.

6 P. J. Dowling. *The Hedge Schools of Ireland.* The Mercier Press. Cork. 1968. p. 35.

7 William Carleton, 'The Hedge School', *Stories from Carleton* : with an introduction by W. B. Yeats, Walter Scott, London, 1889. pp. 241-242.

8 Yeats. 'Hanrahan and Cathleen, the Daughter of Houlihan.' *Stories of Red Hanrahan, Mythologies*. p. 237.

9 Yeats. 'The Death of Hanrahan' *Stories of Red Hanrahan' Mythologies*, p. 261.

10 *The Letters of W. B. Yeats*, ed. Allan Wade, Hart-Davis, London 1954. p. 421 (Letter to Lady Gregory, dated January 2. 1904).

11 W. B. Yeats. *Autobiographies*, Macmillan. London 1961. p. 439.

12 Yeats acknowledged Lady Gregory's help. See *Mythologies*, p. 211.

13 Augustine Martin. 'The Secret Rose and Yeats's Dialogue with History,' quoted from page 19 of the author's ms, shortly to be published in *Ariel.*

14 W. B. Yeats. 'The Pot of Broth.' *The Variorum Edition of the Plays of W. B. Yeats*, ed. Russell K. Alspach. Macmillan, London, 1966, p. 239.

15 Ibid.. p. 254.

16 Richard Ellmann, *The Identity of Yeats*, Macmillan. Newport. 1954. p. 275.

17 *Letters*, pp. 785–786 (Letter to Olivia Shakespear dated November 23, 1931).

18 I draw here upon information given by A. Norman Jeffares, *W. B. Yeats Man and Poet*. Routledge and Kegan Paul. London. 1966. p. 256.

19 *Letters*, p. 758 (Letter to Olivia Shakespear dated March 2 (1929).

20 John Synge. *Poems and Translations* (Dublin : Maunsel, 1912), p. 44, cited in full in Jeffares, note 11a, p. 333.

21 *The Life and Correspondence of M. G. Lewis*, Henry Colburn. London. 1839. vol. 1, pp. 188–189.

22 See Maurice Johnson, *The Sin of Wit*, Syracuse University Press, Syracuse. 1950, p. 134.

23 Augustus John. *Chiaroscuro*, Cape. London, p. 102.

24 Yeats. 'Hanrahan and Cathleen, the Daughter of Houlihan.' *Stories of Red Hanrahan, Mythologies*, p. 234.

Lester I. Conner

25 *Letters*, p. 788 (Letter to Olivia Shakespear, December 15 (1931)).
26 Cited. as being in a letter from Yeats to his wife, by John Unterecker. *A Reader's Guide to William Butler Yeats*, Noonday Press, New York. 1959. p. 226.
27 T. S. Eliot, '*Ulysses*, Order, and Myth,' *The Dial*, November, 1923, p. 48.
28 Yeats, 'The Death of Hanrahan,' *Stories of Red Hanrahan, Mythologies*, p. 260.

ROMANTIC IRELAND

DENIS DONOGHUE

Normally when we come upon a phrase, we ask what it means, unless the meaning is so clear that we think the question redundant. In many contexts we are willing to see the phrase replaced by its meaning or reference: we find the phrase not sufficiently gripping to make us hold it in its own character or refuse to exchange it for another. Sometimes, but less often, we question it not for its meaning but for its character or status: it may point beyond itself to something in the world at large, representing the object by an epitome; or it may denote an idea in the mind of the person who utters it. We say, without much dispute, that the phrase 'Romantic Ireland' denotes such an idea; or at least that it denotes such an idea before denoting anything else. Most of our political vocabulary consists of words and phrases which denote ideas in our minds before denoting anything in the world at large, if indeed they ever do: they are ideas, and if they acquire any power in the world, or if they seek such power, we turn them into ideologies. But there are other words and phrases which denote not an idea but a desire. We utter them not to refer to something but to release a desire for it, a certain tenderness, as we invoke a lost cause.

We say, then, that the phrase 'Romantic Ireland' denotes an idea, but that the idea is compounded mostly of desire and loss. So when we ask what the idea means, we are asking still more pesistently what desires are appeased by speaking the phrase, uttering its syllables. We might interrogate with equal force such phrases as 'Merrie England' and 'The Golden Age': the chief character of these phrases is that they are uttered when England is felt to be no longer merry, the age no longer golden, Ireland no longer romantic. Thoreau wrote in his journal: 'The lament for a golden age is only a lament for golden men'; or, as we would say, a lament uttered at a time when men are seen to be no longer golden but iron, leaden, brazen, or otherwise inferior in their mettle. But there is a distinction to be made, or an old one to be recited. If such phrases as Romantic Ireland, Merrie

17

England, and the Golden Age express our desires, the desires can't be particular or highly individual, they must be desires that have already been felt by other people. We share these desires, but we have not invented them, we are not the first to feel them. If we are willing to express our desires in these standard phrases, it is because they denote the general category of the desires rather than the particular or intimate form in which you or I feel them. What each phrase expresses, then, is a genre of desire. The old distinction we need is of course between myth and fiction. We say that a consciously invented form or structure is a fiction if it has these qualities: we do not claim for it any practical or applicable truth; we produce it solely upon our own authority; we do not live by it or act upon it; we value it because it helps us to be more conscious. A myth may be equally fictive, but it has these quite different qualities: we have not invented it; we have received it from its use by other people: in many cases it may already be a force in the world at large. We say, perhaps glibly, that a poem is a fiction but that anti-Semitism is a myth; and we mean that people act upon anti-Semitism but not upon poems. Our meaning begs the question while it claims to answer it; but that is another day's discrimination. For the moment it is enough to say that 'Romantic Ireland' is a myth rather than a fiction, a distinction that may be verified by thinking of modern Irish history as a drama at once romantic and revolutionary. I do not need to prove that people have acted upon the genre or category of desires which we call Romantic Ireland.

Partly to annotate these remarks and partly to carry them further, I shall refer to some of Yeats's poems which use the vocabulary of Romance. The word itself turns up in the poem 'King and No King', where the No King is allowed to become King at last because, as Yeats has it,

> . . . Old Romance being kind, let him prevail
> Somewhere or somehow that I have forgot.

Romance is given the character of being Old, presumably, to say that it has seen a lot of human life and many deaths, and that it is correspondingly patient. If the poet's mood were religious rather than pagan, he would call Romance Providence, meaning to emphasise its lenient character. When we refer to the ostensible force embodied in human life as such, we call it Destiny if our thought is neutral, Fate if it is melancholy, Providence if it is buoyant in faith, and Romance if we think it somehow responsive to our desire. Indeed, we can go far enough to say that Romance is a function of our desire, so far as the function is felt as a power in the land. Yeats says that the power is kind, meaning that it likes to arrange that our endings will be happy rather than miserable. In a story, the happy ending is the native form of our desire, unless our desire has sophisticated itself to the point of disowning the naivete of its native character. If you say that our desires are more elaborate than those which are appeased by happy endings, I answer that the genre of literary Romance has always recognised that our desires are elaborate, and has ministered to their character also in that respect. In Yeats's poem, Romance is the force in the world which eventually appeases our desire, after delays and frustrations which make our satisfaction, when it comes, more complete.

When the phrase 'Romantic Ireland' appears in the poem 'September 1913', it comes with the additional force of being, in three of the four stanzas, a refrain:

> Romantic Ireland's dead and gone,
> It's with O'Leary in the grave.

If what I have been saying is at all valid, to say that Romantic Ireland's dead and gone is to commit a redundancy; its character of being dead and gone is already given in its being Romantic Ireland. The line about John O'Leary is an attempt to rescue the first line from tautology; it is not Romance in general but the particular version of it which takes O'Leary for its tragic or romantic hero. If the first line of the refrain invokes a myth, the second gives it a specifying force that concentrates the desire and makes it personal; it directs the feeling toward the personal invention of fiction. A more elaborate account of the lines would involve something like the theory of the 'concrete universal'. The first line recites the universal, but lest the universal remain remote in its security, it is given a concrete accompaniment, a personal image to elect one of the many possible forms of Romance and give it a personal aura, the glamour of one heroic instance. The refrain is then ready to answer in its own terms the wretched money-grubbers fumbling in a greasy till. Romantic Ireland is declared to be everything that modern Ireland is not:

it is not Catholic, bourgeois, or otherwise circumspect.

Having named O'Leary in the first stanza, Yeats goes on to speak of 'the names that stilled your childish play,' without yet naming them. They were the objects of the hangman's rope, they had no time to pray or save: 'And what, God help us, could they save?' The phrase 'God help us' is both Irish and Catholic, so I assume that Yeats is using it to shame Irish Catholics out of the money-grubbing attributed to them in the first stanza. The refrain comes now as if with the force of a truth as familiar as it is inescapable; which is mostly how refrains come.

The third stanza is full of names; the Wild Geese, Fitzgerald, Robert Emmet, Wolfe Tone, enclosed in a phrase that nearly floats free from its syntax, 'All that delirium of the brave.' I once tried to persuade Conor Cruise O'Brien that the reference to delirium makes Yeats's sense of revolutionary courage more complex than it would otherwise be; that it qualifies what otherwise seems total endorsement of nationalistic fervour. But he would not be persuaded, and I suppose he was right: delirium, in Yeats's context, is a word of praise, as in saying that someone was driven crazed for something he loved we would intend respect, admiration, perhaps a desperate sense of the price such people are willing to pay. In the last stanza a different source of delirium is indicated, another kind of desire, but the moral judgment, 'they weighed so lightly what they gave', applies to each about equally. The poem ends with the refrain displaced into

> But let them be, they're dead and gone,
> They're with O'Leary in the grave.

The cadence is not as Yeatsian as I have sometimes thought: or it is Yeatsian in a sense that marks its continuity with Moore's Melodies, songs that invoke Romantic Ireland so memorably that it is impossible to distinguish between the songs and their burden of reference. 'But let them be' exchanges for Romantic Ireland the funereal decency of silence as we stand at the graves of those heroes whose names, except for O'Leary's, we are admonished not even to breathe. Romantic Ireland becomes a place or a scene of tragic heroes, opposing to the limit of their deaths the casual comedy that has displaced them.

I have hesitated between saying 'place' and 'scene'. Ireland is indeed a place, but it does not follow that Yeats's Ireland is a place: it could be a scene as in a theatre, a scene of romance and tragedy in which the locale scarcely matters, or matters only because it is the point of conjunction between our desires and their symbolic form. Even if we leave Yeats aside for a while, we find little reason to think of Ireland as place and only place. I recall that some years ago I brought Frank Kermode to see, in Dublin, some of the portraits Yeats described in the *Autobiographies,* including Sargent's portrait of President Wilson. Kermode remarked that Ireland, more than most countries, is seen through a haze of reference, mainly literary, musical, and pictorial: it seems perverse to try to see it more directly than its received forms allow. Kermode did not remark something equally true, that to see Ireland through its received artistic forms is mostly to see it as a lost cause. Richard Blackmur once said of Ford Madox Ford that his special concern is with lost causes known to be lost. The phrasing makes a difference. Lost causes are often known by others to be lost, but not by ourselves: we may think there is still time. But when we give ourselves to a lost cause which we know to be lost, we do so from a different structure of desires and needs; perhaps because we dwell in impossibility and would not live elsewhere even if we could. Even when we have accepted the loss, we have not released ourselves from it; or not necessarily. In an essay called 'Two or Three Ideas' Wallace Stevens wrote of these desires as a secularist on principle if not entirely at heart, and he said that 'to speak of the origin and end of gods is not a light matter':

It is to speak of the origin and end of eras of human belief. And while it is easy to look back on those that have disappeared as if they were the playthings of cosmic make-believe, and on those that made petitions to them and honored them and received their benefits as lengendary innocents, we are bound, nevertheless, to concede that the gods were personae of a peremptory elevation and glory. It would be wrong to look back to them as if they had existed in some indigence of the spirit. They were in fact, as we see them now, the clear giants of a vivid time, who in the style of their beings made the style of the gods and the gods themselves one.

Stevens prefers to speak of giants than of gods, because it eases somewhat the question of believing in them. But it makes little difference, in Yeats's context, whether we speaks of gods, giants, heroes, fighting men, or golden men: under any sign it is to speak of a peremptory glory and elevation. And if there is any question of an indigence of spirit, the indigence is now and in Ireland rather than then and in the other Ireland, the country sustained by the desire and need of it. Where Stevens speaks of gods and giants of a vivid time, Yeats speaks of Romantic Ireland, but the speech is continuous; it issues from the desire to be more and better than ourselves. It is only natural, or if not natural then cultural, to express such desires and to propose as their fitting object such men as gods and giants, and to set such gods and giants in a landscape fit to receive them. Doing so, we draw the attendant feelings toward ourselves and hope to claim something of their elevation and glory.

We are moving toward Romance in a different sense, the sense we think of as having much to do with Romanticism. Yeats referred to it in a swift account of literary history called 'Three Movements':

> Shakespearean fish swam the sea, far away from land;
> Romantic fish swam in nets coming to the hand;
> What are all those fish that lie gasping on the strand?

Presumably these lines ask us to think that the freedom of Shakespearean fish was real, true to the element that sustained it: the freedom of Romantic fish was a delusion, they were already a lost cause though ignorant of their state; they merely felt and thought themselves free. And the modern fish know that they are lost, and feel it through sand and the loss of their element. That page in the *Collected Poems* is fixed upon loss and diminution, the thinning out of 'Spilt Milk', the loss of the great song and the rueful accounting of what we still have in 'The Nineteenth Century and After', God's fire upon the wane in the poem 'Statistics'. I have said that Romance and Romanticism are different, but there are continuities between them: in both cases the gods and giants act as though they were immortal, which they are in one special sense; they live as long as there are enough people to desire that they live, but when the people lapse from that desire, the giants and gods die; and the people dwindle with them.

In some such mood, Yeats wrote 'Coole Park and Ballylee, 1931', where after five stanzas of nostalgia and hauteur he took up the adjective 'romantic' and made a noun of it:

> We were the last romantics – chose for theme
> Traditional sanctity and loveliness;
> Whatever's written in what poets name
> The book of the people; whatever most can bless
> The mind of man or elevate a rhyme;
> But all is changed, that high horse riderless,
> Though mounted in that saddle Homer rode
> Where the swan drifts upon a darkening flood.

I would read these lines somewhat narrowly. The 'we' to whom Yeats refers are probably best taken as Lady Gregory, Synge, and Yeats, to begin with, and then such of their associates at Coole and the Abbey Theatre as maintained the true Irish themes. They were the last romantics in the sense that they attended upon Romantic Ireland, kept the sense of it alive by sustaining in themselves and a few others the desire for such glory and elevation. According to that sense, traditional sanctity and loveliness are the property of gods, giants, and fighting men, the book of the people, some chapters of which Yeats and Lady Gregory collected by talking to the few people left in the neighbourhood who still had memories and fidelities. Homer is Yeats's example partly because his unchristened heart had a place for gods, giants, and beautiful women. The stanza can be interpreted otherwise if we think of Yeats's friends not only in Coole Park but in London and make a context of predicament and loss which will include them all. But I choose the narrower reading, mainly because the poem looks back to 'Meditations in Time of Civil War' and other poems local in provenance however wide in reverberation.

I have been maintaining that we come upon Romantic Ireland more tellingly if we feel the desires its syllables appease rather than if we enumerate its constituents. Indeed, our notion of Romantic Ireland is all the better if it is boundless and without contour, because such vagueness testifies the better to the limitlessness of desire. Somewhere in the *Per Amica Silentia Lunae* Yeats says that the desire that is satisfied is not a great desire; and to this we may add that the desire that is strictly defined is compromised by the definition. What Yeats meant by Romantic Ireland is indicated well enough by thinking of *The Celtic Twilight* and *The Secret Rose,* the *Stories of Red Hanrahan,* many of the early poems, Lady Gregory's *Cuchulain of Murthemne* and *Gods and Fighting Men,* the first volume of Standish O'Grady's *History of Ireland,* and nearly anything we remember of Davis, Mangan, and Ferguson. The distinctions of theme and quality between these works are of no account in the present context: it is all the better if they merge or even fade into one another to make a pervasive blur of loss. But if we insist on keeping the constituents of Romantic Ireland as clear as the endlessness of desire allows, we may choose to represent them in a passage from the introduction to O'Grady's account of 'the heroic period' in Irish history:

> Now it is not to be supposed that the heroes and events of this wonderful period are to be lightly passed over – a period which, like the visible firmament, was bowed with all its glory above the spirit of a whole nation. Those heroes and heroines were the ideals of our ancestors, their conduct and character were to them a religion, the bardic literature was their Bible. It was a poor substitute, one may say, for that which found its way into the island in the fifth century. That is so, yet such as it was under its nurture, the imagination and spiritual suscepti-bilities of our ancestors were made capable of that tremendous outburst of religious fervour and exaltation which characterised the centuries that succeeded the fifth, and whose effect was felt throughout a great portion of Europe. It was the Irish bards and that heroic age of theirs which nourished the imagination, intellect, and idealism of the country to such an issue. Patrick did not create these qualities. They may not be created. He found them, and directed them into a new channel.

O'Grady took the same occasion to distinguish his treatment of the early Irish sagas from Keating's in the *History of Ireland.* Keating could not love a story unless he thought it was true. O'Grady was indifferent to the question of true or false: what mattered in a story was its epic and dramatic force, the nature of the feelings it expressed. So he was not troubled by the obligation of saying where fact ended and epic invention began. Yeats was of O'Grady's party in this dispute, as he was of Oisin's party in every dispute with Patrick. In each case Yeats speaks up for what he called, in an early letter, 'the revolt of the soul against the intellect'.

O'Grady used the words 'bardic' and 'heroic' almost interchangeably, and I think Yeats meant much the same thing or things in using the phrase 'Romantic Ireland'. The values he found in the early Irish legends, or ascribed to them from a mixture of ignorance, knowledge, and desire were those he later called 'antithetical' as opposed to the punier values he called 'primary'. Northrop Frye's essay on *A Vision* gives a fairly considerable list of terms under each heading, but the list is incomplete. It rightly includes personality as opposed to character, tragedy superior to comedy, discord superior to concord, lunar to solar, Michael Robartes opposed to Owen Aherne; but it does not include Parnell's superiority to O'Connell, or conflict between Irish voice and English print. Nor does it include the most heartbreaking conflict between Romantic Ireland and the modern Ireland that achieved shoddy victory by a conspiracy of precaution and forgetfulness. Was it for this the wild geese spread the grey wing upon every tide?

Even if we argue that Romantic Ireland existed for Yeats only in his need of it and his desire for it, his quarrel with modern Ireland persists unchanged. The difference it makes is that in one version Yeats's contemporaries in Ireland are accused of ignoring their history, the values and sacrifices undertaken by heroic ancestors so that magnanimity would not die. In another version they are accused of repudiating the noblest forms of desire in favour of the shoddiest. Instead of the bardic poems, we hear only 'money's rant'. But this is to look toward Yeats's middle and later poems, in which the defeat of heroic Ireland is taken for granted, – at least till 1916, – and the poetic mood is correspondingly bitter. In the early years, Yeats assumed, or hoped against hope, that the values of Romantic Ireland might still prevail. The Irish Literary Revival is predicated upon that hope: in poetry, the scholarship of translation, the Gaelic League, in the gathering of Irish stories and songs, the teaching of Irish dancing, the fostering of Irish games, we find the same hope, that the broken tradition of Ireland may still be mended, that past and present may still be brought into league. O'Grady's phrase comes again to mind: the heroic period which, 'like the visible firmament, was bowed with all its glory above the spirit of a whole nation'. In political terms,

Denis Donoghue

it is a vision of 'a nation once again', freedom from Britain. In aesthetic or spiritual terms, it is a sense of nationhood which depends upon memory; or rather, upon being mindful of the responsibility of the present to the past and future. Remember that I have remembered, Ezra Pound said, with a sense of responsibility different from Yeats's in its circumstance but not in its essential character. Yeats's desire was to stir people into a sense of their participation in an Ireland that had expressed itself long before Patrick directed the Irish imagination into one channel.

What can we say of this predicate upon which the Irish Literary Revival was sustained? It is easy to say that the attempt to arouse a sense of national unity by appealing to a common origin was childish; that it was based upon the absurd assumption that several hundred years of dissension can be transcended by stimulating the 'emotion of multitude'. It is just as easy to say that the three Yeatsian unities make only a dream, and then a frustration: unity of race, unity of culture, unity of being. But the question is far more difficult than these sentences suggest. I propose to come upon them by making a little detour. We are still annotating Yeats's sense of Romantic Ireland and the values proposed by the phrase, but the harder question turns upon Yeats's own relation to those values, not as themes of propaganda but as the motifs of his own early experience.

The detour I propose to make is by way of Schiller's essay on naive and sentimental poetry. The difficulty in reading the essay arises mainly from the necessity of clearing from our minds the normal meaning of these words, 'naive' and 'sentimental'. The gist of the distinction is that, as Schiller says, the poet either *is* nature or he will *seek* her. If he is nature, he is of the naive mode of poetry; if, lacking nature, he seeks her, he is of the sentimental mode of poetry:

So long as man is pure nature, he functions as an undivided sensuous unity and as a unifying whole. Sense and reason, passive and active faculties, are not separated in their activities, still less do they stand in conflict with one another . . . (But) once he has passed into the state of civilization and art has laid her hand upon him, that *sensuous* harmony in him is withdrawn, and he can now express himself only as a *moral* unity, that is, as striving after unity. The correspondence between his

26

feeling and thought which in his first condition *actually* took place, exists now only *ideally;* it is no longer within him, but outside him, as an idea still to be realized, no longer as a fact in his life.

I shall interrupt Schiller's sentences only to say that the naive and the sentimental modes of poetry correspond to these two conditions, respectively. In the naive mode the poet has a simple, direct relation to nature, and his only task in poetry is to imitate or transcribe it. In the sentimental mode, the harmonious cooperation of the poet with nature is only an ideal, not an actuality, and poetry can only be the representation of that ideal. As Schiller says

> Since the naive poet only follows simple nature and feeling, and limits himself solely to imitation of actuality, he can have only a single relationship to his subject and in this respect there is for him no choice in his treatment. (The sentimental poet, on the other hand) *reflects* upon the impression that objects make upon him, and only in that reflection is the emotion grounded which he himself experiences . . . (He) is thus always involved with two conflicting representations and perceptions – with actuality as a limit and with his idea as infinitude; and the mixed feelings that he excites will always testify to this dual source.

Schiller's example of the naive mode in poetry is Homer, and his example of the sentimental mode is Horace; but the names do not matter to us. What matters is the distinction between two ways of being present in the world. In the naive way, the poet is possessed by the object of experience, there is no gap between them, no ambiguity, no shadow or guilt. In the sentimental way there is every form of shadow, because the poet is of necessity more directly related to the idea than to the object. Self-consciousness obtrudes: no object can be seen free of the shadow of reflection.

What then do we find in Yeats, if not a sentimental poet trying to persuade himself, to begin with, and his readers, thereafter, that a naive relation to nature is possible? For what else is Romantic Ireland but the assertion that a naive relation to an original or aboriginal Ireland is indeed possible? If many of

Yeats's early poems are sickly, it is because they are trying and failing to maintain the pretence that a sentimental poetry can at the same time achieve naivete. Matthew Arnold produced as one of the distinctive marks of the modern element in literature 'the dialogue of the mind with itself'. Yeats tried to convince himself, by recourse to Irish legends and myths, that a dialogue of the mind with objects, unperturbed by self-consciousness, was possible, and that many favours would drop from practising it. He may have been encouraged in this belief by the diverse examples of Blake and other Romantic poets who insisted that nothing was impossible to the human imagination. As we know, he retained his concern with Romantic Ireland all his life: from the early plays and poems to *The Death of Cuchulain,* he continued to recite these themes. But I think it could be shown that he gave up the ambition of naivete and settled for the complex fate of being in the sentimental mode of poetry by historical determination as much as by a poetic temper self-reflective through and through. He continued to invoke Romantic Ireland for occasions of praise and blame; that is, he continued to use it for its ideological force, and to direct that force against his timid compatriots. But he did not continue to practise the repellent art of *faux-naiveté.* I put in evidence for this view such poems as 'The Man and the Echo' and 'The Circus Animals' Desertion' which take full responsibility for self-consciousness, and practise it upon certain masterful images from Oisin and Cuchulain to Maud Gonne. In those poems Yeats stands in judgment not only upon his soul but upon its rhetoric. The effect is not to repudiate the old themes or to dispose of them as compounded of vanity and dreams, but to confess that one's relation to them must register the lateness of the hour. At the end, everyone feels himself native of a dwindled sphere, and acts upon this feeling with patience or with hysteria; in Yeats, often with hysteria and its violence. But I have found no evidence that Yeats turned against the values of Romantic Ireland, or indeed expressed any attitude in regard to them except regret that in modern practice they are likely to fail.

We are considering naivete in both the ordinary sense and the technical sense prescribed by Schiller. I shall not go beyond a general reference to the relation between naivete, the desire for a naive relation to the world, and the various forms they have taken in pastoral literature. I note that Jacques Derrida has remarked, in his meditation on Nietzsche, that all great noise makes one imagine happiness in calm and in distance. Noise, and the desire to escape from it, may have as much to do with Yeats's early poems as the other constituents we have ascribed to them. In any case, so long as we think of the spiritualising of passion, and of silence as the necessary condition of spirit, we are in Yeats's world, so far as the early poems invoke it.

But it would be naive on my part, naive in the ordinary sense, to leave the subject in a terminology of desire, calm, and distance. So far as naivete is present, there is always a corresponding desire to rebuke its folly out of existence. In contemporary criticism we refer to this activity as deconstruction, which proposes to show that our motives are mainly pathetic and childish. But there is no need for us to deconstruct the ideology of Romantic Ireland; the work of irony and scepticism has already been done by Joyce. Answering in 'The Holy Office' not only Yeats but the entire tradition of Romantic Ireland, he wrote: –

> But I must not accounted be
> One of that mumming company.

And a few lines later he associated himself with the poet in his role as victim and scapegoat:

> But all these men of whom I speak
> Make me the sewer of their clique.
> That they may dream their dreamy dreams
> I carry off their filthy streams.

In 'Gas from a Burner' the mockery is more specific:

> O Ireland my first and only love
> Where Christ and Caesar are hand and glove!

and one of the last romantics becomes 'Gregory of the Golden Mouth'.

A full account of Joyce's work in the deconstruction of Romantic Ireland would go from these poems to the little tetchiness between Gabriel Conroy and Miss Ivors on the subject of Ireland and the Irish language in 'The Dead', and from there to

29

many telling passages in the *Portrait, Ulysses,* and *Finnegans Wake*. Such an account would eventually begin to deconstruct itself, and would find Joyce baptised by desire, as deeply as by revulsion, in the naivete he would officially expose. It is a conclusion almost foregone and foretold; that Romantic Ireland is a set of values espoused, promoted, bought and sold in the market-place, subjected to an adversary rhetoric from Joyce to Austin Clarke, endlessly deconstructed, and yet, even now, not entirely annulled. Sequestered, rather. In law, the state may order a property to be sequestered, removed for a time from the dispute of the parties concerned, so that it may be preserved for a quieter time, a future available to justice.

THE WILDNESS OF CRAZY JANE

BARBARA HARDY

'Crazy Jane and the Bishop', 'Crazy Jane Reproved', 'Crazy Jane on the Day of Judgment', 'Crazy Jane and Jack the Journeyman', 'Crazy Jane on God', 'Crazy Jane talks with the Bishop', 'Crazy Jane Grown Old looks at the Dancers', 'Crazy Jane on the Mountain'.

CRAZY Jane has several disadvantages. She is crazy, she is a woman, she is old, or for most of the poetry she appears to be old, and she is poor. Yeats turns all these human disadvantages into poetic advantages, creating Crazy Jane to fulfil both local and general needs in his poetry. She was born in 1929 and had a short life, appearing first in *The Winding Stair,* and, despite Yeats's attempt to exorcise her, surviving until *Last Poems.*

Yeats describes the conception of Crazy Jane in some letters to Olivia Shakespear written between 1929 and 1933 when the Crazy Jane poems appeared in 'Words for Music Perhaps'. Yeats provisionally called the sequence 'Twelve Poems for Music' – 'no[t] so much that they may be sung as that I may define their kind of emotion to myself. I want them to be all emotion and all impersonal.'[1] In a later letter he indicated the psychological context in which these poems were written; the ' "Crazy Jane" poems . . . and the little group of love poems that follow are, I think, exciting and strange. Sexual abstinence fed their fire – I was ill and yet full of desire. They sometimes came out of the greatest mental excitement I am capable of.[2] Elsewhere[3] he puts it slightly differently and talks as if they were inspired by the excitement of recovery and convalescence, stressing the stimulus of deprivation and desire. These are poems which Yeats wrote out of sexual need, and yet they answer his desire for impersonality. In a later letter he tells Olivia that Jane is founded 'upon an old woman who lives in a little cottage near Gort. She loves her flower-garden . . . and [has] an amazing power of audacious speech. One of her great performances is a description of how the meanness of a Gort shopkeeper's wife over the price of a glass of porter made her so despair of the human race that she got drunk. The

31

incidents of that drunkenness are of an epic magnificence. She's
the local satirist and a really terrible one.'[4] Jane maintains her
audacious speech and terrible satire from beginning to end.

Jack the Journeyman, Crazy Jane's lover, appears first in a
little poem in the play *The Pot of Broth* (1902). In a note to this
play, Yeats explains that he took both the words and the air for
that song, which brings Jack the Journeyman into its refrain,
from an old woman called 'Cracked Mary', a seer of visions.
Perhaps the most puzzling comment Yeats makes about Crazy
Jane is about the poem 'Crazy Jane and Jack the Journeyman',
which he says was inspired by a particular and repeated mystical
experience. Like most mystical experiences, it can not be fully
and lucidly uttered in words. Unlike all the previous comments,
which clarify the purpose or effects of the Crazy Jane poems,
this passage is arresting rather than illuminating:

> The night before letters [?] came I went for a walk after dark
> and there among some great trees became absorbed in the most
> lofty philosophical conception I have found while writing *A
> Vision*. I suddenly seemed to understand at last and then I
> smelt roses. I now realised the nature of the timeless spirit.
> Then I began to walk and with my excitement came – how shall
> I say? – that old glow so beautiful with its autumnal hint. The
> longing to touch it was almost unendurable. The next night I
> was walking in the same path and now the two excitements
> came together. The autumnal image, remote, incredibly
> spiritual, erect, delicate featured, and mixed with it the violent
> physical image, the black mass of Eden. Yesterday I put my
> thoughts into a poem which I enclose, but it seems to me a poor
> shadow of the intensity of the experience.[5]

In this passage, and in the earlier letters, Yeats is indicating a
combination of extreme emotional experiences: sexual abstinence, sexual desire, philosophical excitement and a sense of holy
and unholy ecstasy.

Crazy Jane provides one of the images of wildness Yeats
speaks of in 'Those Images':

> Seek those images
> That constitute the wild,
> The lion and the virgin,
> The harlot and the child.

Crazy Jane does not fit neatly into the category of harlot but, of course, she resembles the harlot as well as the lion, the virgin, and the child, in being fierce, simple, singleminded, and subversive.

Like 'Cracked Mary' the name 'Crazy Jane' is a traditional term of abuse. (The abusive term 'Crazy Jane' is even found in *Scenes of Clerical Life* by George Eliot.[6]) In England as well as Ireland, it is one of those names that are given to old women, notorious women, beggars, outcasts and outsiders. Yeats ironically identifies her by the abusive label, and uses, examines and expresses her craziness from the inside. She represents some essential things in the originality, irrationality, licence, wisdom and innocence of the Fool and the lunatic. Shakespeare collocated lunacy, love and poetry in *A Midsummer Night's Dream,* ('The lunatic, the lover and the poet are of imagination all compact'), and Yeats in Crazy Jane, and her male counterpart Tom the Lunatic, and some of the fools in his poems and plays, is making the same kind of association. He is also presenting us with what Blake identified as the Fool's persistency in folly: 'If the fool would persist in his folly, he would become wise.'[7] Crazy Jane consistently, persistently, and resourcefully pursues wisdom through folly, stability through waywardness. Like Genet's outcast prisoners, she has the advantage of inferiority and poverty, and is placed honourably below hierarchies, establishments and heroisms.

Yeats bears in mind the poet as well as the lover and the lunatic, and lays a special, almost technical, stress on the importance of wildness, using it to suggest something natural, erotic, abandoned and ecstatic in poetic experience. Many things in the poems are wild, or run wild, or grow wild.[8] In the early poems there is mad King Goll who finds a 'tympan' in a wood and sings 'wildly' to its accompaniment. There are all the wild creatures in Yeats's bestiary -- geese, hares, swans, gulls. Amongst other functions, they have that of representing the spontaneity of the subjective animal world. But the heart of man is wild too, and so is his imagination. There are wild summers, wild infancy, wild beauty and wild youth. The moon is wild and grows wilder in 'Solomon and the Witch'. At the end of 'The Tower' there is the jackdaw's nest – 'her wild nest' which stands, amongst many images, for Yeats's own sense of artistic brooding and making. The nest is wild, being part of nature within a civilised structure.

It is wild because made from odds and ends. The mother bird, like the artist, contemplates what she has made:

> As at the loophole there
> The daws chatter and scream,
> And drop twigs layer upon layer.
> When they have mounted up,
> The mother bird will rest
> On their hollow top,
> And so warm her wild nest.

In 'A Man Young and Old' there is the lament for 'wildness lost' in 'The Death of the Hare', the departed wildness of Madge in 'The Friends of his Youth', and the poem 'His Wildness'.

On a number of occasions Yeats speaks about the imagination being driven to a state of extremity or wildness. 'The Cold Heaven' provides us with a paradigm for this experience of inspirational wildness. First there is a strongly visual image from the external world:

> Suddenly I saw the cold and rook-delighting heaven
> That seemed as though ice burned and was but the more ice,

and this image drives the imagination wild:

> And thereupon imagination and heart were driven
> So wild that every casual thought of that and this
> Vanished, and left but memories . . .

There is the fiat or initiating image, followed by the wildness. (Perhaps fiat is not the best word here, since the emphasis is placed on the passivity in which imagination and heart were driven wild.) Yeats presents the consequences of the process: to be driven wild is to be pitched into concentration. All that is 'casual' in the mind, all the odds and ends of attention, disappear. In this instance there is an invocation of a particular vision – that of sexual remorse. It gives place to a vision of death. The first is a vision of physically shattering memory, the last of physically terrifying fantasy. This poem, like many, shows Yeats's ability to be poetically reflexive and introspective without falling into analytic coldness, dryness or impersonality. 'The Cold

Heaven' describes and dramatises an entire emotional history of poetic inspiration. Yeats puts into his poetry the creative process of imaginative abandon, but this is to state the matter too dryly. The poem enacts the process, becomes wild and gets wilder. In it the imagination catches fire from the sensation, gets wilder as it remembers, and finally abandons itself to a literally wild speculation about the afterlife.

In 'Towards Break of Day' Yeats and the woman who lies beside him share a dream. The dream is preceded, perhaps precipitated, by the process of 'growing wild'. The 'I' of the poem is driven wild, on this occasion, because he is contemplating what cannot be touched. It is a piece of the natural world, tangible as phenomenon, but inaccessible because loved in the past, the 'waterfall/ Upon Ben Bulben side'. What makes his heart ache and then grow wild is the impossible longing to return to the unplumbable experience of the past. Love exists still, but can no longer touch what is loved. The word 'ponderable' is unusually complex and witty, having the double sense of weighing and reflecting:

> I grew wild,
> Even accusing Heaven because
> It had set down among its laws:
> Nothing that we love over-much
> Is ponderable to our touch.

The wildness partakes of rage, but once more there is the stimulus of image, then abandonment, and once more contemplation leads to the concentration of wildness. The man sleeps, and in dream, but only in dream, can he return to 'The cold blown spray' which in dream, but only in dream, he can touch. Dreams can be more solid than memories. The bridge from memory to dream is wildness.

In 'Nineteen Hundred and Nineteen' the creative stimulus discussed in the poem comes from literature. A moralist, or a mythological poet, compares the solitary soul to a swan, and Yeats says in one of his marvellously calm lines, 'I am satisfied with that', but moves from 'satisfaction' to wildness:

> The swan has leaped into the desolate heaven:
> That image can bring wildness, bring a rage
> To end all things . . .

35

Barbara Hardy

This poem, like 'The Cold Heaven' and 'Towards Break of Day', pivots on the experience of growing wild. The image of the leaping swan precipitates energy, rage, despair and desolation. It is a bitter vision, a vision of annihilation. Once more wildness is essential, and in this poem is startlingly contrasted with scholarly calm approval. Then follows the sudden exuberant take-off from calm contemplativeness to wildness and its consequent vision. It is like a move from theory to practice.

Perhaps the most celebrated example of Yeats's imagination being driven wild comes in 'Among School Children'. It arrives conveniently and elegantly in the middle of the poem. Once more there is the process of image, abandonment, wildness, and vision. Once more we have the history of an emotional experience. There is a surface calm and a deeper uneasiness. The speaker in the poem does not like being a 'sixty-year-old smiling public man' and as he looks uncomfortably around the schoolroom he is seized by involuntary memory. Once more memory and imagination go hand in hand. He suddenly remembers how the woman he loved told him about some childhood incident which had brought about for her a fit of grief or rage, and his recall of her memory precipitates the main emotional action of the poem. First of all the memory is simply a way of tolerating and handling the experience of being in the classroom with the children. This is a daunting psychological collision of the fixity and falsity of public identity with the fluidity and vagueness of innerness. He looks upon the children and desperately imagines a relation between their childhood and that of the woman, so bridging the abyss between the sense of social person and that of central self:

> I look upon one child or t'other there
> And wonder if she stood so at that age –
> For even daughters of the swan can share
> Something of every paddler's heritage –
> And had that colour upon cheek or hair,
> And thereupon my heart is driven wild:
> She stands before me as a living child.

This image of the past invokes the image of the present:

36

> Her present image floats into the mind –
> Did Quattrocento finger fashion it
> Hollow of cheek as though it drank the wind . . .

Then the poem takes off from this vision into the elaborate contemplation of form and substance, vision and reality. This poetic action turns upon wildness.

These poems are reflexive; and they tell us about the nature of lyrical inspiration and lyrical generation. The process Yeats expresses also explores the larger human experience. The abandonment of the imagination is not an experience confined to poets, and what we have in Yeats is the fusion of a special poetic experience and a common emotional experience which goes beyond poetry.

A deceptively short journey leads from 'Among School Children' to 'A Bronze Head'. In the later poem the wildness is complicated because of the complexity of the things he remembers. The 'I' remembers, and remembers imagining. Amongst the things that are remembered is a sense of the woman's wildness, which is part of her beauty, a part of her courage, and a part of what he imagines to be her terror. There is an astonishing image of her as a race-horse 'at the starting-post, all sleek and new', which is physically and emotionally right for beauty, youth, energy, pressure, and nervous vulnerability:

> But even at the starting-post, all sleek and new,
> I saw the wildness in her and I thought
> A vision of terror that it must live through
> Had shattered her soul.

After this he remembers how he imagined her vision, and continues:

> Propinquity had brought
> Imagination to that pitch where it casts out
> All that is not itself . . .

This concentration is like the process of getting rid of the chaotic and casual in 'The Cold Heaven'. Here too is intensification through wildness:

37

> Propinquity had brought
> Imagination to that pitch where it casts out
> All that is not itself: I had grown wild
> And wandered murmuring everywhere, 'My child, my child! '

The feeling shuttles surprisingly from wildness to gentleness. In this image of compassion coming out of imagined terror we have, as in 'Among School Children', a sense of enlargement. Yeats contemplates not only his past and her past, but the present state of his world. In terms of poetic creation, there is inspiration, abandon, new concentration and enlargement. Again the process is recognisably not confined to poetry. It is the process of love's abandonment, concentration and caring.

One last example from the poem-cycle, 'A Woman Young and Old'. At the end of the cycle there is an extract translated by Yeats from Sophocles's *Antigone*. (Oedipus, like Crazy Jane, is an old, outcast, and ecstatic beggar, suffering for passion and wisdom.) Yeats translated Sophocles's great choric invocation to Eros, seen as a bringer of abandonment, wildness, and destruction, and praised as glorious. This is Sophocles's vision of a 'terrible beauty':

> Overcome the Empyrean; hurl
> Heaven and Earth out of their places,
> That in the same calamity
> Brother and brother, friend and friend,
> Family and family,
> City and city may contend,
> By that great glory driven wild.

The Crazy Jane poems are of course clearly related to Yeats's poems about women, through similarity and dissimilarity. It is very tempting, but illegitimate, to assimilate Crazy Jane to other violent women, especially in the lyrics in 'A Man Young and Old' and 'A Woman Young and Old'. There are certainly some poems that have a family resemblance to the Crazy Jane poems; for instance, 'Meeting', which may come to suggest a link between Crazy Jane and Maud Gonne, who once made a celebrated and disastrous appearance on Yeats's doorstep disguised as a beggar: [9]

> Hidden by old age awhile
> In masker's cloak and hood,
> Each hating what the other loved,
> Face to face we stood . . .

A man and a woman in extreme old age, they speak so aggressively to each other that the violence becomes amorous:

> 'Let others boast their fill,' said I,
> 'But never dare to boast
> That such as I had such a man
> For lover in the past;
> Say that of living men I hate
> Such a man the most.'

These characters and their relationship in no sense belong to the experience of Crazy Jane but there is the link in Yeats's dramatic play of love and vituperation, the 'odi' and the 'amo'. And there is the imagery of rags and lunacy:

> 'A loony'd boast of such a love,'
> He in his rage declared:
> But such as he for such as me –
> Could we both discard
> This beggarly habiliment –
> Had found a sweeter word.

This brings together sexual love, old age, rage, and folly. Rage and age are appropriate rhymes for Yeats.

In the Sophocles chorus at the end of 'A Woman Young and Old' and in 'Meetings' there is the image of the beggar. Beggars are frequently old, but Yeats likes to think of old age itself as a state of reduction into poverty and rags, as in 'An aged man is but a paltry thing,/ A tattered coat upon a stick'. He sees too that the soul sings the more ecstatically for the tatters 'in its mortal dress':

> An aged man is but a paltry thing,
> A tattered coat upon a stick, unless
> Soul clap its hands and sing, and louder sing
> For every tatter in its mortal dress . . .

Barbara Hardy

From its beginning Yeats's poetry is full of beggars, old men like Father O'Hart, Father Gilligan, the old pensioner, the old fox-hunter, the old fisherman, and women like Moll Magee and the Old Mother. From its beginnings the poetry also reveals and stresses an aestheticism, which leads Yeats to prefer youth, beauty, and civilised elegance. In 'The Phases of the Moon' Yeats has Owen Aherne say,

> 'All dreams of the soul
> End in a beautiful man's or woman's body.'

In the early poem, 'The Lover tells of the Rose of his Heart' from *The Wind Among the Reeds,* Yeats is aware of the need for rigorous selection in the creation of beauty, in the making of a certain kind of art. He longs to make for his beloved 'a casket of gold' because the world is too full of ugly, old, uncomely and broken things, wronging her image. Although the poem shows Yeats in some ways as moving towards aesthetic seclusion – he sits 'on a green knoll apart' and contemplates making the appropriate casket – the poem itself for more than half its stretch is taken up with the things that have to be excluded. Here, as later in 'Sailing to Byzantium' he imagines the creation of a stylised artefact. Whether in the early golden casket, or in the later golden Byzantine bird, art challenges and competes with nature by imitating it brilliantly but mechanistically or coldly. These concepts of fixity, style, and ornament present the aesthetic context in which Crazy Jane violently forced her appearance. In 'Adam's Curse' a beautiful woman says 'we must labour to be beautiful', and in his images of art and his images of man and woman Yeats is compelled to create and to admire beauty. But in Crazy Jane Yeats creates and admires ugliness, drawing on certain images and feelings always present in the poems, and forming an undercurrent to the aestheticism. Yeats is, of course, changed in his imagination by his ageing. His tendency to admire or over-admire beauty and to confine his images of sexuality to beauty is sternly and harshly but sometimes humorously corrected in *The Tower* and *The Winding Stair*. Sexuality is freed from aestheticism. Age is not protected or freed from sexuality, nor of course at this stage would Yeats have wanted it to be. Perhaps the greatest contrast to Crazy Jane is found in the young man's imagination of age:

When you are old and grey and full of sleep,
And nodding by the fire, take down this book . . .

Yeats, when he was a young man, liked to imagine age, but
imagined it innocently and strangely. When he grew older, he
knew that it did not sleep or nod or contentedly find love in
books.

In 'A Man Young and Old' and 'A Woman Young and Old'
he wants to admit and exult in the sexuality of old age. Sometimes this exultation is part of his capacity for joy and vigour.
(Hence the relevance of that detail about the inspiration of sexual
abstinence in illness and convalescence.) Yeats seems to cease to
distinguish as he used to do between the male and the female.
One of the most refreshing things about 'A Man Young and Old',
'A Woman Young and Old', Crazy Jane and Tom the Lunatic,
is that Yeats wants now to produce a double image. He still wants
to separate man from woman – and it was probably sexually
exciting for him to do this – but he wants not so much to make
distinctions of gender as to show a common experience of survival
in vitality. Sex cannot be aesthetically presented any more. Its
needs seem harsher. The bodies are less beautiful.

Although Yeats first approved of Crazy Jane, he eventually
wrote to his wife, 'I want to exorcise that slut, . . . whose language
has become unendurable.'[10] Even at the start he limits her by
refusing to let her have a poem sequence all to herself. When he
was writing 'A Man Young and Old', into its lyrical and narrative
sequence came a woman young and old, and eventually he gave
in and let the woman have her own sequence. Crazy Jane only
occupies the beginning of 'Words for Music Perhaps', and is not
allowed to have her own spot, her own series. She has to share it
with other images and characters, and she is finally ousted. After
seven Crazy Jane poems, for example, come 'Girl's Song' and
'Young Man's Song'. The modulation works interestingly. The
girl asks 'Saw I an old man young/ Or young man old?' The
young man looks ahead with horror and has a vision of his love
being turned into a withered crone, and yet manages to assert
that it was 'No withered crone I saw/ Before the world was
made.'[11] Yeats preserves some continuity in this group of twenty-
five separate and distinct poems; the key themes of age, instability,
and time are summed up in 'After Long Silence', 'bodily decrepi-
tude is wisdom'. The same themes are kept going throughout the

group, but the sequence is much more like an anthology than a poem sequence, lacking a tightly constructed form and set of characters and images, like those in 'A Man Young and Old' and 'A Woman Young and Old'.

Crazy Jane is ousted by the poet. She initiates the sequence, as a character with her own context of fragmented but sufficiently powerful narrative. Yeats gives us teasing scraps of the story. We know about her antagonistic relationship with the Bishop: she is a highly articulate example of Irish anti-clericalism. We know about one man who had her virginity, whom she continued to love, and by whom she was delectably but unnervingly haunted after his death. We also know that her body is 'like a road that men pass over' and that 'men come and go': Jane is promiscuous and open to sexual adventure, though the adventures are not romanticised. History and dramatic character make the poems separate from the poet's lyrical autobiography, and so in a way 'impersonal'. The poems are also 'all emotion': they are a vehicle for wildness, rage, ecstasy, pride and hatred. Putting the matter less thematically and more affectively, they scream, scoff, attack, defy, praise and adore. I think one can understand why Yeats thought of Crazy Jane as someone or something who had to be exorcised. He appears to have been highly excited by her and into the creation of these images of woman, created by man, may have gone something of the need to make sexual fantasy exciting in cause and in effect. There may well have been something of a pornographic urge behind this poetry, but if it possesses more than usual emotion, it also reveals control and order. Yeats orders the emotions rigorously in the first poem, 'Crazy Jane and the Bishop'. Jane is always controlled and ordered through her language. She does not speak in a rough informal or uneducated voice, and although of course we know from Yeats and other sources that Irish beggar women may speak in a high style, nevertheless into this speech goes rather more than mere social realism.

> Bring me to the blasted oak
> That I, midnight upon the stroke,
> (*All find safety in the tomb.*)
> May call down curses on his head
> Because of my dear Jack that's dead.

Coxcomb was the least he said:
The solid man and the coxcomb.

Nor was he Bishop when his ban
Banished Jack the Journeyman,
(*All find safety in the tomb.*)
Nor so much as parish priest,
Yet he, an old book in his fist,
Cried that we lived like beast and beast:
The solid man and the coxcomb.

The Bishop has a skin, God knows,
Wrinkled like the foot of a goose,
(*All find safety in the tomb.*)
Nor can he hide in holy black
The heron's hunch upon his back,
But a birch-tree stood my Jack:
The solid man and the coxcomb.

Here Yeats is most decorously and formally presenting wildness, rage and sexuality. There is a natural flow, and there is the shrill note in the engaging, almost irrelevant objection:

> Nor was he Bishop when his ban
> Banished Jack the Journeyman . . .
> Nor so much as parish priest . . .

Jane has been endowed, although it is kept fully in character, with a little of Yeats's own sexual snobbery:

> The Bishop has a skin, God knows,
> Wrinkled like the foot of a goose . . .

We tend to think of Crazy Jane as old, but in this poem she seems to be straight and smooth enough to be squeamish about the Bishop's gooselike skin and the humped back. The poem's refrain, though shifting in sense, keeps a firm hold of the feelings, posing the sense of death against the physically exultant praise.

The second poem, 'Crazy Jane Reproved', is the one which critics have found most difficult.[12] It presents certain initial and

inescapable difficulties. It has an ambiguous title which does not
tell us whether she had been reproved or whether she is still being
reproved; we do not know where in the poem the reproof is
being placed, because there are two stanzas which may have
different speakers. The speaker or speakers are not definitely
indicated, as in some of the other Crazy Jane poems, where we
know precisely what Crazy Jane said. The first stanza seems to
have Crazy Jane's characteristic carelessness and recklessness
about it, but the argument in the second stanza does not seem
to come from Crazy Jane's experience or Crazy Jane's brain.
The speakers are opposed, but not explicitly:

> 'Crazy Jane Reproved'
>
> I care not what the sailors say;
> All those dreadful thunder-stones,
> All that storm that blots the day
> Can but show that Heaven yawns;
> Great Europa played the fool
> That changed a lover for a bull.
> *Fol de rol, fol de rol.*
>
> To round that shell's elaborate whorl,
> Adorning every secret track
> With the delicate mother-of-pearl,
> Made the joints of Heaven crack:
> So never hang your heart upon
> A roaring, ranting journeyman.
> *Fol de rol, fol de rol.*

It is possible, as has been suggested,[13] that in the second stanza
Jane is arguing ironically against herself. But it seems likely that
the argument from design, and the rude way of describing the
'roaring, ranting journeyman', comes from some other speaker.
(There seems to be no justification for identifying the speaker
as the Bishop.) In the first stanza Jane seems to be objecting
to any kind of moral imperative that comes from a concept of
providential control and concern. If we could be sure that the
weather comes from the gods then we might live more prudently,
but Jane does not think there is evidence of design, and consistently rejects a Heavenly source of thunder and Zeus the bull.

In the absence of gods, Europa made the bad exchange of a lover for a bull. Now woman rejects man's myth.

The argument in the second stanza seems to be made by some other speaker, holding that every natural object reveals a necessary design, in which heaven is unmelodramatically but surely involved, even at the expense of making its joints crack. Jane is reproved because this is a world in which it is better not to 'hang your heart upon/ A roaring, ranting journeyman'. In both the refrains, one completing Jane's assertion, the other rudely rejecting the reproval, there is Yeats's marvellous use of a kind of gabble or babble: *'Fol de rol, fol de rol.'* Jane makes a rude noise in order to assert her contempt for the reproof, but attached, through her poet's craft and cunning, in *'Fol de rol, fol de rol'*, to a traditional design. The 'fol' has a suitable suggestion of frivolity and folly which reflects on Jane and on her opinion of the opposition.

The next poem, 'Crazy Jane on the Day of Judgment', has also a slightly ambiguous title. Is this the Day of Judgment or is it, as we may well conclude, Crazy Jane anticipating and speaking on the subject of the Day of Judgment. This poem brings in an unnamed man, possibly Jack the Journeyman. Within the poem Jane is not called Crazy Jane but just Jane, which takes on a special emphasis, a freedom from abuse.

> 'Love is all
> Unsatisfied
> That cannot take the whole
> Body and soul';
> *And that is what Jane said.*

Here the refrain moves in the opposite direction from the *Fol de rol* refrain. It makes us, or asks us, to attend seriously and solemnly. The poem does not go on being serious and solemn, and one of the good things about it, I think, is the way in which it moves from the conceptual to the personal. It sounds grand, even sublime, to say that ' "Love is all/ Unsatisfied/ That cannot take the whole/ Body and soul" ', but what it amounts to, in personal and domestic detail, is that you have to put up with everything, however awful. This is what Jane goes on to explain and offer,

> 'Take the sour
> If you take me,
> I can scoff and lour
> And scold for an hour'

He is probably a little abashed as the reduced style suggests:

> *'That's certainly the case,' said he.*

Next comes intimacy, secrecy, mystery,

> 'Naked I lay,
> The grass my bed;
> Naked and hidden away,
> That black day';
> *And that is what Jane said.*

There is a sense here of sexual exposure in nature, but it is something undisclosed, and unnerving, in the nakedness, harshness and blackness. To take all, or give all, is to be naked, and not to be totally brought into the light. The poem, like so many of Yeats's poems, ends in a question:

> 'What can be shown?
> What true love be?
> All could be known or shown
> If Time were but gone.'
> *'That's certainly the case,' said he.*

The final stanza completes the relationship, providing of course a seemingly cold and coarse reception for Jane's ecstasy and speculation. As in all the poems where she is in conversation, the communication is ironic and doubtful. She elaborates, refines, translates, and speculates, whereas the man is confined to the non-commital and terse words of the refrain. It is one of those poems where dialogue shows Yeats's experience in the theatre.

'Crazy Jane and Jack the Journeyman' is the poem referred to earlier, written out of the experience where Yeats's philosophical concentration and sense of an unholy ecstasy – 'the Black Mass of Eden' – came together. It is a poem that is probably about a dreaming back and certainly about two kinds of loving:

46

I know, although when looks meet
I tremble to the bone,
The more I leave the door unlatched
The sooner love is gone,
For love is but a skein unwound
Between the dark and dawn.

A lonely ghost the ghost is
That to God shall come;
I – love's skein upon the ground,
My body in the tomb –
Shall leap into the light lost
In my mother's womb.

But were I left to lie alone
In an empty bed,
The skein so bound us ghost to ghost
When he turned his head
Passing on the road that night,
Mine must walk when dead.[14]

The statement of visionary wildness is plain and frightening. 'A lonely ghost the ghost is/ That to God shall come', Jane imagines in a vivid and not entirely simple image, the dying and coming to God, as a leap into 'the light lost/ In my mother's womb.' It may be the light lost when she got into her mother's womb, or when she got out of it; the image leaves questions ringing in one's mind. The alternative to leaping into light is to be bound to a ghost: 'The skein so bound us ghost to ghost/ When he turned his head/ Passing on the road that night/ Mine must walk when dead.'

In the first version of this poem, Yeats imagined a companionable ghostly afterlife in which the lovers would walk together, 'We would walk being dead.'[14] The final version retains something of a compulsion both terrifying and desired. The use of 'skein' is another beautiful example of Yeats's control of violent feeling. The skein, wound and unwound, is an exact image for the process of tumescence and detumescence; in the second stanza, the skein is like a shed skin of a snake, a mortal coil left upon the ground; finally the skein works as a bond to join the ghosts together. In each image the shape and structure are physically apposite, though the shape changes throughout the poem.

In 'Crazy Jane on God', the fifth poem, we have the very strong sense of her survival. It is both matter-of-fact and mystical, the refrain being traditional, making no claims for Jane's wisdom that are not evasive and elusive.

> That lover of a night
> Came when he would,
> Went in the dawning light
> Whether I would or no;
> Men come, men go,
> *All things remain in God.*

Here we remember that Cracked Mary was a seer of visions. Crazy Jane too is presented as a visionary. The poem begins by dealing roughly and harshly with sex, 'That lover of a night/ Came when he would', and 'Men come, men go;', but presents a series of visions. There is the martial vision of Thermopylae and other battles; in the second stanza, there follows the image that occurs in several poems, and in *Purgatory,* of the sudden illumination of a ruin; in the return at the end, 'I had wild Jack for a lover', we experience one of the few moments in the Crazy Jane poems where her promiscuity is insisted upon::

> That men pass over
> Though like a road
> My body makes no moan
> But sings on:
> *All things remain in God.*

Sexual experience for Jane is harsh and not delectable, though the body's singing is mysterious, seeming to suggest sexual outcry and to assert her claim to the lyrics in which she appears.

The poem that is most assertive, most harsh and most joyous is 'Crazy Jane talks with the Bishop'. Yeats greatly admired D. H. Lawrence's use of obscene language in *Lady Chatterley's Lover*, and he once wrote that 'Those two lovers, the gamekeeper and his employer's wife . . . are poignant in their loneliness, and the coarse language of the one, accepted by both, becomes a forlorn poetry uniting their solitudes, something ancient, humble and terrible.'[15] What Yeats does is to manage to write highly sexual

poetry in highly decorous language. This is partly to do, no doubt,
with the tradition and the time in which he is using his poetic
language. I sometimes feel that Yeats would have liked to write
obscenely, but his restraint in writing about sex is highly effective.
As Yeats knew, if we restrain passion, we feel 'the stirring of the
beast' beneath. Here there is the suggestiveness of restraint. There
is also a particular dramatic advantage in making Jane speak the
same language as the Bishop. The title 'Crazy Jane talks with the
Bishop' draws attention to talk, and she meets him on his own
ground, to hold her own brilliantly and finally to outdo him. Her
theology and her use of Biblical language are more profound and
flexible than his and her characteristic language makes the poem
outrageous, harsh, witty and subtle. The Bishop is given only one
stanza, and Jane has two highly effective ones; she is given the
emphatic and resounding last word, making up for the last words
spoken by the man in 'Crazy Jane on the Day of Judgment':

> I met the Bishop on the road
> And much said he and I.
> 'Those breasts are flat and fallen now,
> Those veins must soon be dry;
> Live in a heavenly mansion,
> Not in some foul sty.

The Bishop is retaliating for the unpleasant things she said about
his loose, wrinkled skin and his crooked back, but she seizes on
his simplicities and complicates them:

> 'Fair and foul are near of kin,
> And fair needs foul,' I cried.
> 'My friends are gone, but that's a truth
> Nor grave nor bed denied,
> Learned in bodily lowliness
> And in the heart's pride.'

Jane has something of the witch about her, but echoes, rather
than repeats, what the witches say in *Macbeth*. They declare
blasphemously that 'Fair is foul and foul is fair', but Jane refrains
from identifying fair and foul, and says something more intelligent, orthodox and metaphysically acceptable: 'Fair and foul
are near of kin/ And fair needs foul.' She backs her generalisa-

tion with the brilliant examples from the grave and the lovers'
bed; she argues whereas he simply abused and preached. She is
really talking to him, fully responding to his advice and assump-
tions, and picking up his allusions and theology.

> 'A woman can be proud and stiff
> When on love intent;
> But Love has pitched his mansion in
> The place of excrement
> For nothing can be sole or whole
> That has not been rent.'

As has often been noticed, 'The place of excrement' is related to
Golgotha and to St Augustine[16], and the rending both to the
virgin's hymen and the veil of the Temple. She is being marvellously outrageous; we feel that she is tempted to dismiss him with
an obscenity, but instead she combines sexual offensiveness with
theological debate, forcing him to hear both theological truth
and sexual truth. She meets him on her own ground, and on
his, replying in the most agile language, picking up the biblical
words that he uses, the 'heavenly mansion', adapting and adopting
it, 'Love has pitched his mansion.'[17] This is Jane's equivalent of
the devil's quoting of scripture and she flouts the Bishop, showing
that her sense of love is larger than his, and that her theology is
very much more complex. Jane's theology, style, orthodoxy, and
Augustinian echoes must not be made to sound too holy. There
is an unholy, even diabolical glee, about her outfacing of the
silent Bishop, and this poem in particular reminds us of Yeats's
reference to the Black Mass of Eden, by which he presumably
refers to the sexualising of the mass. The reference, though
encompassing blasphemy, insists that everything that lives is
holy. It also cunningly argues that if you take the Incarnation
seriously it should be seen as thoroughly carnal. Love pitches his
mansion in the place of excrement, and is necessarily a little
defiled by touching pitch. But as in *The Herne's Egg*, Yeats,
through Crazy Jane, is making out a case for desecration. In
The Herne's Egg he argues outrageously, through a case of
bestiality, excusing outrage by revising myths in a way for
which there is elegant precedent. Donkeys are less dignified than
swans and doves, but neither Attracta nor Jane is pursuing
dignity, and somewhere implicit in the play and in the poetry is

the thought that Bishops are more concerned with dignity than Christ was. Once more we come to the dangerous area where Jane is taken too solemnly. Her outrageousness must not be tamed by commentary. In the humour, the cleverness, the *double-entendre*, and the final flouting, there is wildness.

Yeats said that 'Crazy Jane Grown Old looks at the Dancers' had its origin in a dream. It may have been an excited sado-masochistic dream which he transformed into something appropriate to Jane. This is another example of Jane, the visionary, seeing in that 'daemonic rage'[18] which seems to belong to the excited creation of dream. The dream is a model for art, like the bird's nest, something natural and something purposive. The rage is also here localised, both within the dream and in the spectator's refrain. Like the woman in 'Her Vision in the Wood', Jane is looking at the sexual passion of youth with the aged desire and jealousy that Yeats's own excited ageing needs. The old woman cannot bend her limbs now to the dance. As so often in Yeats, the dance is a splendid image for the wildness, the abandon, the rhythm, the order and the delight of art or sex. Jane watches, as the spectator may contemplate dream, fantasy, art or sex, in that excited reverie – aesthetic or kinetic or a blend of both – which we blur or chill in our current insistence on the idea of 'distance' and our neglect of the concept of 'intimacy'. Jane is tempted to break the dance because it is a dance of death, eroticism carried to a murderous intensity. What stops her is the glamour of art, and the glamour of human passion, joined here inextricably, 'Eyes under eyelids did so gleam'. She comes to the conclusion in the second stanza that there is something complete and so satisfying in the intensity of hatred, even if the dance becomes murderous:

> When she, and though some said she played
> I said that she had danced heart's truth,
> Drew a knife to strike him dead,
> I could but leave him to his fate;
> For no matter what is said
> They had all that had their hate;
> *Love is like the lion's tooth.*

Throughout, the mutations of the refrain, 'Love is like the lion's tooth', pierce differently in each place. In the first stanza

51

the gleam of the eye, perhaps amorous, perhaps destructive, is brought out simply in the simile; in the second it belongs to the emphasis on hatred; at the end, to the lost erotic abandon. It is also a poem whose fierce and reductive refrain fits the jealous mood introduced by the marvellous 'that ivory image', the woman's image for the young dancer. But the poem goes beyond jealousy in its revivals and resolutions of erotic and aesthetic experience.

This poem tells us that Jane has 'grown old'. The process of her ageing cannot be definitely charted because of the doubtful identity of some of the male figures in the poems; the first poem, 'Crazy Jane and the Bishop', must come after the second in Jane's biography, when Jack the Journeyman is still alive. She is obviously getting on in 'Crazy Jane on God', and said to be old in the last two poems in *The Winding Stair*. The last Crazy Jane poem comes in *Last Poems* and seems to be a version of the poem 'Cracked Mary's Vision' which Yeats was persuaded by Pound not to publish with the other Crazy Jane poems because it had the offensive refrain 'May the devil take King George', and King George V was ill at the time.[19] Although this version is linguistically quite different, it does now bring Crazy Jane back into the political arena, and makes an attack on the English monarchy. It looks back at the poems attacking the bishop, takes one last hit at the church in the very abdication of attack:

> I am tired of cursing the Bishop,
> (Said Crazy Jane)
> Nine books or nine hats
> Would not make him a man.

It turns its attention to 'something worse':

> A King had some beautiful cousins,
> But where are they gone?
> Battered to death in a cellar,
> And he stuck to his throne.

Once more Jane has a vision of the lost heroic world. She shares Yeats's own nostalgia and bitterness in the lament for 'Great-bladdered Emer' and Cuchulain, but her vision is particularised. The mythological reference to Emer's victorious feats of urination is an epithet typically physical in content and classically elaborate in manner. Emer comes first because she is a woman. Jane is also linked with the man in 'His Wildness' in 'A Man Young and Old' who, like old Madge, being 'all alone' nurses a stone and sings it lullaby. Crazy Jane is again looking on at full-blooded ghosts appearing in a dream or a vision, and must fall back on sad fetishism, and weep. It is tactful of Yeats to emphasise physicality not through the vexed union of Emer and Cuchulain, but through her great bladder and his troubled violence. The last line's Irishness ('And I cried tears down') completes the present's lamentation for the myth.[20] The myth itself, and 'Crazy Jane Grown Old looks at the Dancers', is brought very close to the dreamer, but is also intact and separate.

The poem which follows is 'The Circus Animals' Desertion', where Crazy Jane does not appear in the list of Yeats's created characters, Oisin, Cuchulain, the Countess Cathleen, 'Lion and woman and the Lord knows what.' Having dismissed and detached himself from the characters of his dreams and art, the poet in the poem creates one more mythological figure, that of the 'raving slut/ Who keeps the till'. There is a link with Jane through the raving and sluttishness (Yeats's revenge, perhaps, for her lascivious hauntings), but the till-keeping is something quite foreign to Jane. (If she is a harlot there is never anything said about the gains.) It is noticeable, however, that she could, like the raving slut, like old Madge, or Margaret Rooney[21] and Winnie Byrne in the *Stories of Red Hanrahan*, lie down in the foul rag and bone shop of the heart.

Like these characters Crazy Jane is imagined for the purpose of contemplating the heroic dream. Like all Yeats's characters, heroic and otherwise, she is not detached and dissociated, but close to her author, resembling him and also meeting his inextricably interwound erotic and poetic needs.

NOTES

1   Letter to Olivia Shakespear, 2 March 1929. (Printed in *The Letters of W. B. Yeats*, ed. Alan Wade. Hart-Davis, London. 1954. p. 758).
2   Letters to Olivia Shakespear, 17 August 1933. (*Letters*, p. 814).
3   Letter to Lady Gregory, 9 March 1929. (*Letters*, p. 759).
4   Letter to Olivia Shakespear, (postmark 23 November. 1931). (*Letters*, p. 786).

Barbara Hardy

5   Same letter, but this time reproduced on p. 785 of Wade. The poem referred to was an early version of 'Crazy Jane and Jack the Journeyman.'

6   George Eliot, *Janet's Repentance*, chapter 14. Dempster says to Janet. 'Then mind and have a dinner provided, and don't go mooning about like crazy Jane.'

7   From 'The Proverbs of Hell' in the *Marriage of Heaven and Hell.*

8   The word 'wild' is used more than a hundred times by Yeats in his poetry.

9   Richard Ellmann. *Yeats: The Man and the Masks*, Oxford University Press, Oxford, 1979, p. xviii.

10 This letter to Mrs Yeats was written sometime during the winter of 1931/2. By her own request the letters of Mrs Yeats are not included in Wade.

11 Cf. 'Before the World Was Made' from 'A Woman Young and Old'.

12 I will not try to summarise the various interpretations; most commentators have disagreed over the poem's ambiguity. Richard Ellmann, in *The Identity of Yeats*, Macmillan, London, 1954, p. 276 and A. Norman Jeffares in *A Commentary on the Collected Poems of W. B. Yeats*, Macmillan, London, 1968, p. 371, have attempted to substantiate the poem by quoting the following passage from *Autobiographies* (p. 249):
    Is it not certain that the Creator yawns in earthquake and thunder and other popular displays, but toils in rounding the delicate spiral of a shell.
    It might be inferred from this passage that the *poet* is reproving Crazy Jane, although it has also been argued that this passage is irrelevant in the context of the poem and that in fact there is no reproval as such. (*see below, footnote 13*).

13 Harold Bloom. *Yeats*, Oxford University Press, New York, 1970, p. 401, argues against Ellmann's and Jeffares's use of the passage from *Autobiographies* (which sees Jane as reproved by herself or by the poet) and claims that rather, in the second stanza, she warns against her own choice of love and that this warning is 'another extravagant affirmation' on her part.

14 The version sent to Olivia Shakespear (see above, footnote 5).

15 Letter to Olivia Shakespear, 22 May 1933. (*Letters*, p. 810.)

16 '*inter urinas et faeces nascimur,*' in Norman O. Brown. *Life Against Death*, Random House. New York. 1961, p. 187.

17 Yeats may have had in mind George Herbert's *Anagram* (ie. Mary/Army): 'How well her name an *Army* doth present,/In whom the *Lord of Hosts* did pitch his tent!' There is a striking coincidence of rhyme and metaphor, though both poets are of course using biblical imagery.

18 'Meditations in Time of Civil War' part II.

19 Ellmann. *The Identity of Yeats*, gives the text, pp. 101–2.

20 It echoes the last words of the story 'Hanrahan and Cathleen, the Daughter of Houlihan' in *Stories of Red Hanrahan*. 'While he was singing his voice began to break. and tears came rolling down his cheeks. and Margaret Rooney put down her face into her hands and

54

began to cry along with him. Then a blind beggar by the fire shook his rags with a sob. and after that there was not one of them all but cried tears down. This follows Hanrahan's singing of a lament for the heroic Irish past.

21 See footnote 20 above.

YEATS AS AN EXAMPLE?

SEAMUS HEANEY

A writer's dedication to his art can entail some kind of hurt for
those who live near and dear to him. Robert Lowell used the
word 'plotting' to describe something that is questionable in the
artistic enterprise:

> I have sat and listened to too many
> words of the collaborating muse,
> and plotted perhaps too freely with my life,
> not avoiding injury to others,
> not avoiding injury to myself –
> to ask compassion . . . this book, half-fiction,
> an eelnet made by man for the eel fighting –
> my eyes have seen what my hand did.

If there is more than a hint of self-accusation in that last line,
there is a strong ring of triumph in it as well, and when Robert
Lowell died I remember some of us toyed with it as a possible
epitaph for him: it seemed to catch the combination of pride
and vulnerability that lay at the roots of his poetic voice.

It would have made a much more rueful tombstone verse than
Yeats's:

> *Cast a cold eye*
> *On life, on death.*
> *Horseman, pass by!*

Where Yeats's eye is cold, Lowell's is warm though by no means
wet, sympathetic to the imperfections of living, the eye of a
pedestrian rather than the eye of an equestrian. Where Yeats's
last poems sang their faith in art and turned in scorn from 'the
sort now growing up' Lowell's final work hesitated, and his
trust in fictions seemed to waver:

Epilogue
Those blessed structure, plot and rhyme –
why are they no help to me now
I want to make
something imagined, not recalled?
. . . .
Yet why not say what happened?
Pray for the grace of accuracy
Vermeer gave to the sun's illumination
stealing like the tide across a map
to his girl solid with yearning.
We are poor passing facts,
warned by that to give
each figure in the photograph
his living name.

'Accuracy' seems a modest aim, even when it is as richly imaged as it is here. Lowell abjures the sublime, that realm where his rhetoric often penetrated, and seeks instead the low-key consolations of the quotidian. He is almost, in Yeats's words, 'content to live'.

Yeats would never have been merely, 'content to live' because that would have meant throwing words away, throwing gesture away, throwing away possibilities for drama and transcendence. From the beginning of his career he emphasised and realised the otherness of art from life, dream from action, until in the end he moved within his mode of vision as within some invisible ring of influence and defence, absorbed as a long-legged fly on the stream:

> That girls at puberty may find
> The first Adam in their thought,
> Shut the door of the Pope's chapel,
> Keep those children out.
> There on that scaffolding reclines
> Michael Angelo.
> With no more sound than the mice make
> His hand moves to and fro.
> *Like a long-legged fly upon the stream*
> *His mind moves upon silence.*

Whatever Yeats intends us to understand by this poem, 'Long legged Fly', we cannot miss the confidence that drive it forward and the energy that underlies it, an energy that exhilarates in the faith that artistic process has an absolute validity. And there is a kind of vitreous finish on the work itself that deflects all other truths except its own. Art can outface history, the imagination can disdain happenings once it has incubated and mastered the secret behind happenings. In fact, we can sense a violence, an implacable element in the artistic drive as Yeats envisages and embodies it. The 'yellow-eyed hawk of the mind' and the 'ancient, glittering eyes' of the Chinaman in 'Lapis Lazuli' and the 'cold eye' of the tomb-inspecting horseman of 'Under Ben Bulben' are suggestive of sinister appetites. If the act of mind in the artist has all the intentness and amorousness and every bit as much of the submerged aggression as the act of love, then it can be maintained that Yeats's artistic imagination was often in a condition that can only be properly described as priapic.

Is this, then, exemplary? Do we altogether assent to the samurai stare and certainty of 'Cast a cold eye/On life, on death'? Do we say yes to this high-stepping tread? How, in other words, do we regard Yeats's affirmation that the man who sits down to breakfast is a 'bundle of accident and incoherence' and that the man reborn in his poem is 'something intended, complete'?

I find much to admire in the intransigence of the stance, as I find much to commend and imitate in the two things that Yeats was so often determined to set at loggerheads, his life and his work:

> The intellect of man is forced to choose
> Perfection of the life, or of the work,
> And if it take the second must refuse
> A heavenly mansion, raging in the dark.

What is finally admirable is the way his life and his work are *not* separate but make a continuum, the way the courage of his vision did not confine itself to rhetorics but issued in actions. Yeats bore the implications of his romanticism into the life of his times: he propagandised, speechified, fund-raised, administered, and politicked in the world of telegrams and anger, all on behalf of the world of vision. His poetry was not just a matter of printed books making their way in a world of literate readers and critics;

it was rather the fine flower of his efforts to live as forthrightly as he could in the world of illiterates and politicians. Beside the ringing antithesis of 'The Choice' we must set this other recognition:

> A poet is by the very nature of things a man who lives with entire sincerity, or rather, the better his poetry, the more sincere his life. His life is an experiment in living and those who come after him have a right to know it. Above all, it is necessary that the lyric poet's life be known, that we should understand that his poetry is no rootless flower but the speech of a man; (that it is no little thing) to achieve anything in any art, to stand alone perhaps for many years, to go a path no other man has gone, to accept one's own thought when the thought of others has the authority of the world behind it . . . to give one's own life as well as one's words (which are so much nearer to one's soul) to the criticism of the world.

* * *

I admire the way that Yeats took on the world on his own terms, defined the areas where he would negotiate and where he would not; the way he never accepted the terms of another's argument but propounded his own. I assume that this peremptoriness, this apparent arrogance, is exemplary in an artist, that it is proper and even necessary for him to insist on his own language, his own vision, his own terms of reference. This will often seem like irresponsibility or affectation, sometimes like callousness, but from the artist's point of view it is an act of integrity, or an act of cunning to protect the integrity.

All through his life, of course, and ever since his death, Yeats has been continually rebuked for the waywardness of his beliefs, the remoteness of his behaviour and the eccentricity of his terms of reference. Fairies first of all. Then Renaissance courts in Tuscany and Big Houses in Galway. Phases of the Moon and Great Wheels. What, asks the reliable citizen, is the sense of all this? Why do we listen to this gullible aesthete rehearsing the delusions of an illiterate peasantry, this snobbish hanger-on in country houses mystifying the fuedal facts of the class system, this charlatan patterning history and predicting the future by a mumbo-jumbo of geometry and Ptolomaic astronomy? Our temptation may be to answer on the reliable citizen's terms, let him call the tune and begin to make excuses for Yeats.

'Well,' we might say, 'when he was a youngster in Sligo he heard these stories about fairies from the servants in his grandparents' house; and then when, as a young poet, he sought a badge of identity for his own culture, something that would mark it off from the rest of the English speaking world, he found this distinctive and sympathetic thing in the magical world view of the country people. It was a conscious counter-cultural ploy against the rationalism and materialism of late Victorian England.' To which the citizen replies, 'Anybody who believes in fairies is mad.'

Yeats would not have thanked us for explaining him. He would want us to affirm him with all the elaborate obstinacy with which he affirmed himself. So for entertainment and instruction, I wish to observe him in action, first as a young poet, and then as an established poet and public figure; and in each case I hope to make clear what I consider to have been exemplary in his bearing.

*　　*　　*

The *Irish Theosophist*, a magazine whose very title is enough to raise the ghosts of the Nineties, carried an interview with Mr. W. B. Yeats in its issue for 15 October, 1893. It had been conducted by the editor, one D. N. Dunlop, who set the scene in his opening paragraphs:

> A few evenings ago I called on my friend, Mr. W. B. Yeats, and found him alone, seated in his armchair, smoking his cigarette, with a volume of Homer before him. The whole room indicated the style and taste peculiar to its presiding genius. Upon the walls hung various designs by Blake and other less well-known symbolic artists; everywhere books and papers in apparently endless confusion.
> In his usual genial way he invited me to have a cup of tea with him. During this pleasant ceremony little was said, but sufficient to impress me more than ever with the fact that my host was supremely an artist, much in love with his art.

Yeats was then twenty-eight, and could deploy that elaborate style he had learned from Pater with as much indolent calculation

on a sofa as in a sentence. If he had not yet formulated his theory
of the mask, he had an instinctive grasp of the potency of his
image; and if he does not altogether ruffle here in a manly pose,
there is nevertheless a bit of a peacock display going on. The
Homer volume was a good touch, and so was the cigarette and
the 'ceremony' of the tea.

The young man whose concern for appearances had led him,
a few years earlier, to ink his heels in order to disguise the holes
in his socks had obviously mastered more complex and sure-footed
strategies for holding the line between himself and the world
around him. He had not, for sure, acquired the peremptory
authority which Frank O'Connor was to see in action decades
later, when the poet could silence an argument or buttress a
proposition with a remark such as 'Ah, but that was before the
peacock screamed,' but he had about him already a definite
atmosphere, a style that declared allegiance to disciplines and
sources of strength not shared by his coevals or contemporaries.
He was an artist, devoted to the beautiful; he was a magician,
adept among hidden powers; he was a Celt, with a lifeline to the
mythological depths; he was a propagandist, with a firm line for
journalists. He was all these things, self-consciously and
deliberately, yet they did not constitute a dispersal or a confusion
of his powers or of his personality; on the contrary, they concentrated one another, grew from a single root, and if they were
deliberate, the deliberation sprang from an inner compulsion, an
energy discovering itself as vision. Yeats's performances, we
might say, then and for the rest of his life, manifested themselves
in the service of creative action. The longer we think of Yeats,
the more he narrows the gap which etymology has forced between
mystery and mastery.

Aspects of the mysterious and the masterful reveal themselves
in one of his coolest strokes during the interview, which was
essentially a conversation about Yeats's connection with the
Blavatsky Lodge of the Theosophical Society. He had been
expelled by Madame Blavatsky, or at least had been asked to
resign, about three years earlier. Dunlop asked him:

'Can you remember anything in the nature of a prophecy,
Mr. Yeats, made by Madame Blavatsky, that might be of
interest to record, notwithstanding the fact that you are yet
awaiting your prophesied illness?'

'The only thing of that nature', replied Mr. Yeats, 'was a reference to England. The Master told me, said she, that the power of England would not outlast the century, and the Master never deceived me.'

It seems to me that Yeats cut a sly swathe with that answer, enlisting the esoteric fringe to serve the nationalistic heartland, hiding the cultural agitator behind the po-faced dreamer, making a cast across the sleeping pool of historical enmity with a line as neutral as theosophy itself, the calm surface of his speech depth-charged with potential rebellion. The remark leaves a broadening wake in the imagination and operates by the perfect camouflaging of judged intention in an aftermath of overlapping effects; and in this way it rehearses in miniature the more complex orchestration of intention and effect which he was to achieve in *The Wind Among the Reeds*, a book which did not appear until six years later but whose title was already haunting his mind, as the conclusion to the interview makes clear:

'And what about your present work?' I asked.
'*Celtic Twilight,* a work dealing with ghosts, goblins and fairies, will be out shortly, also a short volume of Blake's poems,' he replied. 'Then I am getting ready for publication, next spring, a book of poems, which I intend calling *The Wind Among the Reeds* and, as soon afterwards as possible, a collection of essays and lectures dealing with Irish nationality and literature, which will probably appear under the title of the *Watch Fire.*'

In the event, of course, it was six years before *The Wind Among the Reeds* appeared, and *Watch Fire* was never published. His essay on nationality and literature had appeared, however, five months earlier in *The United Irishman* and work on similar themes had been published all through the late 'eighties and continued to be published throughout the 'nineties. He began with his famous championship of Sir Samuel Ferguson's poetry – 'the greatest poet Ireland has produced, because the most central and most Celtic' – and went on to praise James Clarence Mangan, William Allingham and the ballad poets; to sponsor new voices like Katherine Tynan's and AE's; to write for English and Irish magazines bibliographies and readers' guides to the best Irish books; to affirm the validity of that magical world-view implicit in Irish country customs and beliefs, and to rehearse those beliefs and customs in the book he mentions which gave its name to an era, *The Celtic Twilight.*

It was all part of a campaign and the various suggestions in the word campaign are apposite. It was sustained over a long period and was pursued on a number of fronts: journalistic, political, poetic, dramatic, amatory even, if we think of Maud Gonne as leading lady in *The Countess Cathleen;* it was conducted with the idea of conquest, not of territory perhaps but of imagination – though a successful awakening of the people's imagination would allow them to repossess their territory with a new conviction. As he comes to the end of that part of his autobiography dealing with the years 1887–1891, the note swells as he recollects his purpose:

I could not endure, however, an international art, picking stories, which the uneducated classes knew and even sang, and and good luck to aid me, create some new *Prometheus Unbound*; Patrick or Colmcille, Oisin or Finn in Prometheus's stead; and, instead of Caucasus, Cro-Patrick or Ben Bulben? Have not all races had their first unity from a mythology that marries them to rock and hill? We had in Ireland imaginative stories, which the uneducated classes knew and even sang, and might we not make those stories current among the educated classes, rediscovering the applied arts of literature, the association of literature, that is, with music, speech and dance; and at last, it might be, so deepen the political passion of the nation that all, artist and poet, craftsman and day-labourer would accept a common design?

If there is something plangent in this proud recollection, there was nothing of the dying fall in the notes struck by the journalism and controversy of the '80s and '90s as he pursued that 'common design'. For example, after declaring in his 1886 *Dublin University Review* article on Sir Samuel Ferguson that of all things the past bequeaths the future, the greatest are great legends and that it was therefore the duty of every Irish reader to study those of his own country, he went on to make clear that this appeal was directed to the selfless and idealistic young:

I do not appeal to the professional classes, who, in Ireland, at least, appear at no time to have thought of the affairs of their country till they first feared for their emoluments – nor do I appeal to the shoddy society of 'West Britonism'. . . .

That pugnacious thrust never deserted him, although he was to develop a less bare-fisted style, abandoning the short jab in the face in favour of a long reach for the side of the head.

The point is, however, that no matter how much we have been led to think of the young Yeats as a dreamer, we must not forget the practical, driving side of him, driving forward towards his ideal goal. The founding of libraries, the association with political activists, all of this was not undertaken without some resoluteness, some ambition, some expense of spirit. And all of this was by no means the whole story. There were his love affairs, first with Maud Gonne and then with Olivia Shakespear, those enhancing and disturbing events in his emotional life that gave him power in other spheres. There were his more serious literary projects, such as the stories of Red Hanrahan, and those other strange stories, at once robust and remote, which formed the substance of *The Secret Rose*; and there was above all his own secret rose, the poetry itself.

It is easy to admire this young Yeats: his artistic ambitions, his national fervour, his great desire to attach himself to a tradition and a corpus of belief that was communal. For all the activity and push of the enterprise, the aim of the poet and of the poetry is finally to be of service, to ply the effort of the individual work into the larger work of the community as a whole, and the spirit of our age is sympathetic to that democratic urge.

It is less than sympathetic, however, to the next stance we find the poet adopting. Twenty years after the *Irish Theosophist* interview in October 1893, in his poem 'September 1913', Yeats's style had evolved a tone for detaching rather than attaching himself, for saying 'I' rather than 'we'. By then, Romantic Ireland's dead and gone. We are in the presence of a poet in his late forties, the Abbey Theatre manager, scorner of middle-class piety and philistinism, mythologizer of aristocratic ceremony and grace. We are in the presence of a man who believes that the redistribution of the Coole Park estate among its tenants would be a step back, not a step forward, in the life of the country. A man stung into superb attitudes by the rude handling meted out to J. M. Synge's *Playboy of the Western World* and by the refusal of Dublin Corporation to provide a gallery for Hugh Lane's collection of Impressionist pictures. All that. An Anglo-Irish protestant deeply at odds with the mind of Irish catholic society. A man who is remaking himself, finding a style for resisting his environment rather than a style that would co-opt it, at that thrilling stage of development which he calls, in "A Dialogue of Self and Soul', 'the finished man among his enemies.' And that poem goes on to ask about this man among his enemies:

> How in the name of heaven can he escape
> That defiling and disfigured shape
> The mirror or malicious eyes
> Casts upon his eyes until at last
> He thinks that shape must be his shape?

So I want our next image of Yeats to be one that the malicious eyes of George Moore cast into shape when he came to write his classic autobiographical account of the Irish Literary Revival in *Hail and Farewell*. Though 'malicious' is perhaps too severe an adjective. Many of Moore's most quotable jabs at the romantic figure of the poet are more suggestive of affection than of a desire to afflict, as when he describes his laugh as a caw, 'the most melancholy thing in the world,' or when he presents a bedraggled Yeats on the margins of Coole Lake looking like an old umbrella left behind after a picnic. Moore's book is finally more of a testimony to Yeats's genius than a worrier of it, sustained and elaborate in its ironies, corrective, accurate in its own way. The following passage occurs after Moore has given his account of the Lane controversy and has reported the text of his own lecture on the Impressionists, a lecture delivered for the edification of the reluctant burghers:

As soon as the applause died away, Yeats who had lately returned to us from the States with a paunch, a huge stride, and an immense fur overcoat, rose to speak. We were surprised at the change in his appearance, and could hardly believe our ears when, instead of talking to us as he used to do about the old stories come down from generation to generation he began to thunder like Ben Tillett against the middle classes, stamping his feet, working himself into a temper, and all because· the middle classes did not dip their hands into their pockets and give Lane the money he wanted for his exhibition. When he spoke the words, the middle classes, one would have thought that he was speaking against a personal foe, and we looked round asking each other with our eyes where on earth our Willie Yeats had picked up the strange belief that none but titled and carriage-folk could appreciate pictures. . .

We have sacrificed our lives for Art; but you, what have you done? What sacrifices have you made? he asked, and everybody began to search his memory for the sacrifices that Yeats had made, asking himself in what prison Yeats had languished, what rags he had worn, what broken victuals he had eaten. As far as anybody could remember, he had always lived very comfortably. Sitting down invariably to regular meals, and the old green cloak that was in keeping with his profession of romantic poet he had exchanged for the magnificent fur coat which distracted our attention from what he was saying, so opulently did it cover the back of the chair out of which he had risen. . .

The conscious theatricality of this Yeats, the studied haughtiness, the affectation – this kind of thing has often put people off. This is the Yeats whom his contemporaries could not altogether take seriously because he was getting out of their reach, the Yeats whom Maud Gonne called 'Silly Willie' and whom W. H. Auden also called 'silly', in his 1939 elegy:

> You were silly like us, your gift survived it all.

But in setting the silliness in relation to the gift, Auden went to the heart of the matter – survival. What Moore presents us with is a picture of Yeats exercising that intransigence which I praised earlier, that protectiveness of his imaginative springs, so that the gift would survive. He donned the mantle – or perhaps one should say the fur coat – of the aristocrat so that he might express a vision of a communal and personal life that was ample, generous, harmonious, fulfilled, enhancing. The reactionary politics implied by Yeats's admiration of the Coole Park milieu are innocent in the original sense of that word, not nocent, not hurtful. What is more to the point is the way his experience of that benign,

66

paternalistic regime and of Lady Gregory's personal strengths as
conserver of folk culture and choreographer of artistic talent
issued in a poetry whose very music is a guarantee of its humane
munificence. The silliness of the behaviour is continuous with the
sumptuousness of the poetry of the middle period. Yeats's attack
upon his own middle class really sprang out of disappointment:
why were they not taking the lead culturally now that they were
leaders economically? Of course Moore is right to say he belongs
to them, and of course Yeats's pretensions looked ridiculous to
his contemporaries. But this was his method of signifying his
refusal to 'serve that in which he no longer believed.'

When Joyce rebelled, he left by the Holyhead boat and created
his drama by making a fictional character called Stephen Dedalus
point up and repeat the terms of his revolt. When Yeats rebelled,
he remained but he still made a new W.B.Yeats to tread the
streets and stage of Dublin, a character who was almost as much
a work of imagination as Stephen Dedalus. In order to fly the
philistinism of his own class and the pious ignorance of another
creed, Yeats remade himself, associated himself with cold, dis-
dainful figures of whom Charles Stewart Parnell was the
archetype and 'The Fisherman' was a pattern. The solitude, the
will towards excellence, the courage, the self-conscious turning
away from that in which he no longer believes, which is Dublin
life, and turning towards that which he trusts, which is an image
or dream – all the drama and integrity of his poem 'The Fisherman' depend to a large extent upon that other drama which
George Moore so delightedly observed and reported:

> Maybe a twelvemonth since
> Suddenly I began,
> In scorn of this audience,
> Imagining a man,
> And his sun-freckled face,
> And grey Connemara cloth,
> Climbing up to a place
> Where stone is dark under froth,
> And the down-turn of his wrist
> When the flies drop in the stream;
> A man who does not exist,
> A man who is but a dream;
> And cried, 'Before I am old

> I shall have written him one
> Poem maybe as cold
> And passionate as the dawn.'

We are moving from what other people saw to what Yeats himself envisaged: it is time to consider the inwardness of the poems.

The poetry is cast in a form that is as earcatching as the man was eyecatching, and as a writer, one is awed by the achieved and masterful tones of that deliberately pitched voice, its bare classic shapes, its ability to modulate from emotional climax to wise reflection, its ultimate truth to life.

What Yeats offers the practising writer is an example of labour, effort, perseverance. He is, indeed, the ideal example for a poet approaching middle age. He reminds you that revision and slog-work are what you may have to undergo if you seek the satisfaction of finish, and he keeps nagging you with the suggestion that if you have managed to do one kind of poem in your own way, you should cast off that way and face into another area of your experience until you have learned a new voice to fix and stay that area. He encourages you to experience a transfusion of energies from poetic forms themselves, reveals how the challenge of a metre can extend the resources of the voice. He proves that deliberation can be intensified until it is synonymous with inspiration. Above all, he reminds you that art is intended, that it is part of the creative push of civilization itself: from 'Adam's Curse' to 'Vacillation' and on until the last poems, his work not only explicitly proclaims the reality of the poetic vocation but convinces by the deep note of certitude registered in the proclamation itself.

> No longer in Lethean foliage caught
> Begin the preparation for your death
> And from the fortieth winter by that thought
> Test every work of intellect or faith,
> And everything that your own hands have wrought,
> And call those works extravagance of breath
> That are not suited for such men as come
> Proud, open-eyed and laughing to the tomb.
> ('Vacillation')

Malachi Stilt-Jack am I, whatever I learned has run wild,
From collar to collar, from stilt to stilt, from father to child.
All metaphor, Malachi, stilts and all. A barnacle goose
Far up in the stretches of night; night splits and the dawn
    breaks loose;
I, through the terrible novelty of light, stalk on, stalk on;
Those great sea-horses bare their teeth and laugh at the dawn.

                            ('High Talk')

But it is not the vaunting of the special claims of art and the
artist that is finally to be saluted. Rather, it is Yeats's large-
minded, whole-hearted assent to the natural cycles of living and
dying, his acknowledgement that the 'masterful images' which
compel the assent of artist and audience alike are dependent
upon the 'foul rag and bone shop of the heart,' the humility of
his artistic mastery before the mystery of life and death. There
are several poems where this tenderness towards life and its
uncompletedness is at odds with and tending to gain sway over
the consolations of the artificial work. The tumultuousness and
repose of a poem like 'Sailing to Byzantium' come to mind,
although there the equilibrium between the golden bird of art
and the tattered scarecrow of life is just held, as it is held and
held in mind, contemplated and celebrated in 'Among School
Children'. I am thinking, however, of quieter poems, more
intimate, less deliberately orchestrated pieces, such as 'What
Then':

> All his happier dreams came true –
> A small old house, wife, daughter, son,
> Grounds where plum and cabbage grew,
> Poets and wits about him drew;
> *'What then,' sang Plato's ghost, 'What then?'*
>
> 'The work is done', grown old, he thought,
> 'According to my boyish plan;
> Let the fools rage, I swerved in naught,
> Something to perfection brought';
> *But louder sang that ghost, 'What then?'*

And the challenge of Plato's ghost is matched and picked up in
that other uncharacteristically introspective poem, 'Man and

Echo', where the Echo mocks the Man and where the voice of conscience and remorse opposes itself to the artistic choice that the old man has lived out all his life; this voice of conscience which asks 'Did that play of mine send out/Certain men the English shot?' is finally symbolised in the anguished cry of a rabbit:

> But hush, for I have lost the theme,
> Its joy or might seem but a dream;
> Up there some hawk or owl has struck,
> Dropping out of sky or rock,
> A stricken rabbit is crying out,
> And its cry distracts my thought.

I have found two poems particularly sustaining during the past few years, one of which sets the dissatisfied poet in the midst of civil war, the other of which sets the violent hero in the middle of the dead. They ask, indirectly, about the purpose of art in the midst of life and by their movements, their images, their musics they make palpable a truth which Yeats was at first only able to affirm abstractly, in those words which he borrowed from Coventry Patmore: 'The end of art is peace.'

The first is from 'Meditations in Time of Civil War':

The Stare's Nest by My Window

The bees build in the crevices
Of loosening masonry, and there
The mother birds bring grubs and flies.
My wall is loosening; honey-bees,
Come build in the empty house of the stare.

We are closed in, and the key is turned
On our uncertainty; somewhere
A man is killed, or a house burned,
Yet no clear fact to be discerned:
Come build in the empty house of the stare.

A barricade of stone or of wood;
Some fourteen days of civil war;
Last night they trundled down the road
That dead young soldier in his blood:
Come build in the empty house of the stare.

We had fed the heart on fantasies,
The heart's grown brutal from the fare;
More substance in our enmities
Than in our love; O honey-bees,
Come build in the empty house of the stare.

Here the great fur coat of attitude is laid aside, the domineering intellect and the equestrian profile, all of which gain him a power elsewhere, all laid aside. What we have is a deeply instinctive yet intellectually assented to idea of nature in her benign and nurturant aspect as the proper first principle of life and living. The maternal is apprehended, intimated and warmly cherished and we are reminded, much as Shakespeare might remind us, of the warm eggs in the nest shaking at the impact of an explosion. The stare at Yeats's window and the temple-haunting martlet in Macbeth's castle are messengers of grace.

And if the maternal instincts are the first, perhaps they call us back at the very end also. Yeats lies under Ben Bulben, in Drumcliff Churchyard, under that dominant promontory which I like to think of as the father projected into the landscape, and there is perhaps something too male and assertive about the poem that bears the mountain's name and stands at the end of the *Collected Poems.* If I had my choice I would make the end of that book more exemplary by putting a kinder poem last, one in which the affirmative wilful violent man, whether he be artist or hero, the poet Yeats or the headhunter Cuchulain, must merge his domineering voice into the common voice of the living and the dead, mingle his heroism with the cowardice of his kind, lay his grey head upon the ashy breast of death.

I would end with 'Cuchulain Comforted', a poem which Yeats wrote within two weeks of his death, one in which his cunning as a deliberate maker and his wisdom as an intuitive thinker find a rich and strange conclusiveness. It is written in *terza rima,* the metre of Dante's *Commedia*, the only time Yeats used the form, but the proper time, when he was preparing his own death by imagining Cuchulain's descent among the shades. We witness here a strange ritual of surrender, a rite of passage from life into death, but a rite whose meaning is subsumed into song, into the otherness of art. It is a poem deeply at one with the weak and the strong of this earth, full of a motherly kindness towards life, but also unflinching in its belief in the propriety and beauty of life transcended into art, song, words. The language of the poem hallows the things of this world – eyes, branches, linen, shrouds, arms, needles, trees, all are strangely chaste in the context – yet the figure the poem makes is out of this world:

'Cuchulain Comforted'

A MAN that had six mortal wounds, a man
Violent and famous, strode among the dead;
Eyes stared out of the branches and were gone.

Then certain Shrouds that muttered head to head
Came and were gone. He leant upon a tree
As though to meditate on wounds and blood.

A Shroud that seemed to have authority
Among those bird-like things came, and let fall
A bundle of linen. Shrouds by two and three

Came creeping up because the man was still.
And thereupon that linen-carrier said:
'Your life can grow much sweeter if you will

'Obey our ancient rule and make a shroud;
Mainly because of what we only know
The rattle of those arms makes us afraid.

'We thread the needles' eyes, and all we do
All must together do.' That done, the man
Took up the nearest and began to sew.

'Now must we sing and sing the best we can,
But first you must be told our character:
Convicted cowards all, by kindred slain

'Or driven from home and left to die in fear.'
They sang, but had nor human tunes nor words,
Though all was done in common as before;

They had changed their throats and had the throats
    of birds.

THE PLACE OF SHELLS

T. R. HENN

i

I have taken the title of this lecture from the Irish form, *Sligeach*,[1] which means 'the Place of Shells'. Most of us, on holiday at some watering-place or wandering on the shingle of some lake-shore, are, instinctively, beachcombers; we look down to see what may be found, left by some ancient or modern tide. We may use them for decoration or just collect; and we have been familiar from childhood with the sea-roar which we can hear from the convoluted heart of certain larger shells, which is no more than the echo of our own restless blood. The heraldic emblem of Sligo is a shell, a scallop shell, which (as you will remember) is also the badge of the pilgrim to some great shrine, or to the Holy Land. May I remind you of Sir Walter Raleigh's poem?

> Give me my scallop-shell of quiet,
>   My staff of faith to walk upon,
> My scrip of joy, immortal diet,
>   My bottle of salvation,
> My gown of glory, hope's true gage;
> And thus I'll take my pilgrimage.
>
> Blood must be my body's balmer;
>   No other balm will there be given:
> Whilst my soul, like quiet palmer,
>   Travelleth towards the land of heaven;
> Over the silver mountains,
>   Where spring the nectar fountains;
>   There will I kiss
>   The bowl of bliss;
> And drink mine everlasting fill
> Upon every milken hill,
> My soul will be a-dry before;
> But after, it will thirst no more.

73

I would not press the thought that you and I are among the pilgrims to this place, though, indeed, we may well have needed our 'staff of faith' to journey here. My purpose this morning is to invite your attention to the historical energy and momentum that lie behind the centuries; to the turbulence of history that Yeats saw, and which he has dramatised in his characteristic way to inflame his imagination; and to offer some thoughts about the growth of a poet's mind – remembering Wordsworth's *Prelude* – in relation to the music of this countryside in his youth.

ii

If we stand on the summit of Knocknarea – and you must carry a stone with you on your climb to put on the Cairn, else you will have no luck afterwards – we can watch the scene and the centuries mirrored as in some kind of glass. First and perhaps simplest, consider the geographical features which have made Sligo a centre of supreme military importance. For it is a point of passage; like Thermopylae, or Marathon, or the Plain of Esdraelon in Palestine. It stands across one of the great highways between Connaught and Ulster. There are at most only two strategic points where an army can cross; one, at low tide only, just below the lower bridge, and a second just above the upper bridge, opposite the Imperial Hotel, and not far from the spot (so one account says) where the warrior Eoghan Bel has stood upright in his grave, holding his spear ready, throughout fourteen centuries. For a defending or invading force, the eastern flank is protected by Lough Gill, and, if you are a soldier, you will see the road round the Lake is commanded by hills and wooded country eminently suitable for ambush. Westward, of course, you are protected by the Atlantic, moody and terrible; as the galleons of the Armada found when they were driven on the shores of Lissadell Bay. The estuaries, bays, sandbanks make it quite impracticable to outflank your enemy by naval power, as in the Elizabethan and Cromwellian combined operations on the coast of Cork. Between Sligo and Drumcliffe the great plain – where Yeats saw Constance Gore-Booth ride.

'Under Ben Bulben to the meet' –

is a perfect arena for war-chariots, and the set-piece battles of the heroic age. It was on the slopes of Ben Bulben that the Irish version of Venus and Adonis was enacted, the story of Diarmuid and Grania, and Diarmuid was slain by the enchanted ravaging boar. (That story and its symbols are as old as history.) You will see from Drumcliffe the cliffs that lie to the North-West of the Mountain, over which a troop of cavalry were driven to their death. And at least one whom I have spoken with has heard, on a foggy day on the plateau on the summit (you can reach it from the Waterfall at Glencar) the thunder of phantom hoofs, and seen the mountain grass spring up again, a few yards away, after the horsemen had passed. This, I think, stuck in Yeats's mind, for he mentions it twice:

> *What marches through the mountain pass?*
> *No, no, my son, not yet;*
> *This is an airy spot,*
> *And no man knows what treads the grass.*[2]

It was a cavern in the side of Ben Bulben that the giant Dhoya, marooned by the Formorian galleys in the Bay of the Red Cataract (you can visit the great waterfall that plunges into the head of Ballisodare Bay, and remember that Kingsley's Tom the Water-Baby came down the Yorkshire hillside 'like a salmon over the Fall at Ballisodare') sought refuge in a cave beside Glencar, and for a time lived in great happiness with a mysterious daughter of the underworld.[3] And I fancy that it was on the Drumcliffe plain, on the edge of Lissadell, that the tiny, exquisite and difficult poem 'The Death of the Hare' came to being.

> I have pointed out the yelling pack,
> The hare leap to the wood,
> And when I pass a compliment
> Rejoice as lover should
> At the dropping of an eye,
> At the mantling of the blood.
>
> Then suddenly my heart is wrung
> By her distracted air
> And I remember wildness lost

75

And after, swept from there,
Am set down standing in the wood
At the death of the hare.

You remember, too, Yeats's tribute to Constance Gore-Booth:

What voice more sweet than hers
When, young and beautiful,
She rode to harriers?[4]

iii

It is a wild history on which you can look from the great cairn
– which will never, I think, be excavated, and we shall never
know if Queen Maeve really lies there or, as some think, at
Croghan – or perhaps from the tower of one of the churches.
Let us glance at it for a moment. Sligo was invaded in A.D. 1235,
and granted to Fitzgerald, an ancestor of the Earl of Kildare.
He built a castle here in 1245, to serve as a base for his intended
conquest of Tir Chonail; and founded the Dominican Priory,
whose splendid ruins you can visit. Within half a century that
castle was destroyed *four* times by either O'Connor or O'Donnell.
In 1310 a new castle was built, and a new town laid out, by
Richard de Burgh, the Red Earl of Ulster. Five years later the
castle in its turn was destroyed by O'Donnell. In 1414 town and
friary were destroyed by fire, but were rebuilt about 1416 by
Friar Brian MacDonagh. In 1470 Red Hugh O'Donnell took the
castle once again from O'Connor: in 1595 the English, Leicester's
forces, besieged the castle and destroyed the friary. In 1641 both
town and friary were sacked by the Cromwellian general, Sir
Frederick Hamilton. In 1645 the town, having presumably
recovered from the sacking, was captured by Sir Charles Coote.
In 1689 it was seized by the Williamites under Lord Kingstown,
but was retaken by Patrick Sarsfield for King James. Then there
seems to have been a period of the Pax Britannica, and of loyalty
to the Hanoverian cause. At least we know that Sligo raised
three whole regiments of militia – all with carefully designed and
differentiated uniforms, for your soldier is a vain sort of animal
– to repel the French invasion of 1798. I mention these odd
fragments from the past only to suggest to you what a long and

turbulent history this peaceful market town has had; that there are many buried dead about us; and that any place that has been much fought over seems to acquire (as we should expect) the character of being saturated with witnesses from the unseen world. It was Jack Yeats, the painter, who told me of an ancient piece of myth: that where a great mass of fresh water meets the sea by way of a short river as it does beside us here, a kind of magic is generated and spread upon the whole neighbourhood.

iv

These may be some of the influences of place on a poet's mind, and on the kind of poetry he writes. Of this general effect, one accepts it, I think, unconsciously. That the Lake District should have fired so greatly Wordsworth's imagination, that Cowper's poetry and his hymns should be related to the placid and comfortable waters of the Ouse, that Crabbe's grim realism should spring from that 'bold surly savage race' that you still find round Aldeburgh – we take these for granted; just as we see the praise of rivers in the song of poet after poet: Spenser, Marvell, Joyce. We accept (but cannot prove) how much of Warwickshire moulded Shakespeare; or how generations of writers have found themselves and their art in Greece and Italy:

> . . . Whence turbulent Italy should draw
> Delight in Art whose end is peace,
> In logic and in natural law
> By sucking at the dugs of Greece.[5]

But there is a world of difference between reading of the genius of place and meeting that genius face to face with the words moving in our minds. When I first saw the Cave of the Cumaean Sybil, on the south of the little sandy bay where Aeneas landed from Troy, its many mouths were filled with German machine-guns sited to fire on the beach; and it took on a strange metaphysical dimension from them. To see the long-extinct volcano of Solfatera where the ground rings hollow like a drum, with its pools of boiling mud, and to realize that you are walking on one of the classic entrances to Hell, is to understand, suddenly, something of Dante. So in the Bible, above all books. One does not, I think, begin to realize the complexity and energy of its poetry until one has studied a little the geography of the Holy Land; and begun to understand how the great images of its poetry spring naturally from the clash of the desert with the valleys that stand so thick with corn; of the importance of the springing well and the waters of comfort; of whirlwind and thunder; of sudden storms upon Galilee; of the imagery of the threshing-floor and of the scattering of nations like chaff before the wind; of Israel's fear of the sea and of its great beasts that take their pastime in it. These, and a thousand other images, even to the bulwarks that defend or break the nations, spring naturally out of the very inscape of place. 'Perhaps, also, to understand fully these poems one needs to have been born and bred in one of the western Irish towns; to remember how it was the centre of your world, how the mountains and the river and the woods became a portion of your life forever; to have loved with a sense of possession even the roadside bushes where the cotters hung their clothes to dry. That sense of possession was the very centre of the matter. Elsewhere you are only a passer-by, for everything is owned by so many that it is owned by no one'.[6]

But there is another strange feature of the Sligo setting which has not, I think, been mentioned before.

All poetry is built on rhythm. Rhythm is in its turn built on stress, tone, pitch. All poets savour the juice of living words upon the tongue, 'bursting joy's grape against his palate fine' in Keats's phrase. All poets have a stock of words which they taste and relish to a special degree. If we were to take any three or four of the many poets here this morning, and analyse their vocabularies, we should find that they had in common the same large stock of words, but that they were in fact differentiated by a small individual vocabulary, perhaps a hundred or so, of words peculiar to themselves; of which they had, as it were, taken personal possession. We recall immediately some that Yeats was fond of: *wild* (in the Anglo-Irish songs;) *arrogant; fanatic; ungovernable; murmuring* and *murmur; withered; ignorant; mummy* (and *mummy-dead*); *gear; magnanimity*. We should note the polysyllabic proper names that he tastes, rolls upon the tongue: 'the Great Smaragdine Tablet', 'the Mareotic Lake', 'Guidobaldo', 'Michelozzo', 'Rhadamanthus; as well as the place-names round about Coole recorded in the poems of *The Seven Woods*. The list could be much extended. So, too, the nonce-words, those that are only used once in the poet's vocabulary of 10,666 words. But it is of the place-names of Sligo that I want to speak now.

I suggest that he found here a great reservoir of words that sing, as it were, of themselves. When we start to write Greek and Latin verse we are taught to keep note-books of phrases, proper names, synonyms, embellishments of expansions, even clichés, that have once been part of some ancient fabric of poetry, whether hexameters or elegiacs or sapphics; and which may legitimately be used again in our 'imitations'. To use these broken fragments of masonry with wit and precision, and to take advantage of allusions and references in depth, was once the mark of the scholar and of the poet who had served his apprenticeship among the classics. But if, as I believe happens here, the 'names' contain in themselves special rhythmical and musical qualities, if their complex musical values include this tone, pitch, stress so that they sing of their own accord, not only can the poetic craftsman weave them into his verse, but they may even suggest a sort of running tune, strongly remembered from childhood, out of which, or on which, the rhythm of a poem may grow.

Let us glance at some examples:

> Saddle and ride, I heard a man say,
> Out of Ben Bulben and Knocknarea.
> *What says the Clock in the Great Clock Tower?*

Now *Knócknaréa* is, technically, the foot known as a cretic, common in Irish place names because the unstressed syllable -na (of) (as in Lugnagall) is a frequent link between two heavier stresses. *Bén Búlbên* on the other hand is the foot that prosodists call a *bacchius,* a kind of rhythmic foil to the *cretic,* sliding off on to a lighter stress after its two explosive but level initial stresses: *Ben Bulben.* But to my ear the strong n-sounds that follow the stresses give a kind of sinister weight, as of the very mountain itself: and these *n*-sounds are echoed (but with a different cadence, or resolution of the chord) in *Knocknarea.*

In the same way,

> The light of evening, Lissadell,
> Great windows open to the south . . .

Líssâdéll is again a *cretic*, but softened and the initial stress lightened, smoothed down by the liquid l's and resolved in the chord by the sibilants

Liss/a/dâll

– where the drama (as it were) of the rhythm is held up for a moment so that the final stress shall be heavier.

But in 'The Ballad of Father O'Hart' we may examine the last four stanzas:

> And these were the words of John,
> When, weeping score by score,
> People came into Coloney;
> For he'd died at ninety-four.

(a bad line, even with precedents from the *Lyrical Ballads*)

> There was no human keening;
> The birds from Knocknarea
> And the world round Knocknashee
> Came keening in that day.

> The young birds and old birds
> Came flying, heavy and sad;
> Keening in from Tiraragh,
> Keening from Ballinafad.

> Keening from Inishmurray,
> Nor stayed for a bite or sup;
> This way were all reproved
> Who dig all customs up.

Now I hold no brief for this poem, even if we are charitable to it as a ballad by a very young poet, whose words and rhymes do not yet 'obey his call'; but listen to the amazing variety of the place-names:

Côloóney, technically an *amphibrach* (x/x, two short 'arms' on either side of the central stress): wholly different in sound as well as position from *Coolaney*.

Knocknarea, again,

Knôcknâshée ('the hill of the faery folk') where we have lost I think something as contrasted with the sharper e-sound of *Knocknarea,* followed by

Tîrárâgh (an amphibrach like Coolooney)

mated with the complex and lovely *Bállinâfád* which is almost a metrical phrase in itself, and which slides over the two light syllables in the middle, to the strong beat at the end. Or we have the more famous lines from 'The Fiddler of Dooney': where the rhythm of the names seems to prepare us for the dance-setting:

> When I play on my fiddle in Dooney,
> Folk dance like a wave of the sea;
> My cousin is priest in Kilvarnet,
> My brother in Mocharabuiee.

We may note several things: that Yeats has cribbed – quite justifiably – a famous line from Shakespeare's *A Winter's Tale,* where Florizel praises Perdita (note here too those singing names of the lovers)

> When you do dance I wish you
> A wave o' the sea ...

Again, hear the 'names' (I am thinking of 'Longinus') lengthen downwards as it were to the end of the verse.

Doónêy – the ordinary reversed iambic foot, the trochee

Kîlvárnêt – which is a strongly marked amphibrach again.

Móchârâbúiee – so that we end up with a four-syllable beat: [7] and we remember that this, the rhyming of the monosyllable with a poly-syllable, is a most effective technical device in Donne and Marvell.

You will read and, better, hear many other examples:

Drómâháire is a cretic, like *Knocknarea,* but the heavier stress on the last syllable gives it a different pitch –

He stood among a crowd at *Dromahaire.*

Inîsfrée, the 'isle of heather', is of this form, but with a light accent on the first syllable which again gives a different effect: while in the line

> Castle Dargan's ruin all lit,
> Lovely ladies dancing in it.

81

– the peculiar harshness of the open a's gives yet another effect to what is technically two trochaic feet of the order of / x | / x.

vi

Now I do not think this is idle speculation. I believe that Yeats learnt, as so many poets have done, something of his word-music from Spenser. His essay on that poet, and the *Selection* he made from him, have received too little attention. Look where you will, you will find these singing names in *The Faerie Queene*: Phaedra, Acrasia, Scudamore, Britomart, Florimell, Cymoducé; and those of all the renaissance ghosts that jostle each other out of Ovid's *Metamorphoses*. We remember too Milton's great catalogue of the battles that saved Western civilization, as Satan reviews those superb troops of Hell:

> And what resounds
> In fable or romance of Uther's son
> Begirt with British and Armoric knights;
> And all who since, baptised or infidel,
> Jousted in Aspramont, or Montalban,
> Damasco, or Morocco, or Trebisond,
> Or whom Biserta sent from Afric shore
> When Charlemain with all his peerage fell
> By Fontarabbia.

You will remember, too, Wordsworth's

> To lie and listen to the mountain flood
> Murmuring from Glaramara's inmost caves . . .

And I remember from my own boyhood days in Clare other mysterious and exciting names: Glenavarra, a long dark pool on a trout stream; Clondagad, with a ruined church and graveyard near it: Lough Lomáun, Thrummeragh, Clonderlaw, Gort Glas. . . . Later in life Yeats fancied himself more in the Greek world, ready to

> Choose Plato and Plotinus for a friend . . .

We have 'the great Smaragdine Tablet'; one can almost taste the name like a pistachio-nut; 'the many-headed foam of Salamis', the Mareotic Lake; all the names of poets, sculptors, painters that flit through the works: Guidobaldo, Michelozzo, Veronese, Mantegna. So Michael Angelo, out of which he extracts two wholly different rhythms (the second a kind of resolution of the chord)

> Michael Angelo left a proof
> On the Sistine Chapel roof . . .

as against

> There on that scaffolding reclines
> Michael Angelo.

I do not think this fanciful, and your ears will note these subtle discriminations of sound: as they will have been trained to do by Shakespeare and Donne and Keats and Bridges. I suggest one caution only.

In Prosody, that ancient science, we can go just so far only. We may gesture towards stresses and accents, vowel and consonantal combinations, and sometimes profit by such exercises. Only by these devices can we explore, for instance, Milton's exquisite counterpointing, by a kind of secondary rhythm, the primary wavemotion of the iambic line. But in the last resort we have no valid language for the critical discussion of rhythm, either in verse or in the movements of a play, though we commonly speak of rhythm as an aspect of dramatic structure, of the advance and retreat of sympathy, or participation, or alienation. In poetry there is one test only: your own ear, and what it tells you of the energy, momentum, the finality of the line. And that is why part of our study should concern (as Jon Stallworthy has shown)[9] the fragments from Yeats's workshop, the perpetual testing of the music by the ear, so that we may, if we are lucky, know for ourselves that perfection and finality that we call great poetry.

vii

And here I want to attempt to lay one heresy by the heel. Sometimes my young men come and say to me: 'O we aren't interested now in what the poem *sounds* like, we're only interested in how it *looks* on the page'. Granted that interesting and perhaps valuable effects can be achieved by typography, that the angels' wings of the Seventeenth Century or the experiments of, say, E. E. Cummings, have their place, the poet has always traditionally been the singer as well as the maker, the seer, the visionary, the unacknowledged legislator of the world. And for all those the voice seems to me essential.

It is for this reason (which Yeats would have approved) that Sligo has insisted that poetry is, among much else, music; and that it should be read aloud, interpreted, discussed, in terms of the human voice. Here of course we are in a mysterious country, and a numinous one; the word or the Word, and its power, on Sinai or beside the Lake. And it may well be that we are in danger of losing our sense of the capacity of the voice to transmit meaning, and the subtle qualities of emotion that go with this kind of meaning; as well as the modulations of which a most delicate instrument is, after due training, capable. We know that Yeats's own experiments with 'Speaking to the Psaltery' were not successful. Whenever I have heard attempts to read poetry against some kind of musical background I have nearly always been disappointed, even frustrated. I would even say that, with a few superb exceptions which we all know, poetry and music do not form too happy a union. A strong music allows you to get away with murder as regards the poetry itself, and this the Elizabethan song-writers knew and often exploited in those often vapid and embroidered verses for madrigals. To interpret by reading aloud has from the beginning been a feature of Sligo, not only in the public readings of Yeats, and by poets of distinction, but by the students themselves. It is the first path to understanding. And one who has helped us so greatly is Mary Watson, the best reader of poetry whom I have heard.

You see, many people come to Sligo with, as it were, empty hands, saying in effect:

'I don't know much about Ireland, or Yeats, or indeed poetry. But I want to learn about these things.'

And Sligo has always held such people to be immensely important. We have not yet had to impose any entrance test for registration. We have instead provided seminars, centre of discussion, where we can learn. It would have been only too easy to have pitched the standard at a level where we had only professors, university teachers, advanced students; and many Summer Schools and Conferences do just that. It seems to me entirely fitting that a proportion here are not, and do not want to become, professional students of literature or 'to cough in ink'; but have come to get to know Ireland, and Sligo, and poetry. How many is, I believe, irrelevant. No teacher ever knows where the seed falls, or what grain may chance from it. No one can ever tell when the ripples from the stones thrown into the pool will end on some farther shore.

So we have lectures at a high level (probably from the most distinguished scholars in two Continents), seminars at all levels, and discussions – wherever you will. Nothing is more admirable than the way in which students, in this sort of setting, begin to *teach one another*; and themselves learn as they do so. And if the time is short, a mere thirteen days, it provides at least some of the tools (such as those in our Bibliographies and other papers) for those who want to use them in the future. No university course, in whatever subject, can be more than a springboard for the future; unless indeed we were to return to the happy days of the Druid Bards, and prescribe a fourteen years' course for the final examination.

viii

This is, perhaps a time at which we might reflect, not only on the Place of Shells, and on music, and poetry, and history; but upon the fact of this International School. If it had been pre-planned instead of growing up spontaneously because of the character of the Town and of the Society, it might have been more logical to have held it in one of the great Irish universities; where accommodation, administration, transport and the like would have lain to hand. It is not, I think, a secret that several American universities would have gladly caught it up into the resources of their wealth and scholarship. But this bad world seems to me (at times) to be over-planned. One of you said to me last year: 'This is the only place left where a poet can read his poetry without feeling self-conscious and over-organized.' I suspect that that was – is – only partly true: yet I know that many of the Poetry Competitions, Festivals and such-like have not been altogether happy

places. I like to think that here we are still casual, carefree, with
no papers to write for credits, no prizes to compete for; and that
we use to the full this unique and magical and very ancient place.
Yeats's father boasts to his son of his family "We have given a
tongue to the sea-cliffs". But the son gave more than that to sea,
mountain, lake.

ix

Yet I would not have it thought that one of our functions is
less than that of providing a meeting-place for the most advanced
and famous scholars. We are indebted to very many who have
taught here over the past decade, and to those who are not with
us whose inheritance we use. Among these last are my own
friends. Among them, Joseph Hone, the first of the Yeats
biographers; Una Ellis Fermor, whose account of the Irish
Dramatic Movement remains a classic; my friend and pupil Peter
Allt.

x

Yet there is so much more to be done: in scholarship, and in
teaching. One day there must be a definitive edition, properly
edited and cross-referenced to the plays and poems, of the Collected Prose. Remember two things; that Yeats's work, like
Shakespeare's, or Milton's, or Arnold's, must be seen as a unity:
and also that the volumes of essays, papers and prefaces that you
know and use differ in some respects from their originals. When
all the manuscript materials of *A Vision* are made available it
will be possible to make a calm assessment of two important
books, round whose walls so many scholars of note have marched
blowing on a variety of rams' horns. When Warner's long-
promised edition of Cornelius Agrippa is completed some new
light will be thrown on Yeats's so-called 'magical' preoccupations
being the end of the long road that led back from Blake through
Swedenborg and Boehme; though I myself would question Yeat's
contention that there was a time when Agrippa was familiar to
every Irish farmer.

xi

Such scholarship is vital; yet there is always the danger that Sligo might be tempted to keep its eyes fixed too closely on the sea-shore, on the smaller shells (however delicate) at its feet. We dare not view a great poet in a lesser setting than that of his time, his friends, and his age, his predecessor and contemporaries; and, ultimately, against the tradition of Western Europe. It would be only too easy, here, to fall into some kind of bardolatry, to let the appetite sicken, surfeit, die. Some form of dilettanteism is an ever-present danger. So far we have tried (and it is my hope that we shall continue) to set beside him some of his great contemporaries: 'A.E.', Synge, George Moore, James Stephens, Lady Gregory. Nor would it be wrong to predict that, as well as hearing them read their own work, some of the living here may join that tradition. Among the host of excellent books there is as yet no 'great' one to lead us through the whole labyrinth of the Irish Literary Revival. I use the word labyrinth with deliberation; for surely there is no literary movement or history of which the setting is so complex, the shifts of emphasis so pronounced with the veering of its intrinsic history and politics, the friendships and hatreds so intense. Out of that comes, of course, the energy of the time; for – again –

> Out of Ireland have we come.
> Great hatred, little room.

xii

The mystery of Sligo remains, and I would have it remain a mystery: as of something which has grown organically, and (as some would say) by chance; out of a map of the 'Yeats Country' in a chemist's shop, a request for a single lecture at the height of the tourist season. It has grown as the ancient universities have done. Some years ago the Yeats Society consulted me about the possibility of a University here. As I remember, my estimate of the cost of such a foundation today closed the discussion. But indeed with all the money and plant, the power of buying professors, you cannot make a University. This some have lately found; to their cost. Here at Sligo I would like to think that men and women will continue to come, as they have come from the time of Plato's academy onwards, to sit at the feet of famous scholars and poets. That, and not a degree or a diploma, is the essence of education. Granted that the time is all too short (though this may be one aspect of its strength); granted that many things are lacking in materials and accommodation (though there may be one day a worthy building[10] for us and the Museum); there is yet this fact that, year after year, men and women of the greatest eminence have come here to make this School. And I can find no reason other than the charity of great minds, the certainty of unjealous friendship and a passion for poetry, and the genius of the Place of Shells, of its people, and of the Society who have made a reality of what was once no more than a 'surmised shape', a living memorial.

NOTES

1 Sligo: The opening lecture, 1968. First published in T. R. Henn's *Last Essays*, Gerrards Cross & New York, 1976.

2 'Three Marching Songs', II. Yeats notes that airy 'may be an old pronunciation of eerie. But we also use it of 'high places', and of their numen.

3 See *John Sherman and Dhoya*, ed. R. S. J. Finneran, New York, 1969.

4 'Easter, 1916'.

5 'To a Wealthy Man . . .'

6 From an essay by Yeats on William Allingham: quoted by Finneran. Preface to *John Sherman and Dhoya* (v. supra). For Palestine, see T. R. Henn. *The Bible as Literature*, London, 1971.

7 The pronunciation that Yeats gives in a footnote is not (in my experience) quite accurate.

8 *The King of the Great Clock Tower*. See also the *Variorum Edition of the Poems of W. B. Yeats*, London, 1957, p. 733.

9 *Between the Lines*, Oxford, 1963; *Yeats's Last Poems*, London, 1968.

10 This came to pass, by the generosity of the Allied Irish Banks, in 1973.

HOW GOES THE WEATHER?

JOHN HOLLOWAY

Local people in the Yeats Country – Sligo or Clare – are conscious of how the south-west is the prevailing wind, and the weather comes from the sea; but they will sometimes tell you, all the same, that it is the south or south-east wind that will bring the worst rain. Incidentally, when I write about the wind in those parts, it is fitting that I should record the melancholy and perhaps historic occasion when a County Mayo farmer, a middle-aged man, was speaking to me about the weather, and spoke of the 'wind', pronouncing that word to rhyme with 'find', not 'finned'; but was immediately corrected by his eleven-year-old son. Be that as it may, local people in the West may not know why the worst weather comes on those winds, but they are quite in the right on the matter. The cyclones come in from the ocean on the prevailing south-westerly airstream, but the local winds in a cyclonic system blow anti-clockwise, in towards the centre of the depression. So the onset of a south-east wind is a clear sign that within a few hours, the centre of a depression will pass more or less overhead.

Another way of understanding this is to have in mind that the wind always veers (that is, changes in a clockwise direction) three points on the passing over of a warm front – which is what produces the long steady rain. So, on the Irish coast, the wind in advance of the rain is always likely to be more southerly than the prevailing south-westerly wind. Often, though, the exact direction will depend on the site of a mountain mass or a mountain pass. The West is a land of micro-climates, and often enough, I have watched almost continuous rain falling all day, at a distance of about three miles, and stayed dry, though outdoors, myself.

In this open, spacious country, you can hardly fail to notice a change in the wind; and changes are frequent, and often sudden. Within a few moments, if you are well out in the open, everything around you becomes subtly but wholly different. If you were walking with a north-east breeze behind you, the air has been chill, the cloud-level a hard, iron grey, sharp but featureless, the

89

hills standing out razor-edged but almost black. You notice that
the air has somehow changed, it is still now; suddenly, it is warm;
then, almost at once, the endless yellow tick-tock, tick-tock of the
buttercups and the hawkweeds will start up again, but this time
the flowers will be nodding and bowing towards you. All day long,
right across the meadows and the bog, these flowers will have been
bowing up and down one way; now they change, and do it the
other.

Before long, the likelihood is, the wind will begin to rise, the
clouds go more silvery, their edges begin to soften, you think the
rain has begun and feel a few spots of it coming on the wind.
Yet usually there will be a succession of seeming beginnings, the
cloud-bank will flow over some southern hill lower and faster, the
breeze feel soft and clammy; but then, that breeze will go a touch
lighter, and the cloud momentarily harden and shift higher in the
sky. As, in the end, the wind begins to rise good and proper, you
hear it everywhere around, about the house if you are indoors,
and right inside the house too, it seems, if you are in one of the
old houses. It may bring the deeper, rougher sound of the sea,
that always comes surprisingly close, it seems near at hand even
though you know the sea is, maybe, two or three miles away.
Soon you hear the rain too, if you are in a one-storey house. Its
at first almost shy rustle on the roof turns to quite a sharp hiss as
it thickens, though not to the heavy thud and patter of eastern
rain. Out of doors, on the road or the puddles, you hear it too;
or more lightly, there comes a faint sound, a kind of shushing
sound, from the leaves and plants everywhere under the rain, it
fills the air just as the rain does.

As the wind veers westerly the rain becomes denser, though it
may become finer too; the cloud-table lowers, all the hills are
blotted out by a single sheet, silver-grey and formless but the
whole width of the sky. You will think this rain too gentle, too
much like simply a kind of mist, to make you wet; but if you are
long outdoors, you will be soaked to the skin unless you are
properly clad. Oilskins are no good unless you are covered in
them to the shoes. What will fall on your coat like a mere distilla-
tion of cloud will soon be rivering abundantly down, and your
trousers will be as if you had stepped into the lake. When it is
like this, the air fills with a pale mist, or often with tall vertical
bands of rain, a few feet at a time, and interspersed with what
looks like emptiness, but in fact is only a little less wet), the whole

way across the valley. These minute cycles, or wave-formations, are the small version of the true rise-and-fall cyclically over a whole belt of rain, often on a period of about twenty minutes or so.

When it is like this, the whole landscape will be silvered over, or the distance or indeed the middle distance may be blotted out; and if you look closely, every spicule of the flowering grasses bears what looks like a minute drop of dew ('Abounding foliage moistened with the dew', 'Vacillation', *Collected Poems,* p. 282); and the scent of vegetation mixed with wetness can be overpowering. You have a strange sense that it is not simply a 'soft day' at all, but that you are deep within some pregnant, potent, secret part of the planet where the ordinary weather for the rest of the world is primordially made. This comes first to mind as an idle fancy. Then you realize that, speaking by and large, it is true.

A real gale of wind, usually from the south-west (but I have known gales from the north or the north-east, and then they are cool or cold as well as tempestuous) seems to weight the air, to give it not only a great motion but also a heaviness, as if it were going to become solid. Out of doors there is noise everywhere, not the noise ubiquitous but gentle of a 'soft day', but self-willed and strident, shrill. Or more, it is like that while the wind is still boisterous and rising but at the height of a storm it is all-consuming, settled, in deadly earnest over something you cannot put a name to. The climaxes of wind come recurrently, I think on a longer rhythm than with the lighter rain. When Yeats begins 'A Prayer for My Daughter' with the words 'Once more the storm is howling . . .' this rise-and-fall must be what is in his mind, he is not likening the storm in the poem to some storm of a week, or a month, before. The noise of wind runs through all his verse: '. . . how bitter is that wind/That shakes the shutter' (*CP,* 151); '. . . that haystack and roof-levelling wind/Bred on the Atlantic' (*CP,* 211); '. . . this desolate lake/What wind cries in the sedge' ('He Hears the Cry of the Sedge', *CP,* 75); 'These winds that clamour of approaching night' ('Nineteen Hundred and Nineteen', *CP,* 235); 'I woke in an old ruin/That the winds howled through' ('The Curse of Cromwell',*CP,* 351). I have never seen a haystack levelled, but I have seen the big haycocks, in a wide meadow on a far hillside, toppled slowly, almost gracefully over, one by one, and swept into the hedge below, in spite of the twisted hay-rope or *sougan* they were made fast with. In winter on a day of heavy

91

rain the cloud cover may be so thick that the air, even at midday, can take on an almost brown tinge, and the rain seem to be falling at late evening not at noon-day. But that is a thing for late autumn or winter rather than summer.

On any day of continuous rain, the light is so pale and pearly that you fail to realise how little light there is; until towards evening (this is usually the time) the breeze begins to fall and the rain gets lighter, fluctuating in waves of rain and then rainlessness. The level of the clouds imperceptibly lifts until the bases, and then the lower slopes of the mountains appear again, but still monochrome grey. Rough forms begin to re-appear in the unbroken grey plane of cloud that has been overhead for maybe a couple of days. As the warmer air comes in from the west, the drenched soil gives its moisture back into the air, first from the tree-branches, that take most of whatever wind still blows, then from the bushes and rain-soaked plants of the bog – what is in the ground itself is already fast running away in the noisy, clucking gullets and glaishes. Then, the moist air rises because it is warm, and the wet condenses again in long, bold sweeps and swirls of grey, especially before the western face of a mountain, where the slope is forcing the wind upwards:

> A mist that is like blown snow is sweeping over all . . .
> . . . a puff of wind
> And those white glimmering fragments of the mist pass by.
> ('Meditations in Time of Civil War', *CP,* 231)

These broad swathes of misty cloud can make it look as if a whole mountain is smoking and smouldering, a great smouldering bonfire. Little by little, as the weather-change goes on, they will fade away, and one by one the hill-tops will appear, and the clouds will break here and there. Yeats's lines (those I have just quoted from 'Meditations in Time of Civil War') are about Thoor Ballylee and northern County Clare. Among the Sligo Mountains, mist that forms when there is a wind will shape itself into wreaths and wraiths and plumes, take its place as one feature in a landscape, and, through contrast, make the hills it floats among look as black as ink.

As the weather brightens, clear sky will appear in a band of blue, slowly opening up and spreading out from the cloud, and broadening, out to sea. You will wait for it to arrive on the wind,

only to find that it never does. As the upper air begins to come
in over the land, it is chilled; besides that, the air is driven up-
ward by the coastal hills, and it rises, so that it is chilled again.
Part of its moisture condenses steadily out, hour after hour all
day, into cloud. So there will be a grey edge of cloud, stationary
and out at sea; and that band of blue will remain, remote, beyond
it, and the sun not appear, although the rain is over, until lateish
in the evening. But when it has westered enough to come out
below that grey line, it will rapidly, suddenly suffuse the whole
landscape. You see the dark line of the front edge of the sunlight
racing across the ground to the west of you, then it flashes by, and
you are bathed in light. This orange-yellow evening light, warm
and wet-seeming, makes the landscape somehow greener than
ever.

At these times the day, of course, grows much brighter even
though it is drawing to a close; and where the blue sky is appearing in the far west, if there is turbulence over the ocean, in the
upper air, huge clouds, forming and mounting at a great distance,
will be lit into a dull, almost lurid greyish-orange.

> These are the clouds about the fallen sun . . .
> ('These are the Clouds' *CP,* 107)

Or, seeming nearer in to the land, there will be shafts of light, all
diverging from the invisible point of the sun, still hidden behind
the long wall of the nearer clouds. These volumes and spaces, far
out to sea and seeming of immense height, and motionless, may
explain the legends of holy isles, out beyond the sealine of the
west, the blessed home of those who have departed this life of
clouded and rainy places:

> . . . when the west
> Had surged up in a plumy fire. . . .
> (*The Wanderings of Oisin II, CP,* 429)

In fine weather, big showers come in quickly from the sea, they
can be boisterous, it is almost melodrama, at these times the sky
is full of violence and variety and seems to be alive. Fair-weather
clouds and rainclouds can sweep across each other. I have seen
a towering cumulus cloud, of great size by inland standards, a
true cloud of summer weather, and only after a moment or so

realized that its background was not the open sky, but an enormous cumulo-nimbus storm-head, rising greyly to a vast height, feathering out at the top into storm-cirrus that went out across almost the whole sky, and totally dwarfing its abundant summery neighbour.

Such clouds rarely produce thunder as they might do inland, but sudden intense showers, with rising wind and a lot of noise from the rain on the plants everywhere – loudest on the tree-leaves. Often at such times, there will seem to be contrary winds in the sky, clouds moving at right angles to each other, or the vertical growth of a storm-head spreading directly against the movement of the lower clouds, or the direction of the wind on the ground. Especially at evening, when the sun is low out at sea, these heavy showers produce rainbows of brilliant brightness, even the secondary bow is clear and sharp, and you can see the primary bow easily even at the bottom edges, where it spreads its colours out across the bog. If you are on high ground that falls away towards the rainy side, you can see the rainbow as more than a half-circle. Once in the West, looking down from a hill-top, I saw the complete circle, a whole iridescent ring motionless in the rain-filled air, but this was a mist-bow not a rainbow.

Occasionally, in summer, the West will be like Greece, with cloudless sky and blazing sun all day, and some of the local people will begin to predict that it is the beginning of a change in the climate. The sea will have scarcely a ripple, and will lap and swill almost in silence at the edge of the great pale strands ('. . . the white border of the murmuring sea': 'Fergus and the Druid', *CP*, 36). The mountains seem soaked in light but curiously drained of colour. All the colour will be in the low land, where you find '. . . noon a purple glow'), 'The Lake of Innisfree', *CP*, 36). But one must take it, I think, that 'purple' in that line has its archaic poetic sense, what one can find in Thomson or Akenside, coming from Latin and meaning colourful in general rather than any one colour. Distances begin to collapse, and the eye is confused. As the sun goes down, the hazy valleys begin to lose the light and, at a distance, shapes in them dissolve. The unlit slopes, as evening wears on, turn a deep, rich blue, lustrous yet velvety, and if the sun is fully behind the slope, the ridges have a thick sharp fringe of gold capping their silhouetted outline.

When the nights are clear, you will be conscious of the crescent moon, not just as somewhere in the sky, but as following round, after the sun, in some kind of long and spacious monthly order. It goes on its slow, slanting flight down into the west, down into where the sun has set already. Then, after a few days, it will be the full moon, rising from some certain, remembered place over the eastern mountain slopes. Always it seems enormous when it rises, and you sense how it is rising near the place of sunrise; but if you see the full moon setting, down behind the south-western hills late in the night or a little before dawn, it will seem small and remote. Perhaps you will begin to think of how, crescent or full, what is making the moon rise is the turning of the earth from west to east. But since, at the same time, the moon itself is describing an orbit about the earth, it is later, every evening, that the moon at last appears above the hills in the east . . . our point on the surface of the earth has each evening to rotate further round, before the moon is overtaken. In a town, when the night sky is glimpsed only occasionally, and then among glaring lamps and neon signs, all that is forgotten. Here, in the 'formless fathomless darkness', ('Two Songs from a Play' II, *CP,* 239), in a landscape in some places still without power lighting, the moon-rise of the moon near the full is an event, solemn, splendid and portentous. First, while it is still unrisen, you see it slowly brightening and yellowing the clouds; then, little by little, its circle rises above some hillside and (on a clear night) its light covers the ground and spreads across the landscape, sharp and luminous. All at once, if you are walking, you can put away a torch, step out as you would by day.

Above all it is the steady getting later of the moonrise that brings the month together into one, and, away from a town, gives a pattern and design even to the year. 'Twenty and eight the phases of the moon', is a truth that shows itself before you, in a grand yet familiar simplicity, every night. Even in thick cloud there will often be a vague light, a submerged brightness, that will tell you of the moon being up although you cannot see it, and will fit this cloudy night into the changing rhythm of the month.

Nor is this the only nightly movement that, in such an open and unlighted place, becomes familiar. On a cloudless and moonless night the stars will appear in astonishing brilliance, right down to the horizon. 'There midnight's all a-glimmer' ('The Lake Isle of Innisfree', *CP,* 44) is an understatement by far. The two-branched Milky Way, that spectacle of the largest example of foreshortening known to man, becomes a well-known and inescapable sight;

95

and far southern stars, Procyon or Antares, that are too near the horizon to be often seen where there is more man-made light and less purity in the air, become familiar too. More memorable is the nightly rotation of the stars, dark counterpart to the rotation by day of the sun. The polarity of the Pole Star (Homer and the Milesians, three thousand years ago, were without it – for them the centre of the heavens was blackness) at last becomes meaningful if you are out for long by night, because you see all the other stars wheeling steadfastly about it, to make up so marvellous a unity in the sky that 'the zodiac is changed into a sphere' ('Chosen' *CP*, 311) inevitably comes into the mind, although by those words Yeats meant something else. The distinction between constellations like Orion that you can watch rising or setting (in places related orderly, of course, to where the sun and moon do so) and those like the Bear that are too near to the Pole ever to set ('That was in ocean stream yet never wet', wrote Spenser, learning the fact, perhaps, in this unlighted land, though further east and south), fixes itself in the mind; and among all the stars, gradually, you come to have a feel for the planets too, as they 'wander' (what their name means): Mars, reddish; Venus, whether in twilight or at dawn, always low in the sky; Jupiter, it seems, always high in the sky, and golden and enormous. All of them move a fraction on, every night, from where they were before. Mercury I have seen, rare and faint, only once or twice, between dawn and sunrise, between Venus and the Sun.

When the rain is continuous there are no birds to be seen, the traveller asks himself if more than usual – more than ever – died the previous winter; but as fair weather spreads back, they re-appear. Wheatears will flash their patches of white at you as they fly by starts ahead, keeping their distance; or the aptly-named stonechats re-appear among the low whins, fearless almost as a robin, and continually giving their brief call, that seems so intimate and sounds like tapping two pebbles together. Little groups of linnets will drop down out of the air with a gay chatter, and not only the evening be 'full of the linnet's wings' ('The Lake Isle of Innisfree', *CP*, 44) as they come 'dispensing round/Their magnanimities of sound' ('A Prayer for my Daughter', *CP*, 213). Or perhaps there will be a charm of goldfinches or a family of greenfinches, that whistle as if they were filled with a kind of unassuming curiosity. If a ruined house stands fairly away by itself ('. . . an old ruin that the wind howls through'; 'The Curse of Cromwell', *CP*, 351) it is sure to have several pairs of jackdaws quick with their jocular clacking but slow to leave as you come near. High in the sky, and flying a long straight course as if they came from far away and still had distant business, maybe a pair of ravens will pass over, uttering their beautiful croak, deep and affable. Ravens mate for life. Over many years, in the part of the West that I know best myself, there have been three ravens that always flew together: a pair, doubtless, with one solitary young. This year there were four. Herons nest in the occasional scraps of oak-wood ('Because we love bare hills and stunted trees'; 'Hound Voice', *CP*, 385) – remnants, it may be, of remote times even before the first forest-burning, by the Norsemen: between the heron and the magpie, unending war. Wind may bring rarer species, a short-eared owl hunting over the bog in broad daylight, the almost black flash of a merlin, or the wild geese. Curlews feed in numbers along the strand ('O curlew, cry no more in the air,/Or only to the water in the West'; 'He Reproves the Curlew', *CP*, 69), along with dunlin, ringed plover and the pied oyster-catcher. Just out beyond the breaking waves the black-and-white terns or 'sea-swallows' (rightly called) patrol effortlessly for fish and drop like bombs into the water when they see one. Farther out – you see them if you take a boat to one of the islands maybe – the gannets follow the same hunting pattern on a bigger scale. I have seen them plummet maybe two or three hundred feet on to a shoal – mackerel I suppose.

In 1919, Yeats wrote:

> I am thinking of a child's vow made in vain
> Never to leave that valley his fathers called their home.
> (Under Saturn', *CP*, 202)

– 'in vain', maybe. But if Yeats's vow had been never to forget the West-of-Ireland landscape and its rain and sun, its day and night, its living creatures, its endless wind and immense scale – that would not have been vowed in vain.

YEATS AND THE WRONG LEVER*

A. NORMAN JEFFARES

I

Yeats made an early – and oblique – reference to Charles Lever in an article published in the *Providence Sunday Journal* of 2 September 1888.[1] This piece, 'The Poet of Ballyshannon', was based upon William Allingham's *Irish Songs and Poems* (1887), and Yeats once claimed that one needed to have been born and bred in a western Irish seaboard town to understand these poems. Originally, he had formed an ambition of writing about Sligo as Allingham had about Ballyshannon. But he had his reservations about Allingham. Though he is always Irish, he said, he is no way national, and 'this widely effects (*sic*) his work'.[2] Allingham created isolated artistic moments; he had a need of central seriousness: 'Like Lever and Lover he does not take the people quite seriously'.[3] This damaging description, this yoking together of Lever and Lover was repeated later in this piece for the *Providence Journal* with even more damaging comments:

> What a sad business this non-nationalism has been! It gave to Lever and Lover their shallowness and still gives to a section of Dublin Society its cynicism! Lever and Lover and Allingham alike, it has deprived of their true audience. Many much less endowed writers than they have more influence in Ireland. Political doctrine was not demanded of them, merely nationalism. They would not take the Ascendancy – and had to go to England for their audience. To Lever and Lover Ireland became merely a property shop and to Allingham a half serious memory.[4]

Yeats continued his incidental sniping in an essay on 'Popular Ballard Poetry of Ireland'[5] published the following year, but probably written in 1887:

> Lever and Lover, kept apart by opinion from the body of the nation, wrote ever with one eye on London. They never wrote

* Part of this essay was given as a lecture in Sligo in 1976.

for the people, and neither have they ever, therefore, in prose
or verse, written faithfully of the people. Ireland was a metaphor to [Thomas] Moore, to Lever and Lover a merry harle-
quin, sometimes even pathetic, to be patted and pitied and
laughed at so long as he said 'your honour', and presumed in
nowise to be considered a serious or tragic person.[6]

Yeats did not discuss the poetry of Moore, Lever or Lover in this
piece – though he thought the English reader might be surprised
that there was no mention of them. But 'they were never poets of
the people'.[7]

In his Introduction to *Representative Irish Tales* Yeats spelt out
his idea even more clearly:

Charles Lever, unlike Lover and Croker, wrote mainly for
his own class. His books are quite sufficiently truthful, but
more than any other Irish writer has he caught the ear of the
world and come to stand for the entire nation. The vices and
virtues of his characters are alike those of the gentry – a gentry
such as Ireland has had, with no more sense of responsibility,
as a class, then have the *dullahans,* thrivishes, sowlths, bowas
and water sheries of the spirit-ridden peasantry.[8]

In view of his admission that Lever's books were 'quite sufficiently
truthful', it is perhaps not so surprising that Yeats, in an article
entitled 'The Young Ireland League', printed in *United Ireland,*
3 October, 1891, recommended that reading-rooms should be
established by the Young Ireland societies, to be stocked with
libraries containing 'not only the best Irish books, but the masterpieces of other countries as well'.[9] And he suggested that these
libraries should include:

Mitchel, Mangan, Davis, both prose and verse, all the Irish
ballad collections, the radiant and romantic histories of
Standish O'Grady, the 'Celtic Romances' of [P.W.] Joyce, the
poems of Sir Samuel Ferguson, the poems of William Allingham
the best novels of Carleton, Banim, Griffin and Lever, three or
four of the Irish stories of Miss Edgeworth, the folk-lore writing
of Hyde, Croker, and Lady Wilde, Moore's Melodies, and some
of the best translations from the old Celtic epics.[10]

In passing, Yeats attacked a list of the 'hundred best Irish books' which had appeared in *The Freeman's Journal,* and then been published in pamphlet form in 1886. He made his own list of thirty books, included in a letter to the Editor of the Dublin *Daily Express* of 27 February, 1895; these books were ones which seemed to him 'necessary to the understanding of the imagination of Ireland'.[11] He had excluded every book in which there was strong political feeling. In the section 'Novels and Romances' he included as the eleventh item out of thirteen in this section of his list Lever's *Charles O'Malley,* and described it – along with 'Father Tom and the Pope', 'Barney O'Reirdon' and Carleton's *Traits and Stories of the Irish Peasantry* – as being 'also in a sense true records but [which] need no recommendation, for the public has always given a gracious welcome to every book which amuses it and does not let it take Ireland seriously. . . .'[12]

This business of the list arose out of Yeats's controversy with Professor Edward Dowden over 'Irish National Literature'. In *The Bookman* Yeats pursued the matter further. Four articles appeared in July, August, September and October 1895. In the last article Yeats gave another list, this time of forty titles and this time Lever's *Charles O'Malley* again appeared eleventh in the section *Novels and Romances,* which now included eighteen titles.

He then seems to have left Lever alone until 1908, when, in the course of attacking nineteenth century Irish novelists for having an English influence running through them, he makes a slight exception for Lever:

> Here and there, of course, one finds Irish elements. In Lever, for instance, even after one has put aside all that is second-hand, there is a rightful Irish gaiety, but one finds these elements only just in so far as the writers had come to know themselves in the socratic sense.[13]

Two more remarks about Lever are to be found, both in the section of *Autobiographies* entitled 'The Trembling of the Veil'.[14] The first contrasted Lever with the Wildes: 'The Wilde family was clearly of the sort that fed the imagination of Charles Lever, dirty, untidy, daring, and what Charles Lever, who loved more normal activities, might not have valued so highly, very imaginative and learned'. The second described some of the youthful

Yeats's Dublin enemies: 'There were others with followers of their own, and too old or indifferent to join our Society. Old men who had never accepted Young Ireland, or middle-aged men kept by some family tradition to the school of thought before it arose, to the Ireland of Daniel O'Connell and of Lever and of Thomas Moore, convivial Ireland with the traditional tear and smile.[15]

There are problems here. How many of Lever's thirty-three novels had Yeats actually read? And how right was he in his critical view of Lever? We could argue that, since he put *Charles O'Malley* into his reading list, he regarded that as 'the best of Lever'. But what was the nature, the range of Lever's novels from which he could select? And who was Lever, anyway?

II

Charles James Lever was born in Dublin in 1806. His father, James Lever, a builder's apprentice who came to Dublin from Manchester, became a successful builder and contractor, who built the Custom House, the General Post Office, the Round Church and St. George's Church. He adapted the Parliament building when it became a bank after the Act of Union. He married a Miss Candler, from County Kilkenny, of Cromwellian stock. Lever sent his two sons to Trinity College, remarking that they could not live the lives of idle gentlemen. He gave them 'a fair start in life but nothing to deprive them of the pleasure of making their fortunes'.[16] John, the elder brother, entered the Church of Ireland, and Charles drew his early knowledge of the West from visits to him at Portumna in County Galway. Charles went to small schools in Dublin, John tutored him, and he entered Trinity in 1822. Here he had a full life of party-going, riding, sailing, drinking and hoaxing; he also read widely, enjoying Terence, Molière, Shakespeare, Cervantes, and Le Sage – and the classic Anglo-Irish writers, Swift, Sterne, Goldsmith, Sheridan. . . . A graduate in 1827, he set off for the wilds of Canada and New York state. He was held captive by an Indian tribe, rescued by a squaw, with whom he may have had a love affair, and then walked the streets of Quebec 'in the moccasins and, with the head feathers' (His novels *Con Cregan* and *Arthur O'Leary* draw on his North American experiences). He brought back an Indian canoe which he used in the Grand Canal on his return to Dublin.

101

From Dublin he went to Paris and to Germany, where he studied at Gottingen, and then went to study at Louvain. He was destined for medicine; he graduated M.B. in 1831, but failed the College of Surgeons' Fellowship examination and so gave up his brief attempts to become a successful Dublin doctor, choosing instead the post of a dispensary doctor in County Clare, and experiencing the horrors of a cholera epidemic there for four months. Next he spent five years in Derry at Portstewart, again as a dispensary doctor. While here he married Kate Baker, with whom he had fallen in love as a schoolboy in Dublin and whom he loved all his life. It was a secret marriage, as her father, a schoolmaster who had moved to Navan, and Lever's father both disapproved thoroughly of the idea, James Lever because Kate had no money.

Provincial life – and the tiresome nature of his employers, the Poor-Law guardians – bored him. He went to Brussels where he built up a promising practice and had a highly enjoyable social life. Then in 1842 he gave this up and returned to Dublin: he had decided to live by his pen. He was offered the editorship of the *Dublin University Magazine* on condition he contributed part of a story each month, and he was given what was then a very good salary of £1200 a year. He lived at Bridge House, Templeogue (in more recent times the residence of the poet Austin Clarke) and entertained lavishly there.

What had led to this change? Largely the success of *The Confessions of Harry Lorrequer,* the first instalment of which had appeared in the *Dublin University Magazine* in 1837. Here was a hero whose life was a round of dining, drinking, dancing, riding, steeple-chasing, pigeon shooting and tandem driving; this energetic life, that of a property owner, was matched to a curiously dreamy character who plays a Hamlet-like role, translated into pure farce against the comic background of the garrison's social life.

Lever had begun his novel in imitation of William Hamilton Maxwell, author of *Wild Sports of the West* and *Tales of the Peninsula War,* who had encouraged him to write. Lever was surprised by his success, *Harry Lorrequer* being published in three volumes, and his future work eagerly sought by rival Dublin and London publishers.

There followed *Charles O'Malley,* written in Brussels when Lever was very low with fortune, and the success of a new venture was pretty much as eventful to me as the turn of the right colour at rouge et noir. At the same time I had then an amount of spring in my temperament, and a power of enjoying life, which I can honestly say I never found surpassed. The world had for me all the interest of an admirable comedy.[16a]

This novel, obviously considered Lever's best by Yeats, was strung together somewhat more effectively than the picaresque *Harry Lorrequer*. There is a picture of ascendancy life, of governmental corruption, of electoral malpractice, and of riotous undergraduate behaviour in Trinity College, Dublin, personified by Frank Webber (founded on the man who had shared rooms in Trinity College with Lever). The hero leaves the university for the army, and, having had more than his share of the Peninsula War, returns to his uncle's estate, which he runs efficiently, only to come back to the army when Napoleon escapes from Elba. Finally he marries one of the heroines and settles down in the west.

Lever describes the topography of the battles superbly; he inserts comic situations and anecdotes freely; and he conveys, notably in the excellent account of Waterloo, his disgust at the waste of war. There are lively characterisations, emphasised by a caricaturist's sense of dominant humours, and Lever casts a sharply satiric look over landlords, undergraduates, military men, and servants alike. The whole story, punctuated by songs, rattles along at a fine speed, and was enormously successful. *Harry Lorrequer* had been written to amuse but *Charles O'Malley* deliberately showed what pre-Union Ireland was like in one of its aspects.

For three years Lever edited the *Dublin University Magazine,* writing several novels, amongst them *Tom Burke of Ours* and *The O'Donoghue* which not only described military life but set it in a historico-political background.

When he left Ireland again, in 1845, Lever moved from Brussels to Bonn, then he rented a castle in the Tyrol; after this he tried Zurich and Lake Constance, and then moved to Florence. He lived high in Florence, his horses and equipage being notable, his expenses vast. In Hood's phrase, he said he was sipping champagne on a tight rope,[17] his royalties declining. In the 1850s he tried to get some public posts but his hopes vanished with the fall of Lord Derby's ministry. In 1854 he visited Ireland and was depressed by his reception, writing that he received as much ridicule as was consistent with viceregal politeness to bestow, and the small wit of A.D.C.s to inflict. *The Martins of Cro' Martin* demonstrates Lever's increasing awareness of Ireland's political problems; it shows the effect of rapid social change and the emergence of a new middle class. He saw English rule of Ireland as tragic in its consequences, and, as his view of life deepened, resented the fact that his role seemed to be taken by the public to be that of jester rather than of tragedian.

Already depressed by what he knew of government politics and diplomacy, he was appointed vice consul at La Spezia in 1858. His spendthrift son died in 1862, and with him died the remains of Lever's social ambitions. He had escaped from his middle class situation in Ireland only to find high society empty, vain, and selfish. And a visit to London in 1856 had led him to dislike also the literary world there, 'a self-perpetuating clique passing promisory notes on one another'.[18] In 1867 he was promoted to the post of consul at Trieste. It did not greatly please him to be in this Dalmatian exile, and his depression deepened when his wife became ill in 1869 and died in 1870. He himself died two years later.

The dedication of his last novel, *Lord Kilgobbin,* shows us something of the fierce affection he had for her, and the novel demonstrates the equally fierce dislike he had formed for English rule. His novels from the 'forties onward show this increasingly critical spirit, a sense of impending disaster no less acute than Yeats's own. And yet Yeats and most Irish critics have labelled him a mere creator of the stage Irishman, a hearty, a garrison writer. The only conclusion one is forced to is that they accepted the fashionable labels and read no further than *Harry Lorrequer* and *Charles O'Malley.* They got hold of the wrong Lever.

III

In Lever's thirty-three novels we have a fascinating insight into eighteenth and nineteenth century Irish life – history and politics as well as social, economic, military and sporting details, in addition to interpretations of Irish character in speech and action, for Lever, like all Irishmen, was deeply conscious of the different ways the Irish and the English speak and think. These novels were written by a man who travelled widely, was well read and highly intelligent, and knew rural Ireland's poverty and bravery as perhaps only a dispensary doctor could. Lever came to understand how government, or rather British party politics, worked; he wanted – increasingly – to put his own point of view, and provided a rich range of character as well as historical background and physical locale in his writings. He created convincing examples of both the dashing, feckless ascendancy and the self-deluding romantic, being himself a subtle blend of romantic and realist.

It is clear to a contemporary reader approaching *Charles O'Malley* detachedly that Lever ran into unduly sensitive nationalist attitudes. Even Shaw, who paid handsome tribute to Lever, and whose criticism ought to be taken as an antidote to Yeats's, has recorded some misgivings or reservations about Mickey Free, O'Malley's servant. But is the stage Irishry of this character so different from the stage cockney of, say, Sam Weller? It is possible that the excessively nationalist bias of critics neglected the harsh criticism of Irish political life and social life dropped incidentally in this novel. While the faked death of Charles O'Malley's uncle is primarily amusing it also reflects upon typical attitudes of landowners to debt and mortgages, when an incidental passage shows the casual attitude young officers adopted to the bills they ran up with tradespeople.

However, the first sign of direct criticism of English attitudes to Ireland comes in *Jack Hinton* (1843) where Lever placed a young Englishman in Ireland as an A.D.C. This was a device originally developed by Maria Edgeworth, from whose novels – and whose advice – Lever learned so much. Jack Hinton is shown the wretchedness of Ireland, and told that it is caused by English misrule. The English, argues Father Tom Loftus, do not know, or will not know the Irish: 'More prone to punish than prevent, you are satisfied with the working of the law and not shocked by the accumulation of crime; and, when broken by poverty and paralysed by famine, a gloomy desolation spreads over the land, you meet in terms of congratulations to talk over tranquillized Ireland'.[19] The priest argues that English laws and institutions are inadequate and unsuitable for Irish conditions, and maintains that the Irish see them as sources of their misery and instruments of tyranny. The picture is Swiftian in its analysis, because it argues that the Irish do not help themselves. Dublin is shown as it was after the Union, with a nostalgic look at the glories of the late eighteenth century 'when the names of Burke, Sheridan, Grattan and Curran start up'.[20] The heroine's father, Sir Simon Bellew, deals with

> 'the brightest period in Ireland's history – when wealth and genius were rife in the land, and when the joyous traits of Irish character were elicited in all their force by prosperity and happiness. It was then shone forth in all their brilliancy the great spirits whose flashing wit and glittering fancy have cast a sunlight over their native country, that even now in the twilight of the past, continues to illuminate it. Alas! they have had no heritors to their fame – they have left no successors behind them'.[21]

The Viceregal court is degenerate – when drunk, the Viceroy knights O'Grady's servant Corny Delany (an event based on a real incident). The social life of Dublin is being invaded by *nouveaux riches*. But there is a larger aim behind the novel which Lever later described. Provoked by characteristically disparaging remarks on Ireland and Irishmen in the London press, he decided not only to show an Englishman misjudging Irish people but also to demonstrate that the Irish squire, priest and peasant were unlike anything in the larger island, that the Dublin professional men, officials and shopkeepers had traits and distinctions entirely their own. He saw Irish habits of quizzical speech playing on the credulity of visitors[22]; he stressed the virtues of Irishwomen who were not overcome by 'the fatigues of fashionable life' and retained an enjoyment of society. Lever, his youth affected by the loss of the capital's former vitality caused by the effects of the Union, had come to see that Dublin had not necessarily lost so much. His hero speaks of 'the supercilious cant and unimpassioned coldness of London manners'.

Jack Hinton is, relatively speaking, an early novel, begun in Brussels. What of those which Lever wrote while in Dublin, while editing the *Dublin University Magazine?* If we read *Tom Burke of Ours* we find this so-called garrison writer taking as his hero a 14 year old orphan who is caught up with loathing for British rule in Ireland, witnesses the savagery of the yeomanry after 1798, and escapes from trial in Dublin to arrive in France, join the Polytechnique and become an officer in Napoleon's army. Disgusted by the arrogance of the French in victory and the suspicion attaching to him, he resigns his commission and returns to Ireland. Here he is again arrested, and is lucky to be acquitted. His trial reveals the duplicity and the degradation of informers and *agents provocateurs*. He returns to France to fight for Napoleon and the romantic ends, of what is largely a military-historical novel, are tied up. This is an anti-Castle, anti-British novel. Although the hero is befriended at several points in the story by an eccentric English officer the latter is shown as someone who utterly misunderstands the Irish as a race.

In 1845 Lever also published *St Patrick's Eve,* which deals with the cholera epidemic of 1832, as it affected the population around Lough Corrib. Here we find Lever describing the poverty, 'the same dull routine of toil and privation', of small farmers and peasants, punctuated by faction fights. He illustrates the relations between landlords, their agents and the tenantry. There is both sympathy for those in adversity and a stern warning that prosperity has its duties.

In the 1872 Introduction to *The O'Donoghue* (1845) Lever doubted whether it had been right to extinguish the old feudalism which bound peasant to landlord before preparing for the new relationship of gain and loss currently coming into being.[23] And he wrote a superb account (in the same preface) of this feudal aristocracy, wondering whether they could change:

Between the great families – the old houses of the land and the present race of proprietors – there lay a couple of generations of men, who with all the traditions and many of the pretentions of truth and fortune, had really become in ideas, modes of life, and habits, very little above the peasantry around them. They inhabited, it is true, 'the great house', and they were in name the owners of the soil, but crippled by debt and overbourne by mortgages, they subsisted in a shifty conflict with their creditors, rack-renting their miserable tenants to maintain it. Survivors of everything but pride of family, they stood there like the stumps, blackened and charred, the last remnants of a burnt forest, their proportions attesting the noble growth that had preceded them. What would the descendants of these men prove when, destitute of fortune and helpless, they were thrown upon a world that actually regarded them as blameable for the unhappy condition of Ireland?[24]

107

Here Lever attacks 'duty work',[25] and the exaction of 'gifts' by unscrupulous agents which led to 'the great man' being felt to be an oppressor.[26]

This novel repeats Lever's increasing contempt for 'Castle society'[27] and for the administration.[28] In *The Knight of Gwynne* (1846) he showed how the Union and the destruction of the Irish parliament in Dublin, once decided upon in England, had been pushed through by 'gross corruption' and 'trafficking for title and place'. Here Lever picked out as a reason for the fall of the Ascendancy, a 'fatal taste for prodigality'. The gentry were 'reckless, wasteful, extravagant'; they lived beyond their means; they were without foresight or prudence – which they would have regarded as meanness – while believing they were sustaining the honour of the country, they were sapping the foundations of its prosperity. The English in England, however, were also to blame. For instance, they simply had not faced the reasons for the disastrous famine of the mid-century. In *The Dodd Family Abroad* (1854) one of Lever's characters attacks the English view that the peasantry's laziness had caused the famine:

> Ask him, did he ever try to cut turf with two meals of wet potatoes *per diem* . . .
> . . . The whole ingenuity of mankind would seem devoted to ascertaining how much a bullock can eat, and how little will feed a labourer. Stuff one and starve the other, and you may be the President of an Agricultural Society and Chairman of your Union [workhouse].

Lever continued his analysis of the Ascendancy's situation in *The Martins of Cro' Martin* (1854), where he again dealt with the cholera epidemic of 1832, giving affectionate praise to the 'poor famished and forgotten people' of Clare. In this novel he pictured the old relationship between landlords and tenants collapsing and estrangement between the two classes deepening. Despite mistakes, however, he thought more generosity and forbearance was emerging on both sides.[29] Later he saw the post-famine period as one of transition, and in his preface to the 1872 edition he wrote that

> There was not at that time the armed resistance to rents, nor the threatening letter system to which we are afterwards to

become accustomed, still less was there the thought that the Legislature would interfere to legalize the demands by which the tenant was able to coerce his landlord; and for a brief interval there did seem a possibility of rewriting once again by the ties of benefit and gratitude, the two 'classes whose real welfare depends on concorn and harmony'.[30]

In *Barrington* (1862) Lever further explored the Ascendancy in decline. Barrington, a former pre-Union Dublin parliamentarian, and his sister, a belle in Castle Society, try to manage an Inn in the country, she apparently accepting her role as hostess of a little wayside inn, he romantically pretending that the clients are guests, and pouring the remnants of their money into useless law suits. The return of brother and sister to the once fashionable and now decaying Reynolds Hotel in Dominick Street in Dublin echoes Maria Edgeworth's picture of the former capital's faded glories in *The Absentee*. Lever, however, treats this Anglo-Irish nostalgia for the past with detachment.

His steadily increasing dislike of English administrators and Dublin Castle Society emerges here and there in *Sir Brook Fossbrooke* (1865), a novel with a complex plot and increased depth in portrayal of character. He includes in this novel attacks on jobbery, police spying, the use of informers, the invention of 'treason-felony'. Lever had developed his capacity for irony; and he also continued to speculate on the differences between Irish and English characters:

> Plodding unadorned ability, even of a high order, meets little favour in Ireland, while on the other side of the Channel Irish quickness is accounted as levity, and the rapid appreciation of a question without the detail of long labour and thought, is set down as the lucky hit of a lively but very idle intelligence.[31]

He expressed direct scorn for those English officials in Ireland, from whose rudeness he had himself suffered:

> Is it fancy, or am I right in supposing that English officials have a manner specially assumed for Ireland and the Irish – a thing like the fur cloak a man wears in Russia, or the snow-shoes he puts on in Lapland not intended for other latitudes, but admirably adapted for the locality it is made for? . . . I do

not say it is a bad manner – a presuming manner – a manner of depreciation towards those it is used to, or a manner indicative of indifference in him who uses it. I simply say that they who employ it keep it as especially Ireland as they keep their Mackintosh capes for wet weather, and would no more think of displaying it in England than they would go to her Majesty's levee in a shooting-jacket.[32]

Lever's last novel – and the best of them – *Lord Kilgobbin* (1870) illustrates in sombre fashion how Ireland was misgoverned and ready to explode, in his words 'uneasy disquieted and angry'. Here are the views of Molyneux and Swift given fresh life: here is fierce indignation at the ineptitude of English politicians who vacillated between repression and submission to terrorism; here, too, is a vacuum, for the Anglo-Irish had lost their power, indeed their will to govern the country. The landlords were decadent, the Fenians inefficient, and he disliked the new citified commercial class that was emerging out of the poverty of the country people, so weakened by the effects of famine and by continuing emigration. Despite anger and despair, despite his feeling of impending catastrophe, Lever loved his country; he surveyed its politics sardonically, at times detachedly; he was Anglo-Irish in his enjoyment of scenery and complexity of character; and he had a sharp awareness of differences in Irish and English sensibilities. How could Yeats (and a horde of lesser writers after him) have got hold of the wrong Lever?

NOTES

1 Reprinted in William Butler Yeats, *Letters to the New Island,* Ed. Horace Reynolds, Oxford University Press, London, 1970, pp. 163–174.
2 Ibid, p. 168.
3 Ibid, p. 168.
4 Ibid, p. 173.
5 Published in the *Leisure Hour,* November 1889, p. 35; reprinted in *Uncollected Prose by W. B. Yeats,* ed. John P. Frayne, Macmillan, London, 1970, I pp. 146–162.
6 Ibid, p. 162.
7 Ibid, p. 161.
8 W. B. Yeats (ed). *Representative Irish Tales,* G. P. Putman's Sons, New York and London, 1891, pp. 5–6, Colin Smythe, Gerrards Cross, 1979, p. 27.
9 From reprinted version of *United Ireland* article. *Uncollected Prose,* I, p. 207.

10 Ibid. p. 208.
11 *The Letters of W. B. Yeats,* ed. Allan Wade, Hart-Davis, London, 1954,
    p. 246.
12 Ibid, p. 248.
13 'First Principles' *Samhain:* 1908, included in W. B. Yeats, *Explorations,*
    Macmillan, London, 1962, p. 235.
14 W. B. Yeats, *Autobiographies,* Macmillan, London, 1956, p. 138.
15 Ibid, p. 207.
16 Charles Lever, Introduction to *Charles O'Malley,* 1897 edition, I, p. x.
17 Edmund Downey, *Charles Lever, His Life in his Letters,* 2 vols, 1906,
    I, 308.
18 Ibid, I, 337.
19 Charles Lever, *Jack Hinton,* New Edition with Autobiographical
    Introduction, n.d., p. 240.
20 Ibid, p. 257.
21 Ibid, p. 257.
22 Ibid, p. 2.
23 p. xiv.
24 Ibid, p. xv.
25 Ibid, p. 143.
26 Ibid. pp. 142–4.
27 Ibid, p. 344.
28 Ibid, p. 275. This was also developed in *Roland Cashel* (1848), I, 38 &
    209–210.
29 *The Martins of Cro' Martin,* 1854, I, pxx.
    p. ix.
30 Preface to Charles Lever, *The Martins of Cro' Martin,* 2 vols, 1872,
    p. ix.
31 *Sir Brook Fossbrooke,* nd., p. 277.
32 Ibid, p. 280.

THE VISITOR

BRENDAN KENNELLY

He strutted into the house.

Laughing
He walked over to the woman
Stuck a kiss in her face.

He wore gloves.
He had fur on his coat.
He was the most confident man in the world.
He liked his own wit.

Turning his attention to the children
He patted each one on the head.
They are healthy but a bit shy, he said.
They'll make fine men and women, he said.

The children looked up at him.
He was still laughing.
He was so confident
They could not find the word for it.
He was so elegant
He was more terrifying than the giants of night.

The world
Could only go on its knees before him.
The kissed woman
Was expected to adore him.

It seemed she did.

I'll eat now, he said,
Nothing elaborate, just something simple and quick –
Rashers, eggs, sausages, tomatoes
And a few nice lightly-buttered slices

112

Of your very own
Home-made brown
Bread.
O you dear woman, can't you see
My tongue is hanging out
For a pot of your delicious tea.
No other woman in this world
Can cook so well for me.
I'm always touched by your modest mastery!

He sat at table like a king.
He ate between bursts of laughter.
He was a great philosopher,
Wise, able to advise,
Solving the world between mouthfuls.
The woman hovered about him.
The children stared at his vital head.
He had robbed them of every word they had.
Please have some more food, the woman said.
He ate, he laughed, he joked,
He knew the world, his plate was clean
As Jack Spratt's in the funny poem,
He was a handsome wolfman,
More gifted than anyone
The woman and children of that house
Had ever seen or known.

He was the storm they listened to at night
Huddled together in bed
He was what laid the woman low
With the killing pain in her head
He was the threat in the high tide
At the back of the house
He was a huge knock on the door
In a moment of peace
He was a hound's neck leaning
Into the kill
He was a hawk of heaven stooping
To fulfill its will
He was the sentence tired writers of gospel
Prayed God to write

113

Brendan Kennelly

He was a black explosion of starlings
Out of a November tree
He was a plan that worked
In a climate of self-delight
He was all the voices
Of the sea.

My time is up, he said,
I must go now.

Taking his coat, gloves, philosophy, laughter, wit,
He prepared to leave.
He kissed the woman again.
He smiled down on the children.
He walked out of the house.
The children looked at each other.
The woman looked at the chair.
The chair was a throne
Bereft of its king, its visitor.

YEATS AND VICTORIAN IRELAND

F. S. L. LYONS*

We have become so accustomed to the spectacle of Yeats making and remaking his life and his work throughout his long career that it is easy to forget that almost half that career was spent in the reign of Queen Victoria. Like most who grew up in her imposing shadow he never quite lost the marks of his early experience, but if Yeats remained in some senses a Victorian to the end, he was a Victorian with a difference. The difference was largely determined by his divided allegiance. This was only partly an allegiance divided between the two islands of Britain and Ireland, it was much more an allegiance divided between the various cultures which co-existed in the country of his birth. His encounters with these cultures in his first fifteen years as a writer are the main themes of this lecture.

First, however, I must briefly outline what late Victorian Ireland was like. In some rather obvious ways it seemed hardly more than an extension of late Victorian England, though in this, as in much else, Irish appearances could be misleading. When Yeats was born in 1865 Ireland had long been linked to Britain by the political union which in 1800 had demolished the Irish parliament. Unpopular at the time, the union had been sporadically opposed during the nineteenth century by both violent and peaceful means. In the very year of his birth the Fenians, a not very secret society who believed in the sacred right of insurrection, were conspiring in Dublin to achieve an uprising intended to lead to the establishment of an independent Irish republic. Although there was an abortive rebellion two years later the conspiracy was easily penetrated by the police and in 1865 some of the leading Fenians were seized, tried and sentenced to long terms of imprisonment. Among them was a Tipperary Trinity student turned journalist, John O'Leary, who was to exercise a profound influence upon the young Yeats.

Flamboyant but ineffectual revolution was not the only path towards undoing the union with Britain. At intervals during the nineteenth century political parties had been formed to present the Irish case in the House of Commons. When Yeats was beginning to be published in 1885 and 1886 this constitutional movement was reaching its climax in the drive for Home Rule headed by Charles Stewart Parnell, who also was to become a symbolic figure for Yeats at certain crucial moments in his life. If I stress these political considerations at the outset it is because they were an essential part of the Ireland with which Yeats as a writer had to come to terms. They occupied so much of the foreground of Irish life that other things, intrinsically no less important, seemed of little account beside them. Indeed, Yeats himself fully recognised this when he later insisted that it was only after the fall and death of Parnell in 1890–91 that a path opened for the kind of literary movement he sought to found.

Yet this continual preoccupation with regaining independence should not mask the fact that in most matters dependence was the norm. Ireland was an integral, if backward, part of the United Kingdom economy. She was governed from London by English ideas and methods. Above all, in an age of cheap and rapid transport she was subjected to an incessant flow, not only of English goods, but of English customs and modes of thought and speech, English education, English clothes and fashions, English sports and pastimes, English drama, music and art – in short of English culture in all its manifestations from the highest to the lowest.

This ascendancy of English culture was the underlying reality of Irish life, compared with which the political ideas of an O'Leary or a Parnell seem curiously superficial. There was, it is true, one area in which the Irish appeared to assert their individuality. This was the struggle by the tenant-farmers to regain possession of the land. That struggle, too, was getting under way during Yeats's childhood and by the turn of the century it had achieved almost complete success with the acceptance by the British parliament of the need to legislate for the break-up of the great estates and their transference to the small farmer-owners who to this day remain the masters of the Irish countryside. But this was a profoundly conservative revolution. Irish farmers, long conditioned to regard the ownership rather than the development of the land as their highest ambition, did not generally shine as agriculturalists. Moreover, they remained wedded to the idea of the family as a socio-economic unit, dedicated to adding field to field and at all costs avoiding the sub-

116

division of holdings which had been such a disastrous feature of Irish rural society on the eve of the great famine of the 1840s. In the typical peasant family the land passed from husband to wife and then to one son who would marry only when he was assured of the succession. For the rest of the family there remained either lifelong celibacy or emigation and both solutions were widely adopted. Life on the land was hard and primitive and though Yeats and Lady Gregory were soon to idealise it, over most of the country the outlook of the farmer and his family was dourly materialistic. Although there were times when the old stories and the old music reasserted their influence, even these traditions had begun to fade as the ancestral Gaelic culture retreated in the face of English pressures to the remoter western regions.

The farmers shared with the commercial classes of the country towns an attitude towards the outside world which was affected both by a sentimental nationalism and by the teachings of the Catholic Church. Sometimes, and especially when the land war was at its height, nationalism and Catholicism threatened to collide, for if nationalism looked towards independence, the Church stood, by and large, for obedience to the civil authority, having been indeed one of the principal anglicising agencies during the nineteenth century. Further, although the Church, through its ritual and discipline, gave a certain form and colour to the otherwise drab existences of farm and market, it upheld rigorously the family-based life of these communities and lent its authority to the accepted pattern of late marriages, large families and sexual abstinence for those unfortunates for whom marriage was economically impossible or undesirable.

It seems, therefore, that while the life of the Irish Victorian countryside was very different from that of the English Victorian countryside, it was steadily ceasing during the nineteenth century to have any clearly defined cultural autonomy. As the century progressed and transport improved, the rural market for English products and ideas steadily increased so that the farmers and the shopkeepers shared with the population of the larger towns an absorption into the sphere of influence of the English culture in its grosser and more material forms.

Only, as I have suggested, along the western seaboard did there linger the vestiges of an antique Gaelic culture. There, Irish was still the staple language; there, life was still of an elemental simplicity; there, ancient beliefs, whether in fairy-tale or legend or of Druidic origin, co-existed with an almost fatalistic Catholicism; there, the old music, the old folk-arts, still survived. But all this was poised upon the brink of destruction. This beautiful part of Ireland was also the poorest and it was visibly dying from emigration. As the young people departed all hope of continuity for the future was threatened, so that those who went to Donegal or Sligo, to the Aran Islands or Kerry, in the closing years of the nineteenth century were virtually the last to see this doomed culture in all its pristine innocence.

There remain two other strands to be woven into the pattern. One need be mentioned but briefly since it impinged little on Yeats or his work, though in ignoring it as they largely did he and his friends greatly over-simplified their view of Ireland. I am referring to the Presbyterian-dominated culture of the north-east of Ireland. This region, the only large-scale centre of modern industry in the whole island, was in some respects closer to Britain than to the rest of Ireland and Belfast was as much a product of the industrial revolution as were Glasgow or Liverpool. Though small and compact, the region was torn by racial and religious rivalries. Its prevailing ethos, however, was that of a stern Calvinist Puritanism where god and mammon were worshipped with an equal seriousness. The British connection was valued in both political and economic terms and Ulster Unionism was, during Yeats's youth, becoming a formidable obstacle to Home Rule. But in cultural terms it was a self-contained province which went its way without much regard for the rest of Ireland. 'As for Willie Yeats and his fairies', a modern Ulsterman has written, 'factory chimneys and fairies were assumed to cancel one another out; if you had one, you couldn't have the other, and we had the factory chimneys.'[1]

Such wilful isolation was far from typical of the last strand, which historians have agreed to call Anglo-Irish. Although the term only emerged in the present century, and then mainly in a literary context, it has come to denote a distinct cultural tradition. The Anglo-Irish were the descendants of the Norman and later English settlers who had colonised Ireland at intervals from the twelfth century onwards. By Victorian times, when the land war and the rise of nationalism had sapped their strength, they were identified in most people's minds with the wicked, often absentee, landlords who ground down their tenantry by excessive rents and evicted them ruthlessly when the rents were not paid. This crude stereotype will no longer serve. There were, no doubt, bad landlords as well as good, but the involvement of many of the class with their estates was close and beneficial. They suffered, indeed, from a chronic shortage of capital, and long-standing laws and customs made it difficult for them to introduce improvements when these were resisted by their conservative tenantry. Nevertheless, some of them never gave up trying and the resolution of the land question early in the twentieth century was largely due to the initiative of one of them, Lady Gregory's nephew, Captain John Shawe-Taylor.

The life-style of these landlords was of course conspicuously different from that of their tenants. Most, though not all, were Protestant in religion and Unionist in politics, and in externals they seemed largely indistinguishable from their counterparts across the Irish Sea, with whom they frequently inter-married; indeed, some of them had estates and business interests in both countries. Almost without exception they sent generation after generation of their sons to the armed forces of the Crown and many achieved high eminence in the service of the Empire.

Despite these resemblances they were a separate race and followed a separate destiny. The fact was that they were anachronistic and beginning to realise it. They lacked the security of the English landed class and they had to wrestle with a different land system, a different climate, an inferior mode of agriculture. Most of all they had to recognise that however closely they might seek to identify themselves with their local communities the gap between the Big House and the cottage was unbridgeable, deriving as it did from the implacable resentment of a subject race to which the landlords remained at bottom an alien garrison. Yet the irony of their position was that the Anglo-Irish never ceased to regard themselves as being Irish and their attachment to the countryside where they had been born and raised was deep and genuine. At the same time few of them could conceive of an Ireland which had any future outside the Empire and they felt no incompatibility between their Irish and their imperial roles. In cultural terms, as was natural from their usually English education and their experience of the wider world, they looked to England as their metropolitan country and for most of them the revival or development of a separate Irish culture would have seemed a naive, not to say ludicrous, presumption.

119

The Anglo-Irish, however, did not consist solely of the landlord class. There were distinctions to be drawn, not only between the greater and lesser landed families, but also between country and town. In the towns, and especially in Dublin, there was a Protestant middle class which, while never large, exercised power and influence far beyond its numbers. It was prominent, if not dominant, in the learned professions and it played an important part in the world of business. Moreover, this Anglo-Irish middle class had its own seat of learning, Trinity College, Dublin, which not only trained the clergy of the Anglican Church of Ireland, and turned out graduates for more lucrative careers, but also supplied a steady stream of young men to the civil service in Britain or overseas.

Trinity in the late nineteenth century was not only rich and exclusive, it also had a reputation for scholarship not far behind those of Oxford and Cambridge. Its ethos was Unionist in politics, cosmopolitan in culture. It looked outwards to England and beyond, but paid little attention to the Irish society immediately outside its gates. Yet because it was a real university, it was not a monolith and in the last quarter of the nineteenth century it produced a number of graduates who reacted against their mentors and began to explore the possibility that a new Ireland might be created where instead of cultural friction cultural fusion might be achieved and where, especially in the lull that followed the death of Parnell, the search for a national identity in a fresh and less insistently political direction might be undertaken.

It was into this circle of Anglo-Irish Protestants, eager to break with the defensive mentality of their seniors, that W. B. Yeats was born. As is well known, his had been a Trinity family for several generations and his father, J. B. Yeats, the artist and himself a graduate, had been somewhat disappointed that Willie elected to go to art-school instead. Perhaps, though, it was as well that he did, for, as we shall see, Trinity College became for him the embodiment of one part of Victorian Ireland which proved indifferent to his enthusiasms and impermeable by his ideas.

Nevertheless, it was one of the Trinity dissentients, Charles Oldham, who founded in 1885 two institutions that directly and permanently influenced Yeats's career. One was the *Dublin University Review,* in which much of his early poetry was to be published. The other was the Contemporary Club which had rooms just across the road from the Front Gate of Trinity. It was a discussion group where any subject might come up and nearly every point of view was likely to be expressed. Willie and his father were frequent attenders and it was there, in 1885, that the poet met John O'Leary, 'the one indispensable man', as he afterwards called him.[2] After his arrest in 1865 O'Leary had endured a term of harsh imprisonment and then had spent a longer period in exile in France. Returning to Ireland in 1885 he soon showed that although still only in his mid-fifties he had ceased to be a positive political force. His influence upon Yeats and others was an influence primarily of character. 'He had', as Yeats later wrote, 'the moral genius that moves all young people and moves them the more if they are repelled by those who have strict opinions and yet have lived commonplace lives.'[3] O'Leary was president of a Young Ireland society to which Yeats also belonged and acquaintanceship ripened into friendship when for a short while he lodged in O'Leary's house. 'From these debates, from O'Leary's conversation, and from the Irish books he lent or gave me has come all I have set my hand to since', Yeats recorded in his *Autobiographies*.[4] This was an exaggeration, for when Yeats was writing the *Autobiographies* he was also constructing a myth, but it had a foundation of truth. The older man taught his young disciple a conception of nationality he was never to abandon and to the end of his days he was content to describe himself as O'Leary's pupil.[5]

At the core of O'Leary's personality was a kind of stoicism. He had engaged in the Fenian conspiracy as a prelude to war against Britain. He had never renounced that as the ultimate solution to the Irish problem, but he despised the hit-and-run violence practised by the men who had succeeded the Fenians of his generation. 'He had grown up', wrote Yeats, 'in a European movement when the revolutionist thought that he, above all men, must appeal to the highest motive, be guided by some ideal principle, be a little like Cato or like Brutus, and he had lived to see the change Dostoievsky examined in *The Possessed*. Men who had been of his party – and oftener their sons – preached assassination and the bomb; and, worst of all, the majority of his fellow-countrymen followed after constitutional politicians who practised opportunism, and had, as he believed, such low morals that they would lie, or publish private correspondence, if it might advance their cause.'[6] O'Leary's was an austere nationalism but he clothed it in a few memorable phrases that Yeats treasured all his life. 'No gentleman can be a socialist', he would say, adding with a thoughtful look, 'He might be an anarchist.' 'My religion', he proclaimed, 'is the old Persian, to pull the bow and tell the truth.' And again: 'There are things a man must not do to save a nation', replying, when Yeats asked what things, 'To cry in public'.[7]

O'Leary repaid Yeats's devotion by doing what he could to promote his poetic career. There was a certain irony here, for O'Leary himself had learnt his patriotism from the Young Ireland movement of the 1840s and had been deeply influenced by its chief poet, Thomas Davis. Davis, a Trinity graduate, had preached a reconciling nationalism, hoping to transcend sectarian and racial differences by recalling to Irishmen of all persuasions that they shared a common heritage, the ancient Irish civilisation, and laying it down as the work of the next generation that it must recover the language, the literature and the history of that fabled past. Unfortunately, because he was so emphatically a man with a message, Davis's poetry, and that of his collaborators, tended to be weighed down with the propaganda which indicated that for them politics took precedence over art. O'Leary, to do him justice, when he pressed the verses of Davis and his group upon Yeats, did not claim that they were good poetry, and this restraint was wise, for even at the outset of his career Yeats was not prepared to subordinate his critical standards to political expediency.

Young Ireland was a necessary beginning, no doubt, but though Yeats was soon to discard this scaffolding he did so not only because of its inadequacy but because he had other means of support. He was beginning to discover the world of Irish fairies, of Irish legend, of Irish ballads, and also to ascribe to Irish peasants virtues and qualities they would have been surprised to learn they possessed. After his family's return to England in 1887, and when he was desperate to make a living, we find him not only sinking deep into journalism and book-reviewing, but producing his own supernatural book, *The Celtic Twilight,* and editing various collections of Irish fairy and folk tales.

Much of this was hack-work, but from it he derived two essential ideas. One was that national traditions, to be effective, must not be immured in libraries, 'but living in the minds of the populace'. And the other was that people and poets should be at one – that there should be no separate literary class with its own viewpoint and its own conventions. 'This condition', he wrote as early as 1887, 'Ireland has long had – whatever the people were the poets have been more intensely. They were one with the people in their faults and their virtues – in their aims and passions.'[8] As for the people themselves, they were still open to the influence of the unseen world. 'The ghosts and goblins', he insisted, 'do still live and rule in the imaginations of innumerable Irish men and women, and not merely in remote places, but close even to big cities.'[9] And in 1891, welcoming Douglas Hyde's collection of Irish folk-stories, *Beside the fire,* he observed that it was small wonder the book was beautiful, 'for it is the chronicle of that world of glory and surprise imagined in the unknown by the peasant as he leant painfully over his spade'.[10]

Yeats's preoccupation with fairies and the legendary past was much more than the exploitation of a novel and colourful literary property.[10a] It has to be seen alongside his equal preoccupation with Indian philosophy, with theosophy and with the whole occult world of magic. Since at the same time he was becoming deeply involved with the works of William Blake, it is clear that he was groping for a system or synthesis which would link him as a poet to sources of inspiration which lay far outside the world of rationality. 'If I had not made magic my constant study', he wrote to O'Leary who had chided him for following such outlandish practices, 'I could not have written a single word of my Blake book, nor would *The Countess Cathleen* have ever come to exist. The mystical life is the centre of all that I do and all that I think and all that I write . . . I have always considered myself a voice of what I believe to be a greater renaissance – the revolt of the soul against the intellect – now beginning in the world.'[11]

At first sight this seemed to contradict his other dogma of this time – that Irish themes were alone the proper business of Irish writers. He got out of this dilemma adroitly by proving, to his own satisfaction at least, that there was no conflict between these dogmas, since it was a characteristic of the Celts to desire 'the things that lie beyond the actual'.[12] Ireland might thus be well suited to be the theatre for the revolt of the soul against the intellect since it had preserved 'a gift of vision which has died out among more hurried and more successful nations'.[13]

In a sense Yeats was swimming with a tide that was already flowing strongly elsewhere. Not merely was the rediscovery of the occult a common phenomenon of the nineties, but the work then being done on the comparative history of religion by Sir James Frazer and others encouraged Yeats in his belief that Ireland still preserved traces of the ancient natural religion that had once been world-wide and now persisted only, and even then imperfectly, in parts of the east. 'The earliest poet of India and the Irish peasant in his hovel nod to each other across the ages and are in perfect agreement.'[14] Indications of this ancient religion still survived in what remained of the ancient legends of Europe and these legends must therefore be the source for literature. 'I will say', he wrote in a famous essay on 'The Celtic element in literature', 'that literature dwindles to a mere chronicle of circumstance, or passionless fantasies and passionless meditations, unless it is constantly flooded with the passions and beliefs of ancient times, and that of all the fountains of the passions and beliefs of ancient times in Europe, the Slavonic, the Finnish, the Scandinavian and the Celtic, the Celtic alone has been for centuries close to the main river of European literature.' ' "The Celtic movement" ', he continued, 'as I understand it, is principally the opening of this fountain, and none can measure of how great importance it may be to coming times, for every new fountain of legends is a new intoxication for the imagination of the world.'[15]

His problem was how to ensure that this revivifying fountain should play in all its fullness upon the complacency of late Victorian Irish materialism. What one man could do Yeats certainly did. Not only was his own writing centred firmly on these timeless Irish themes, but he was constant in his encouragement of others, both in reviewing their books and in editing anthologies where the new poets could be represented. But no one man could carry the renaissance on his shoulders and Yeats, who for most of his life was an inveterate founder and joiner of societies, used the political lull that followed the death of Parnell to launch in 1892 the Irish Literary Society in London and the National Literary Society in Dublin. He wished to encourage the study of Irish history and language, to organise lectures on Irish subjects, to establish reading-rooms and local libraries and perhaps even a travelling theatre to familiarise the people with Irish works of the imagination and with the masterpieces of other countries.[16] Essentially, his purpose, as he said, was to 'teach to the writers on the one hand, and to the readers on the other, that there is no nationality without literature, no literature without nationality'.[17]

Almost at once, however, he had his first important lesson in the power of conservative nationalism. Among his most cherished schemes was a project to publish a New Irish Library rather on the lines of a similar enterprise which Young Ireland had successfully carried through in the 1840s, with the significant difference that the books selected by Yeats would not be political tracts or verses, but rather would be works contributing directly to the literary revival of which he was already the acknowledged apostle. Unhappily, a distinguished relic of the original Young Ireland movement, Sir Charles Gavan Duffy, had the same idea almost simultaneously, except that his plan was to take up where he had left off nearly fifty years earlier and to use the Library for the political indoctrination of the rising generation.

From Yeats's standpoint to use literature in this way was in effect to abuse it and soon bitter argument began to rage between the two sides. Looking back on the episode twenty years afterwards Yeats affected an attitude of wry amusement: [18]

The cleverer and better educated of those who opposed me did not think the literature of Young Ireland very satisfactory, but it was all Ireland had, they said, and if we were to admit its defects England would take advantage of the admission. The argument would rouse me to fury; England had only bound the hands of Ireland, they would silence her intelligence.

Later, when he was arranging his memories to construct his own version of the literary renaissance, Yeats linked this early battle with the later battles he was to fight on behalf of J. M. Synge. The literature of Young Ireland, he complained, had been obsessed by Irish virtues and English vices. 'All the past had been turned into a melodrama with Ireland for blameless hero and poet, novelist and historian had but one object, that we should hiss the villain, and only a minority doubted that the greater the talent the greater the hiss. It was all the harder to substitute for that melodrama a nobler form of art, because there really had been, however different in their form, villain and victim; yet fight that rancour I must, and if I had not made some head against it in 1892 and 1893 it might have silenced in 1907 John Synge, the greatest dramatic genius of Ireland.'[19]

The truth is that in 1892 and 1893 he made very little head against his diehard opponents. Although he had found the publisher, the series was taken away from him, he was given no final say in the choice of titles and his own projected contributions were quietly dropped. And when the Library began to produce the backward-looking volumes he had always feared, Yeats publicly denounced it in such a way as to close the door inexorably upon any future reconciliation:[20]

> I recognise [he wrote to the newspaper *United Ireland* on 1 September] with deep regret, and not a little anger, that the 'New Irish Library' is so far the most serious difficulty in the way of our movement, and that it drives from us those very educated classes we desire to enlist, and supplies our opponents with what looks like evidence of our lack of any fine education, of any admirable precision and balance of mind, of the very qualities which make literature possible. Perhaps criticism, with as little of the 'great day for Ireland' ritual as may be, can yet save the series from ebbing out in a tide of irrelevant dullness . . . We require books by competent men of letters on subjects of living national interest . . . and, if they are not to be obtained, let us bow our heads in silence and talk no more of a literary renaissance.

When Yeats wrote of 'those very educated classes we desire to enlist', it was not primarily nationalists he had in mind. On the contrary, when living in Ireland he had noticed that it was the Protestants and Unionists who were the best educated people he met. But they were difficult to reach, especially for a young man whose mentor was the Fenian O'Leary, even though, through his father's Trinity connections, he either knew or knew of the leading members of this circle. Perhaps because of his early association with the Trinity dissidents, perhaps in involuntary recognition of the weight of influence exerted by the unversity in one of its great periods, he came to regard official Trinity as the symbol of everything hostile to his attempt to create a national literature and to see in his father's old friend, Edward Dowden, the embodiment of the lofty indifference that always had the power to lash him into enraged controversy.

Dowden was indeed a key figure. He and J. B. Yeats had been undergraduates together in Trinity, but although sporadic attempts were made to keep their friendship alive, changing circumstances had made this impossible. Whereas by the 1880s, J. B. Yeats had dwindled, as it must have seemed, into the role of an impecunious and little sought painter, struggling to raise a young family, Dowden had developed into a scholar of international renown. Appointed to the chair of English at Trinity when only 24, he had written important studies of Shakespeare, Shelley and Browning and was sufficiently alive to contemporary trends to be an enthusiast both for Walt Whitman and for Ibsen. Yet, to the eye of a Yeats, there was something lacking in Dowden. By settling so early in Trinity he had isolated himself from the wider world and especially he had stifled in academia the small but genuine creative talent of his youth. Protestant and Unionist, he grew to be part of the Anglo-Irish establishment, though ironically enough in Trinity itself, the hard core of that establishment, he was never· taken very seriously because he taught English and not the more prestigious disciplines of Classics or Mathematics.

To the younger Yeats he had shown kindness and attention, listening to the early poems and giving judicious encouragement. When *The Wanderings of Oisin* was published Dowden was prompt to write in its praise, while delicately insinuating that the market for poems about fairies was not illimitable. 'I do not expect to get from you as good Fairy poetry in any future volume. You will I suppose advance rather in the direction of the poetry of human romance and passion.'[21] Before long Yeats's early belief in his 'sage' was shaken, mainly by his father's criticism, but perhaps also through his own youthful intolerance of professorial timidity. As early as 1886, in a long and impassioned assessment in the *Dublin University Review* of the poetry of Sir Samuel Ferguson, who a generation earlier had been a pioneer in exploiting the old bardic literature, Yeats claimed that Ferguson – whom he called 'the greatest poet Ireland has produced, because the most central and the most Celtic' – had been unjustly neglected by his fellow-countrymen. 'It is a question', he wrote, 'whether the most distinguished of our critics, Professor Dowden, would not only have more consulted the interests of his country, but more also . . . his own dignity and reputation, which are dear to all Irishmen, if he had devoted some of those elaborate pages which he has spent on the much bewritten George Eliot, to a man like the subject of this article.'[22]

F. S. L. Lyons

Dowden's real crime, however, was that he represented that Anglo-Irish attitude of casual disdain which Yeats instinctively felt to be as grave a danger to the emergence of a new literature in Ireland as the nationalistic piety of Gavan Duffy and his like. And it was quite true that Dowden, judging Irish literature in the perspective of world literature, all too often found it wanting. His ideas were crystallised in a speech he made to the College Historical Society in Trinity in 1883 which was then reworked and published in the *Fortnightly Review* in 1889 and again in 1895 as the introduction to his book, *New studies in literature.* Viewing with alarm the rise of the Home Rule movement, he dreaded lest Home Rule in literature should be a recipe for provincialism. If a national spirit were to manifest itself spontaneously in Irish writing, well and good, but attempts to generate it deliberately seemed to him bound to be self-defeating: [23]

> If national character be really strong and vivid it will show itself, although we do not strive to be national with malice prepense; it will show itself, whether we occupy ourselves with an edition of Sophocles or of Cicero, or with a song of the deeds of Cuchullainn or the love and sorrow of Deirdre. No folly can be greater than that of fancying that we shall strengthen our literary position by living exclusively in our own ideas, and showing ourselves inhospitable to the best ideas of other worlds.

The irony of this was that it was not very different from the policy Yeats himself was shortly to proclaim when launching his literary theatre at the end of the century and from which even in his irascible youth he would not have wholly dissented. But Dowden was a part of the Trinity establishment and that establishment had still to be attacked as representing one of the two kinds of philistinism Yeats was seeking to overthrow. Accordingly, although he may not have seen Dowden's article until 1895, Yeats used the occasion of the Trinity tercentenary celebrations to attack what he called 'Dublin scholasticism'. 'As Dublin Castle', he wrote, 'with the help of the police keeps Ireland for England, so Trinity College with the help of the schoolmasters keeps the mind of Ireland for scholasticism with its accompanying weight of mediocrity. All noble life, all noble thought, depends primarily upon enthusiasm, and Trinity College, in abject fear of the national enthusiasm which is at her gates, has shut itself off from every kind of ardour, from every kind of fiery and exultant life. She has gone over body and soul to scholasticism, and scholasticism is but an aspect of the great god, Dagon of the Philistines.'[24]

It was not, however, until 1895 that the controversy boiled up to its climax. Early that year Dowden had taken part in a discussion on Sir Samuel Ferguson. While conceding that Ferguson had good qualities, Dowden then ran over the list of Irish poets of the nineteenth century and bleakly concluded that few would qualify even for the third rank. They were, he considered, too ensnared by political rhetoric, too addicted to sentimentality, and too uninstructed in the rudiments of technique.[25] For Yeats this was a little embarrassing, since he was acutely aware of the kind of shortcomings that Dowden had identified. But, while admitting their existence, he demanded whether it was not better to join in the work of eradicating them than to stand aside uttering disparaging generalities. 'Professor Dowden', he wrote, 'has been for years our representative critic, and during that time he has done little for the reputation of Ferguson, whom he admires, and nothing for the reputation of these others, whom Ferguson admires.'[26]

Unfortunately, the quarrel did not stop there. During the next few weeks both men published lists of what they regarded as the best Irish books. Yeats's list, predictably, was designed as propaganda for his own movement; Dowden's list, no less predictably, was firmly anchored to the Anglo-Irish tradition and included writers such as Swift and Berkeley whom Yeats would eventually welcome into his own pantheon but for whom he had as yet little good to say. To make matters worse, Dowden added his own remarkable definition of what a national literature should be. 'It must', he said, 'be based on the old Celtic legends, must come from the Celtic people of the country, must have the basis and inspiration of race and racial tradition and must not and cannot be divorced from the philosophy and influences of the Catholic religion.'[27] This would, of course, have effectively excluded Yeats himself, and he immediately protested that Ireland was not wholly Celtic or wholly Catholic, though with these reservations he broadly agreed with the definition.[28]

Typically, however, he could not resist intensifying the quarrel. In the last of four seminal articles on the Irish literary movement which he published in the latter part of 1895 he renewed his attacks both upon the conservatism of Irish nationalism and the indifference of Irish Unionism. He represented them as being really the two faces of a single coin. If old-fashioned nationalists were trapped in the rhetoric of political argument, this was partly because the educated classes were responsible for the lack of perception shown by the masses. 'The most that read Irish national literature read from patriotism and political enthusiasm, and make no distinction between literature and rhetoric.' This in itself, he argued, would have done no permanent mischief, 'were it not that our educated classes are themselves full of a different, but none the less noisy, political passion, and are, with some admirable exceptions, too anti-Irish to read an Irish book of any kind other than a book or jokes or partisan argument'. Then Yeats, who was never one to spoil a controversy by the pedantry of accurate quotation, turned on Dowden for accusing Irish writers of 'raving of Brian Beru' [sic], of 'plastering' themselves 'with shamrocks', and of having neither 'scholarship' nor 'accuracy'. What Dowden had actually said in the article already cited (though there was a contemporary dispute as to whether he said it in the original version or added it later) was this. 'Let the Irish writer show that he can be patient, exact, just, enlightened, and he will have done better service for Ireland, whether he treats of Irish themes or not, than if he wore shamrocks in all his buttonholes and had his mouth full of Brian the Brave.'[29] This was certainly more balanced than Yeats's misrepresentation, but Yeats had at least this much right on his side that as late as 1895 Dowden was still unrepentantly saying that the new Irish writers – in effect, Yeats himself and his friends – were really no different from the old. Such criticism Yeats felt to be deeply unfair and even harmful: [30]

It is too empty of knowledge and sympathy to influence to any good purpose the ignorant patriotic masses, and it comes with enough of authority to persuade the undergraduates and the educated classes that neither the history, nor the poetry, nor the folklore, nor the stories which are interwoven with their native mountains and valleys are worthy of anything but contempt. This would perhaps be no great matter if it drove them to read Goethe and Shakespeare and Milton. . . . It has no such effect, however, but has done much to leave them with no ideal enthusiasm at all by robbing them of the enthusiasm which lay

130

at their own doors. . . . It is only when some young man or young girl is captured by a despised enthusiasm that the vacancy is peopled and the common made uncommon; and to make such captures and at length overthrow and sack Dublin scholasticism is one half of the business of 'The Irish Literary Movement'.

Dowden did not bother to reply and the matter ended there. But though it would be easy to dismiss both this quarrel and Yeats's quarrel with the Young Ireland traditionalists as merely the clash of coterie against coterie, this would be to lose sight of his main objective in his struggle against the prejudice and the materialism of late Victorian Irish society. We may say that the struggle had a double aim. First, it was a sustained effort by personal example and extraordinarily energetic propaganda to create a new school of Irish writers and to obtain for them a hearing in their own country. In this he was largely successful, even though some of the writers soon sank back into the obscurity from which he had ruthlessly wrenched them, and even though the 'Celtic note' that he and his friends struck soon came to seem a little precious and self-conscious. Without the leadership he gave, the voices of Douglas Hyde and AE, as later those of Lady Gregory and Synge and John Eglinton, might not have been so readily heard, nor would the Irish theatre have developed as it did if he had not prepared the way and the audience for it.

But the struggle had a second and more personal significance. We must never forget that throughout this period of furious campaigning and controversy Yeats was becoming ever more deeply involved in his occult studies and ever more anxious to hammer out that unity of being which was his personal holy grail. Central to his thought at that time was the idea of creating an Irish mystical order and devising for it a ritual which might combine Druidic and Christian elements. He and Maud Gonne took this so seriously that they envisaged basing their order upon a disused castle on an island in Lough Key and although this had to be abandoned as too impracticable even for them, Yeats's preoccupation with mystical – more accurately, occult – knowledge remained intense and directly influenced his attitude towards the theatre which he and Lady Gregory and George Moore founded in the last two years of the century. Many influences indeed, some foreign and some Irish, went to the making of that theatre,

131

but for Yeats himself it had a twofold significance. First, it projected into the most public of the arts the ideas about literature he had been preaching in the preceding years. But secondly the theatre, and particularly the early plays which he himself contributed to it, offered a fresh means of interpreting and making explicit his occult doctrines. 'I wished my writings', he recorded later in his *Memoirs,* 'to have a secret symbolical relation to these mysteries, for in this way I thought there would be a greater richness, a greater claim upon the soul, devotion without exhortation and rhetoric.'[31]

The religious overtones here are unmistakable, nor were they merely retrospective. 'The arts', Yeats wrote in 1898, 'are, I believe, about to take upon their shoulders the burdens that have fallen from the shoulders of priests, and to lead us back upon our journey by filling our thoughts with the essences of things, and not with things.'[32] And again, three years later: 'We who care deeply about the arts find ourselves the priesthood of an almost forgotten faith, and we must, I think, if we would win the people again, take upon ourselves the method and the fervour of a priesthood . . . We must baptise as well as preach.'[33]

Such Messianic pronouncements invite two comments. First, they are obviously of high significance for Yeats's own development as a man and as an artist, and especially for his ceaseless strivings towards 'unity of being'. But secondly, and more directly relevant to the main theme of this lecture, they disclose the wide gap which existed between his ambitions for the theatre and how it actually developed. The prospectus he and others wrote for those whom it was hoped to persuade to underwrite the project financially now reads somewhat ironically. In building up a Celtic and Irish school of dramatic literature, it stated, 'We hope to find in Ireland an uncorrupted and imaginative audience trained to listen by its passion for oratory, and believe that our desire to bring upon the stage the deeper thoughts and emotions of Ireland will insure for us a tolerant welcome, and that freedom to experiment . . . without which no new movement in art or literature can succeed. We will show that Ireland is not the home of buffoonery and easy sentiment, as it has been represented, but the home of an ancient idealism.'[34]

These confident aspirations were never really fulfilled. I cannot here pursue the history of the theatre which, in its broad outlines, is probably familiar to many of you, but certain things may be said briefly because they bear directly upon Yeats's involvement with Victorian Ireland. The theatre movement, which was in origin an extension of the literary movement, experienced both success and failure. Its major success was simply that the frail bark which its creators pushed out upon the tempestuous waters of Irish criticism did in fact survive, and in its ultimate form, as the Abbey Theatre, threw up two writers of genius, Synge and O'Casey, achieving thereby a worldwide reputation.

The failure from Yeats's viewpoint was that what developed was very far indeed from the mystical, spiritual theatre that he had envisaged. Being at bottom a tough-minded pragmatic man he acquiesced in the way in which it actually evolved even if he became increasingly disenchanted after the death of Synge in 1909 removed the one towering figure whose work he could unreservedly admire. But the theatre survived, we may say, because of its deviation from Yeats's ideal rather than because of any marked adherence to that ideal, and it survived because it fascinated and sometimes infuriated audiences of real people whose reactions were very different from those he had set out to evoke. Even so, it would be wrong to suppose that the Abbey, still less its literary precursors, was ever 'popular' in any broad sense of the term. While those who worked for it did so with great enthusiasm and for little enough material reward, they were always a tiny minority performing their plays for an audience which was itself a minority.

That audience remained a minority because the preoccupations of most Irish men and women were little affected by what the theatre had to offer. Throughout the nineties and beyond, Yeats was acting on the assumption that the fall of Parnell had liberated new energies that made possible the literary renaissance to which he was himself committed. In the sense that the imaginations of the young were for a time deflected from politics towards the new movement he was correct up to a point. But his analysis was deficient on two counts. On the one hand, it under-estimated the extent to which the idea of a Gaelic revival predated his own movement. And on the other hand, it over-estimated the extent to which there had been a genuine change of attitudes and in particular the extent to which the Parnellite split had created a real vacuum.

I am suggesting, in short, that the different cultural traditions which I sketched at the beginning of this lecture remained as different and separate at the end of the Victorian period as they had been during it. If anything, indeed, the distinguishing features had been multiplying while Yeats was at work. In an article he wrote about the literary movement in 1899, after taking the Parnellite split as his usual point of departure, he listed the various initiatives which had helped to fill what he still fondly regarded as the political vacuum. Significantly, these included not only the two literary societies and the Irish Literary Theatre, but also the Feis Ceoil (the annual Irish festival of music) and what he regarded as more important than all the others, the Gaelic League.[35] He was indeed right to regard it as more important, but it was important for reasons he had scarcely begun to comprehend. The Gaelic League, founded in 1893 to encourage the revival of Irish as a spoken and literary language, was in fact the spearhead of a new Gaelic nationalism which was to imbue the rising generation with a sense of Irish separateness and to lead some of them back into the politics of revolution. Seeking to establish this separate identity for Ireland, the League and its supporters were bound to question the work that Yeats was doing, maintaining as they did that his attempt to create an Irish literature in the English language was a vain, if not fraudulent, enterprise. The League, so far from being a support for Yeats's dream of fusing the existing cultures into something other and higher, contributed rather to an intensification of the existing cultural divide.[36]

For Yeats this might have mattered less if he could have obtained the support he needed from the Protestant educated classes. Even while chastising them for their indifference he had never quite given up hope that he might convert enough of them to his ideas to recruit a leavening minority into his movement. In the late 1890s he thought briefly that this was actually happening. Perhaps this was partly a result of his friendship with Lady Gregory whose influence with the landed gentry he may have over-rated. Certainly it was in part due to his appreciation of the work of Sir Horace Plunkett who at this time was not only launching the co-operative movement amongst the Irish farmers, but through his ownership (until 1900) of the Dublin *Daily Express* opened that newspaper to literature and the arts in such a way as to give Yeats and others – his oppenents as well as friends – almost unlimited scope. In 1899 he paid Plunkett this remarkable tribute: [37]

The last few months have been of extreme importance to the Irish intellectual movement, which began with the break up of the political movement of Parnell, for they have done more than the preceding ten years to interest the Irish leisured classes in Irish thought and Irish literature. Certain political impulses have helped; but the Irish [sic] *Daily Express,* a paper whose policy is under the direction of Mr [sic] Horace Plunkett, has been the chief mover in what had seemed an almost impossible change . . . Now, however, the sons and daughters of the landlords and officials are beginning to read, and at the same time old rancours are dying down; and that sense of something going to happen, which alone gives creative spirits their opportunity, whether in action or in thought, has begun to spread among all classes.

Alas, this was far too sanguine. Although there was a creative element in Irish landlordism it was no more than a small and unrepresentative group. The class as a whole was never touched by Yeats's movement, partly because it was not an intellectual class and was content to immerse itself in country pursuits, but partly also because its grip on reality was far stronger than Yeats's. It was always clear that the struggle for survival would be political far more than cultural, and to the extent that it *was* cultural, that its allegiance was to the traditional mode rather than to any new-fangled amalgam which Yeats and his friends might proffer.

Lacking support among the Anglo-Irish, and failing to carry the Irish-Ireland movement with him, Yeats was thus left in an extremely vulnerable position when he found himself – as he increasingly did in the decade after 1900 – face to face with the powerful but immovable force of Catholic bourgeois nationalism. Whenever the theatre, or his own writings, offended, or seemed to offend against either the morality of puritanical Catholicism, or the stereotypes which the Irish middle class admired in the mirror of their own complacency, the stock reaction he encountered was always the same blank negation, the same outcry against an art which strove to idealise and to separate itself from propaganda.

Though the battles of those Edwardian years are outside my scope, their scars are easily visible in the poetry of *Responsibilities,* which he published in 1914. Yet the bitterness which pervades that volume should not blind us to the extent of Yeats's

135

achievement in the last Victorian decade even if it was different from what he had hoped for when as a young man he had set out with such fiery optimism upon his hard road. It was partly, of course, a personal achievement. His ordeal did not break him. Rather, it matured and toughened him without interrupting his creative flow, so that he emerged from those traumatic years a much more considerable writer than when he went into them, even if the best was still a long way in the future.

But his achievement was much more than personal. Not only did he give his movement its characteristic institutions, not only did he supply it with a criticism at once exacting and sympathetic, but he played a crucial role in encouraging new writers and enabling their work to appear in print and on the stage. True, as I have indicated, many of his discoveries quickly relapsed into the oblivion from which it was almost unkind to have rescued them initially, but enough good work was done for the movement to be regarded in truth as a movement which had something to say and said it with grace and power. Better even than this was the fact that although the wider public remained content with the familiar stale rhetoric, and continued to regard literature either as mere entertainment or else as an extension of politics, the revulsion from nationalistic cliché which Yeats had taught his generation was transmitted to the generation that began to write about Ireland in the aftermath of revolution and civil war. Their new realism might have been, frequently was, repugnant to Yeats and their goals were very different from his. Nevertheless, they brought to literature his sense of the absolute value of the artist's work, and most of them gained encouragement and strength from the fact that their exemplar was himself a great writer who continued to change and grow through all the phases of his life.

He could affect them in this way because, in spite of all, they could recognise in him an Irishman who wrote out of that particular burden and who, despite all other influences and his ever increasing fame, still continued to regard Ireland as the profoundest source of his art. So it was given to him to fulfil in his maturity the declaration he had made in 1888 when the world lay all before him: [38]

To the greater poets everything they see has its relation to the national life, and through that to the universal and divine life: nothing is an isolated artistic moment; there is a unity everywhere; everything fulfils a purpose that is not its own; the hailstone is a journeyman of God; the grass blade carries the universe upon its point. But to this universalism, this seeing of unity everywhere, you can only attain through what is near you, your nation, or, if you be no traveller, your village and the cobwebs on your walls. You can no more have great poetry without a nation than religion with symbols. One can only reach out to the universe with a gloved hand – that glove is one's nation, the only thing one knows even a little of.

NOTES

* This is a slightly expanded version of a lecture delivered to the Victorian Studies Association of Ontario, at Toronto, 12 April, 1980.

1 Denis Ireland, *From the Jungle of Belfast*, Belfast, 1973, p. 18.
2 W. B. Yeats, *Memoirs*, ed. Denis Donoghue, Macmillan, London, 1972, p. 52.
3 W. B. Yeats, *Autobiographies*, Macmillan, London 1955, p. 95.
4 Ibid, p. 101.
5 Allan Wade (ed.), *The letters of W. B. Yeats*, Hart-Davis, London, 1954, p. 869 (hereafter cited as W. B. Yeats, *Letters*).
6 W. B. Yeats, *Autobiographies*, pp. 209–10.
7 Ibid, pp. 211, 213.
8 John P. Frayne (ed.), *Uncollected Prose by W. B. Yeats*, Macmillan, London, 1970, i, 147 (hereafter cited as W. B. Yeats, *Uncollected prose*). This was from an article 'Popular ballad poetry of Ireland' which, though written two years earlier, did not appear in the London *Leisure Hour* until November 1889.
9 W. B. Yeats, *Uncollected Prose*, i, 175.
10 Ibid, i, 189.
10a That Yeats's approach to Celtic Ireland was more gradual than has often been supposed and that it passed consecutively through four literary traditions – ballad, folklore, fiction and ancient myth – has been demonstrated by Mary H. Thuente, 'W. B. Yeats and Celtic Ireland 1885–1900', in P. J. Drudy (ed.), *Anglo-Irish Studies*, iv (1979), 91–104.
11 W. B. Yeats, *Letters*, p. 211.
12 W. B. Yeats, *Uncollected Prose*, i, 108.
13 From the dedication of his book of stories, *The Secret Rose* (1908), cited in Philip L. Marcus, *Yeats and the beginning of the Irish renaissance*, Ithaca and London, 1970, pp. 23–4.
14 W. B. Yeats, *Letters to the New Island*, ed. Horace Reynolds, Oxford University Press, London, 1934, p. 204.
15 W. B. Yeats, *Essays and Introductions*, Macmillan, London, 1961, pp. 185, 186–7; the essay in its original form was written in 1897.
16 W. B. Yeats, *Autobiographies*, pp. 229–30; *Uncollected Prose*, i, 206–8.
17 W. B. Yeats, *Uncollected Prose*, i, 224–5.

18. W. B. Yeats, *Memoirs*, p. 65.
19 W. B. Yeats, *Autobiographies*, p. 206.
20 W. B. Yeats, *Uncollected Prose*, i, 339–40.
21 Richard J. Finneran, George Mills Harper and William M. Murphy (ed.), *Letters to W. B. Yeats*, Macmillan London, 1977, i, 4.
22 W. B. Yeats, *Uncollected Prose*, i, 89. The best modern account of this obscure but bitter quarrel is in Phillip L. Marcus, *Yeats and the Beginning of the Irish Renaissance;* Cornell University Press, 1970, pp. 79–98.
23 Edward Dowden, *New Studies in Literature*, Kegan Paul, Trench, Trübner & Co., London, 1895, p. 19.
24 W. B. Yeats, *Uncollected Prose*, i, 233.
25 *Irish Times*, 15 Jan. 1895; Dublin *Daily Express*, 15 Jan. 1895.
26 Dublin *Daily Express*, 26 Jan. 1895.
27 Dublin *Daily Express*, 28 Feb. 1895.
28 W. B. Yeats, *Uncollected Prose*, i, 351–3.
29 Edward Dowden, *New Studies in Literature*, p. 20.
30 W. B. Yeats, *Uncollected Prose*, i, 384. For a more detailed account of the Yeats-Dowden controversy, though based on essentially the same sources, see Phillip L. Marcus, *Yeats and the Beginning of the Irish Renaissance*, pp. 104–21.
31 W. B. Yeats, *Memoirs*, p. 124.
32 W. B. Yeats, *Essays and Introductions*, p. 193.
33 Ibid., p. 203.
34 Lady Gregory, *Our Irish Theatre*, Colin Smythe Ltd., Gerrard's Cross, 1972 ed., pp. 8–9.
35 John P. Frayne and Colton Johnson (eds.), *Uncollected Prose by W. B. Yeats*, Macmillan, London, 1975, ii, 85–6.
36 See Yeats's letter to the first number of *The Leader*, 1 Sept. 1900 and the reply by its owner-editor, D. P. Moran, on 8 Sept. 1900. Moran, though not uncritical of the Gaelic League, was perhaps the severest contemporary critic of 'Anglo-Irish' literature which he denounced along with much else, in an important book, *The philosophy of Irish Ireland*, Dublin, 1905, *passim.*
37 W. B. Yeats, *Uncollected Prose*, ii, 162.
38 W. B. Yeats, *Letters to the New Island*, p. 174.

HOUND VOICES WERE THEY ALL: AN EXPERIMENT IN YEATS CRITICISM

AUGUSTINE MARTIN

This essay is experimental. It is based on a conviction that the best commentary on Yeats's poems is provided by his other poems. No source outside Yeats is therefore used in the commentary and there are only two significant appeals to his prose.

> Because we love bare hills and stunted trees
> And were the last to choose the settled ground,
> Its boredom of the desk or of the spade, because
> So many years companioned by a hound,
> Our voices carry; and though slumber-bound,
> Some few half wake and half renew their choice,
> Give tongue, proclaim their hidden name – 'Hound Voice'.
>
> The women that I picked spoke sweet and low
> And yet gave tongue. 'Hound Voices' were they all.
> We picked each other from afar and knew
> What hour of terror comes to test the soul,
> And in that terror's name obeyed the call,
> And understood, what none have understood,
> Those images that waken in the blood.
>
> Some day we shall get up before the dawn
> And find our ancient hounds before the door,
> And wide awake know that the hunt is on;
> Stumbling upon the blood-dark track once more,
> And stumbling to the kill beside the shore;
> Then cleaning out and bandaging of wounds,
> And chants of victory amid the encircling hounds.
>
> 'Hound Voice' (1938)

This most neglected of Yeats's last poems can yield one of his most explicit statements on history and individual conviction in

139

the poetry of these final years. Its neglect may be due to its apparent simplicity or, ironically, to its apparent vagueness, or perhaps even to Jeffares's only remark on it in his *Commentary*[1] that it was written 'in a spirit of mockery'. For my own part I have always been appalled by its sanguinary images and the poet's endorsement of some bloody and triumphant personal consummation. Unlike all his other 'apocalyptic poems' the 'I' says yes, and with obvious relish, to the bloodshed. But this is to anticipate; 'Hound Voice' is not normally numbered with his apocalyptic poems, and the blood that is shed, at least at first glance, is that of the huntsmen's normal quarry, fox, deer or hare. Indeed the main images of landscape, sleep, hound and blood – that most complex of all Yeats's words – are so familiar from the poet's earliest work that our first task is to establish their connotations for this particular lyric. All of them wait on our sense of 'We', because by a curious sleight of hand the poet and his elected company are at once the hounds' masters and their voices.

The *hound* as companion appears in his earliest work, notably in 'The Ballad of the Foxhunter' and 'The Wanderings of Oisin'. In the former the dying foxhunter calls for his hounds and asks his huntsman Rody to sound the horn before he expires. It would hardly strain the simple pathos of the ballad – adapted from an incident in Kickham's *Knocknagow* – to note that it is redolent of the aristocratic and traditional, and that it may even symbolise the decay of those values in the Ireland of 1889. But while the hounds in this ballad are 'human' in a metaphorical sense, in 'The Wanderings of Oisin' they are literally so: Finn's aunt, Uirne, had turned into a hound when pregnant and had given birth to the hounds Bran and Sceolan. Apart from this detail – which admittedly plays no part in the long narrative – hunting with hounds is used by Oisin to typify the warrior, and therefore aristocratic life as he reveals it to his opposite, the 'primary' Christian, St Patrick:

> Caoilte, and Conan, and Finn were there,
> When we followed a deer with our baying hounds,
> With Bran, Sceolan, and Lomair.[2]

A further connotation of the hound image occurs towards the end of the first Book of the poem when the lovers, Oisin and Niamh, pass by a 'hornless deer . . . chased by a phantom hound' with one red ear. This image for human desire is later personalised to express the poet's love for Maud in 'He mourns for the Change that has come upon him and his Beloved, and longs for the End of the World':

> Do you hear me calling, white deer with no horns?
> I have changed to a hound with one red ear;

The poet has not only become a 'hound voice', but the occasion is, in the early Yeats style, overtly apocalyptic:

> I would that the Boar without bristles had come from the
> West
> And had rooted the sun and moon and stars out of the sky
> And lay in the darkness, grunting, and turning to his rest.[3]

Equally significant, of course, is the fact that name of his favourite hero, his 'double' and his 'anti-self', Cuchulain, means in Irish 'the Hound of Culan', a name which the boy Setanta assumes by symbolically assimilating himself to the character of the animal which he slays in one of the prefatory tales to the *Tain*. Finally one may mention Yeats's wry use of the tongue hound as metaphor in expressing his aristocratic hauteur for 'certain Bad Poets', his imitators:

> You say, as I have often given tongue
> In praise of what another's said and sung,
> 'Twere politic to do the like by these;
> But was there ever dog that praised his fleas?[4]

The hound imagery in Yeats is consistent from his earliest writings: apart from its specialized sense of erotic desire and pursuit,[5] it connotes courage, nobility, the aristocratic life-style and its historical obverse of warrior culture.

Turning to the *women that I picked* one comes upon difficulties. The most obvious candidates are Maud Gonne and Constance Markiewicz, and in each case one must assume a revisionary impulse in the poet. Constance had certainly spent an aristocratic youth 'companioned by a hound' but that was before her 'voice grew shrill':

What voice more sweet than hers
When young beautiful
She rode to harriers.[6]

Maud, in 'A Prayer for my Daughter' had bartered the horn of
plenty to become an 'old bellows full of angry wind'. Mabel
Beardsley, his ideal of the female 'sprezzatura' in 'Upon a Dying
Lady', could hardly in any vocal sense have 'given tongue' though
her identification ·with 'Grania's shade,/ All but the terrors of
the woodland flight forgot' would indicate her heroic mettle. Iseult
in 'The Death of the Hare' is the quarry not the hound. Though
Olivia Shakespeare certainly 'spoke sweet and low' it is hard to
determine a sense in which she gave tongue.[7] Provisionally I suggest that it is Maud and the Gore-Booth sisters that he has in
mind: all three turned from 'dispensing round Magnanimities of
sound' to revolutionary action. He turns to the sisters for help in
burning time in 'In Memory of Eva Gore-Booth and Con
Markiewicz' and he comes to recognise a pre-ordained destiny in
Maud's fanaticism in the last poems, notably 'A Bronze Head'.

There Maud is imagined as a bird, a goddess and a thorough-
bred horse, all consistent with the pride and mettle – 'wildness' is
his preferred word here – of a higher race looking down upon
'this foul world in its decline and fall'. But she is also described
emphatically as 'a most gentle woman'. Certainly 'that terror's
name' in 'Hound Voice' finds a plausible echo in the vivid
characterisation of Maud in the third stanza of 'A Bronze Head':

But even at the starting post, all sleek and new,
I saw the wildness in her and I thought
A vision of terror that it must live through
Had shattered her soul.[8]

The terror of the imploding gyre, the 'irrational streams of
blood',[9] 'the heart's fullness' and 'the coming emptiness'[10] register
on the elect, those whose values are most obviously at risk. However, if my hunch as to the identity of the women is correct, there
is also the implication that they have the capacity somehow to
fight the terror. Thus we may see here Yeats's final reconcilement
to their defection from the world of privilege to fight the battles
of the time; his return to the mood and stance of 'No Second
Troy' with the huntress image of the 'tightened bow' drawn

against the ignobility of the age – 'Why, what could she have done, being what she is?'

The landscape images are at least initially daunting. The preference for 'bare hills and stunted trees' is altogether consistent with the hunt, and with the warrior culture out of which the aristocratic caste evolves, and the freebooting life implied is consonant with the antithetical values which are currently under threat from the twentieth century. But since *The Wild Swans at Coole* – from as far back as 'Upon a House Shaken by the Land Agitation' – Yeats has as his most persistent theme the celebration of ancestral houses by special virtue of their antiquity: 'Where passion and precision have been one / Time out of mind'.[11] In 'The Tower', 'Meditations in Time of Civil War', 'A Prayer for my Daughter', the Coole Park elegies of 1929 and 1931, later in 'To Dorothy Wellesley' and in the play 'Purgatory' (works contemporary with 'Hound Voice') the values of stable, aristocratic life, of 'custom' and 'ceremony', of 'famous portraits of our ancestors'[12] and of 'gradual Time's last gift, a written speech'[13] are untiringly praised. How, therefore, do we identify the 'We', these reluctant converts to the settled life?

In answering one must invoke what might be called the 'tower' syndrome as distinct from the 'house' syndrome in Yeats's symbology. It is variously significant that Yeats, when he retired to Galway on his marriage in 1917, chose a tower to be his residence and his symbol. The juxtaposition of 'Ancestral Houses' with the tower 'My House' in the first two movements of 'Meditations in time Civil War' is sharply schematic. The ancestral houses represent an autumnal flowering of the aristocratic lifestyle: having been conceived and designed in the first place by 'violent and bitter men' who longed for the 'sweetness' of a settled ease, of 'slippered Contemplation', they are seen as threatened from within by the decay of manliness in their inheritors

> And maybe the great-grandson of the house,
> For all its bronze and marble, 's but a mouse.[14]

This innate threat is reinforced by the menace of the times, the actual Civil War dramatised in section V, 'The Road at my Door' and VI 'The Stare's Nest at My Window'; and by the apocalyptic finale where he envisions the collapse of civilisation and the onset of a new barbarism – 'A glittering sword out of the east.' Indeed the innate threat to the 'stamina' of his caste seems to obsess Yeats through these years, not less in his Senate speeches than in a poem like this. The Tower is accordingly presented as chief among his 'Befitting emblems of adversity.' Before the manor house was built there had to be a fortress. Now that the house is doomed, its inheritors must fall back upon that ancestral resource; greatness can only be renewed out of bitterness.

Consequently the high ground and stunted trees of 'Hound Voice' are foreshadowed in the landscape of the tower:

> An acre of stony ground,
> Where the symbolic rose can break in flower,
> Old ragged elms, old thorns innumerable,
> The sound of the rain or sound
> Of every wind that blows: [15]

The 'man at arms' who first founded there with his 'dwindling band' of 'castaways' are plausible kindred for the mountainy freebooters we have sought to identify for the purposes of our explication. It becomes irresistible that 'Hound Voice' is deeply embedded in Yeats's idea of cyclical historic process, that it is 'apocalyptic' in its vision, and that it invokes an alternative sense of the aristocratic to the elegiac sense in which the great houses are lamented. Also that this alternative sense involves the warrior culture epitomised in Oisin and Cuchulain which has its later counterparts in the soldier ancestry of the Irish Ascendancy. Civilisation, now at the stake, must rely on these warrior atavisms to survive through the contemporary violence and work towards a future renewal of their strength and value.

The possibility of such renewal is best exemplified in the great elegy 'In Memory of Major Robert Gregory'. Gregory had not only fought and died heroically in the Great War but he had embodied in his personality the Renaissance *sprezzatura* which Yeats saw as the hallmark of high civilisation. He was therefore our 'Sidney and our perfect man' combining the gifts of 'Soldier, scholar, horseman'. More relevantly to our theme, however, Gregory rode superbly 'with the Galway foxhounds', he loved the symbolic landscape of 'Hound Voice', the 'old storm-broken trees / That cast their shadows upon road and bridge' and he was born, significantly,

> To cold Clare rock and Galway rock and thorn,
> To that stern colour and that delicate line
> That are our secret discipline
> Wherein the gazing heart doubles her might.

Before dealing with the image of 'blood' it is useful at this point to sketch the historical time-scale which Yeats is assuming in all of these apocalyptic poems of his final period. His key period is five hundred years. The great moments of civilisation have occurred when his subjective or antithetical gyre has reached its fullest extension. From the primary or objective climax of Christianity's founding it took five hundred years to reach a new subjective 'unity of culture' at Byzantium. It then declined while the objective gyre expanded to its fullness in the Middle Ages. From there the subjective gyre grew to its perfection in the Italian Renaissance on 'Urbino's windy hill.' Since then the primary gyre has grown to its fullness and is approaching its disintegration in Yeats's own time with the rise of democracy, socialism and communism the 'levelling spirit' of modern 'mechanical' civilisation. The Christian era is at a close, the 'twenty centuries of stony sleep'[16] are ending and at the inner centre of the old gyre the 'rough beast' of a new antithetical civilisation is beginning to stir. To adapt Synge's remark in the preface to his poems before civilisation can become human again it must first become brutal. This process will take five hundred years and must endure a prefatory period of war and violence as the old dispensation gives way to the new. Looking out upon that violence in the late thirties and looking back at Ireland of 1913, 1916, at the Troubles and the Civil War, looking at Europe of the Great War and of the October Revolution, Yeats is inevitably concerned for those aristocratic values which he cherished and for their survival through this turbulent transition. He naturally harks back to the values, the resources, the virtues that sustained his forbears five hundred years before, in the early days of conquest. It is these virtues that 'Hound Voice' celebrates. But the full force of that celebration cannot be adequately felt before the final term 'blood' is briefly annotated.

There are two sense of *'blood'* in the poem. The simpler is the quarry's blood, shed by hounds and hunters. The hunters are also wounded in the chase or its climax, hence the 'cleaning out and bandaging of wounds' as if after a battle. The hunt must stand for something complex and momentous in human terms. This first sense of blood, frightening enough in itself, is stressed and amplified by the second sense conveyed with that ominous vagueness I mentioned at the outset: 'Those images that waken in the blood.' The most immediate suggestion is that the hunters' blood is up, the hunt is on. But underlying this colloquial import of the word is the ancestral, the genetic, perhaps even the Lawrentian sense of the 'dark gods in the blood'. Yeats had been exulting in 'blood/ That has not passed through any huckster's loin' since the 'Introductory Rhymes' to *Responsibilities* (1914). In 'To a Shade' he had compared the efficacy of fine art to 'gentle blood' passing from parent to child. The same sense of aristocratic blood, of thorough breeding, lurks behind the imagery of his Senate speech on divorce where he describes his Anglo-Irish as 'one of the great stocks of Europe'.[17] Therefore the blood of those who respond to 'those images' – a phrase still far from precise – is the blood of an elite, those with a shared racial memory, who can pick each other 'from afar' and feel within their veins a peculiar 'terror' incomprehensible to the many.

Which brings us to *'those images'* themselves, sensed by the hunters in their sleep, leading them to a bloody consummation 'some day' when they rise before dawn. It would be careless to ignore the short poem entitled 'Those Images' published in March of the same year. The relevant gloss is found in the fourth stanza:

> Seek those images
> That constitute the wild,
> The lion and the virgin
> The harlot and the child.[18]

Images such as these are not ostentatiously relevant to 'Hound Voice' – unless it is read as an apocalyptic poem. But if it is, if it is seen to enact a personal Armageddon, their relevance becomes not just patent but interesting. The most explicit of Yeats's early apocalyptic visions occurs in 'The Adoration of the Magi'. In that story three Irish Magi answer the command of Michael Robartes and travel to a brothel in Paris to kneel by the bed of a dying Irish harlot who gives birth to the avatar of a new savage dispensation.[19] Similarly the 'lion' prowls through Yeats's apocalyptic scenario in a wide range of postures, not only the 'shape with a lion body' in 'The Second Coming' or the 'lion and woman' of

'The Circus Animals' Desertion', but even more significantly through 'The Wanderings of Oisin' where, in Book Three, it forms part of a recurrent motif and refrain:

> O flaming lion of the world, O when will you turn to
> your rest?

If therefore we decide that 'Hound Voice' can bear an apocalyptic reading, if in other words we decide that a Yeatsean apocalypse is somehow possible without a single 'occult' emblem – no sphynx, incubus, fiend, unicorn, brazen hawk, or dragon of air – we are well advised to determine how this version of apocalypse differs from the others.

One can distinguish three phases in Yeats's antecedent sense of apocalyptic change. In the Nineties, notably in *The Wind Among the Reeds* and the 'Secret Rose' stories, the sense of radical historic change was mediated almost exclusively through invented *personae,* or through the third person singular; the tone was mostly one of reverent expectation; the iconography was drawn from the alchemical process and from the allied formulae of Joachim of Flora which defined and foretold a new dispensation: 'the Kingdom of the Father was past, the Kingdom of the Son passing, the Kingdom of the Spirit yet to come.'[20] Thus the narrator of 'Rosa Alchemica' saw alchemy as 'a universal transmutation of all things into some divine and imperishable substance . . . the transmutation of life into art, and a cry of measureless desire for a world made wholly of essences.'[21] It was overwhelmingly the idiom of aspiration and prophesy; manifesting itself without explicit violence;

> Surely thine hour has come, thy great wind blows,
> Far off, most secret and inviolate Rose?[22]

The second phase arose out of the poet's horrified recognition that these prophecies were coming true before his eyes in the process of history, in the Easter Rising, the Russian Revolution, the Black and Tan war and later the Civil War in Ireland. This phase was marked by the threatening nature of the omens which no longer spoke of a fine transmutation but rather declared themselves as dragons, rough beasts, brazen hawks, insolent fiends. The relevant volumes are *Michael Robartes and the Dancer* and *The*

147

Tower. In these apocalyptic visions the narrator, the Yeats figure, is dissociated and terrified: his wits are astray, his sight troubled, he restrains himself from crying vengeance on the murders of Jacques Molay, absolves himself from involvement in 'something that all others understand or share',[23] climbs to his 'proper dark', traffics in mockery.

The third phase is more excited and desperate, it announces itself most clearly in 'Parnell's Funeral' at the opening of *A Full Moon in March* (1935) where he sees the history of his own country yield ignobly to the 'contagion of the throng'. Later in the same volume in 'Meru' the poet acknowledges that civilization is maintained only by 'manifold delusion'. As the gyre staggers and the face of civilisation cracks the poet is forced back upon his old concept of 'tragic joy' which he had first adumbrated as a dramatic theory in 1910:

> What matter? Out of cavern comes a voice,
> And all it knows is that one word 'Rejoice! '[24]

This attitude bespeaks a degree of collusion with the ugliness and the violence, but no involvement. The poet and his surrogates – as in 'Lapis Lazuli – stare on 'all the tragic scene', no longer horrified or afraid because, in the nature of that 'unfashionable gyre' the entire civilization can be built again. The times are ugly and the elite may have to brace their sensibilities as spectators to observe 'this age and the next age / Engender in a ditch.'[25] But they remain spectators; they do not bear a hand in the mayhem; the gross imagery of blood and carnage preclude participation on either side; the poetic self stands, however fearfully, aloof.

But in 'Hound Voice' the poetic self is almost drunk with excited participation in the chase and in the kill. Furthermore the apocalyptic images are no longer drawn from the underworld of black magic or the 'frogspawn of a blind man's ditch'; there are no witches, incubi, no dubious hybrids or occult monsters. Instead there is the open-air exhilaration of the chase, the aristo-cratic verve and vitality, the triumph of the best. If we set this unique version of apocalypse against Yeats's political formula-tions of the time we find that it takes on an even more formid-able implication.

In his last extended essay, *On the Boiler* (1939), Yeats reveals an obsession with breeding. In that section of it entitled 'To-

morrow's Revolution' he prefaces his observations on the contemporary scene with six pages of commentary on selective breeding drawn from Burton, Fernelius, Curtius, Shaw and Cattell and
notes with dismay that since 'about 1900 the better stocks have
not been replacing their numbers, while the stupider and less
healthy have been more than replacing theirs.'[26] He goes on to
note that the 'Fascist countries' who know that 'civilisation has
reached a crisis' are – to his disgust – offering bounties for large
families, thus adding to the universal decline in human excellence.
'Sooner or later we must limit the families of the unintelligent
classes.' In a passage that echoes much of what has already been
said in theme and image he projects the possibility of an aristocratic future:

> Yet we must hold to what we have that the next civilization
> may be born, not from a virgin's womb, nor a tomb without a
> body, not from a void, but of our own rich experience. These
> gifts must return, not in the mediumistic sleep, dreaming or
> dreamless, but when we are wide awake. Eugenical and
> physical research are the revolutionary movements with that
> element of novelty and sensation which sooner or later stir men
> to action. It may be, or must be, that the best bred from the
> best shall claim again their ancient omens.[27]

These prose sentences resemble 'Hound Voice' not only in
language – 'sleep', 'wide awake', 'ancient omens' – but in the
deliberate sense of mystery it creates through its rapt prophetic
cadences. The argument of the essay presses forward to strange
plans of practical action; 'The formation of military families
should be encouraged' to confront 'the disciplined uneducated
masses of the commercial nations.' A hundred such men would
be equal of 'a million of the lesser sort' because 'we have as good
blood as there is in Europe.' This faith in noble blood and its long-
term destiny for Ireland and Europe is reinforced in a frequently
quoted passage from 'A General Introduction for my Work'
(1937) where an ominous vagueness, reminiscent of 'Hound Voice'
gives witness to the poet's apprehension of the years to come:

> When I stand upon O'Connell Bridge in the half light and
> notice that discordant architecture, all those electric signs,
> where modern heterogeneity has taken physical form, a vague

149

hatred comes up out of my own dark and I am certain that wherever in Europe there are minds strong enough to lead others the same vague hatred rises; in four or five or in less generations this hatred will have issued in violence and imposed some rule of kindred. I cannot know the nature of that rule, for its opposite fills the light; all I can do to bring it nearer is to intensify my hatred.[28]

This brings our survey of the poem's background to an end. It remains to read it again in the light of these annotations – drawn exclusively from Yeats's work – and look for the source of its curious power, for the psychic realities which it communicates through its violent and victorious rhetoric.

Immediately it appears that its theme is the awakening of a 'rule of kindred' to encounter and defeat the spawning democracy of the age. This awakening will not occur immediately, may not occur even soon, but 'Someday' the challenge will be presented and the best blood will answer. For now the impulse is dormant, 'slumber bound.' But when it awakes it will marshall all its ancient, ancestral energies, and call upon its friends. The civilities of courtly life where the women 'spoke sweet and low' will reveal their old strength, the passion and violence which had achieved in the first place 'the sweetness that all longed for night and day.' Blood will cry out to blood and for blood; the crucial images that make and break civilisation will beckon to the savage consummation. The seeds of a new high culture will be sown as aristocracy calls upon its warrior heritage to face the new Salamis, Thermopylae, Valley of the Black Pig:

> That civilisation may not sink
> Its great battle lost.[29]

But what makes 'Hound Voice' unique among these poems is the poet's exultant participation. No longer does he merely look on in expectation, dismay or tragic joy. He is magisterially present, not with a 'gift to set a statesman right',[30] but with the poet's instinct to recognise the right cause, the true allies, the crucial moment of test for all his kind. That 'hour of terror' will, it seems, wipe out vacillation and remorse – unlike the options rehearsed in the opening the 'The Man and the Echo' – because

the individual will now finds its sanction in the universal imperative. Stephen Dedalus had spoken of history as a nightmare from
which he hoped to awake. The Yeats voice here aspires to awake,
as it were, *into* the nightmare of history as one of those choice
and master spirits which he had spent his lifetime summoning in
demonic rage – Oisin, Cuchulain, Pearse, Connolly, Robert
Emmet and Wolfe Tone – 'Aye, and Achilles, Timor, Babar,
Barhaim, all/ Who have lived in joy and laughed into the face of
death.'[31] It was inevitable that at some stage the self would want
to become the anti-self, casting off hesitation and scruple, that
the anxious and sedentary poet should wish to assume the hero
'violent and famous' like Cuchulain or live momentarily, like
Oisin among

> Companions long accurst and dead,
> And hounds for centuries dust and air.[32]

It is the one poem in which Yeats gives himself to the blood-
dimmed stream of history and becomes personally 'fighting mad.'
That identification can be interpreted as an imaginative leap into
vicarious violence which he had spent a lifetime contemplating
through a whole range of persona and scenario, fictional,
mythical, historical. Or it can be seen as a dramatic presentiment
of the moment when, in a not far future reincarnation, the poet
would become the swordsman while Cuchulain sang and sewed in
Hades among cowards. In either case it gives us Yeats, however
obliquely, entertaining with relish a rare moment of violence and
triumph on the shore of modern history.

NOTES

1   A. Norman Jeffares, *Commentary on Yeats's Poems,* London 1968,
    p. 500. Professor Jeffares told me that when he asked the poet's widow
    about the poem she replied that Yeats had given her this one cryptic
    comment on it.
2   *Variorum Edition of the Poems of W. B. Yeats,* Allt and Allspach,
    New York, 1973 (hereafter *Variorum*) p. 3.
3   *Variorum,* p. 153.
4   Ibid., p. 262.
5   See note in *Variorum* pp. 806–807 in which Yeats explains that 'This
    hound and deer seem plain images of the desire of the man for the
    woman', and the desire of the woman which is for the desire of the
    man.'

6 'Easter 1916', Ibid., p. 392.
7 Perhaps that spirited gentlewoman, Dorothy Wellesley with her 'Great Dane that cannot bay the moon' being, perhaps ominously, 'sunk in sleep' (p. 580) is also sister of the company.
8 *Variorum* p. 619.
9 'The Gyres', Ibid., p. 560.
10 'I See Phantoms of Hatred', Ibid., p. 564.
11 Ibid., p. 264.
12 'Ancestral Houses', p. 418.
13 'Upon a House Shaken by the Land Agitation', Ibid., 264.
14 'Ancestral Houses' p. 418.
15 'My House', Ibid., p. 419.
16 'The Second Coming; Ibid., 402.
17 *The Senate Speeches of W. B. Yeats,* ed. Donald R. Pearce. Faber, London 1960, p. 99.
18 *Variorum* p. 601.
19 It is perhaps useful, though not necessary, to note here that before Yeats had discovered the gyres, his symbolic 'sesame' to the recurrent cycles of history, he had derived from Blake an antithetical concept of religious process.

> The Mother had a Harlot been
> Just such an one as Magdelen

20 'The Tables of the Law', *Mythologies,* Macmillan. London, 1959, p. 296.
21 *'Rosa Alchemica'*, Ibid., p. 267.
22 'The Secret Rose', *Variorum*, p. 170
23 'I See Phantoms of Hatred', Ibid., p. 427.
24 'The Gyres' Ibid., p. 564.
25 'The Old Stone Cross', Ibid., p. 598.
26 *Explorations,* p. 423.
27 Ibid. p. 437.
28 *Essays and Introductions,* p. 586.
29 'The Long-Legged Fly', *Variorum,* p. 617.
30 Ibid. p. 359.
31 'Her Courage', Ibid. p. 366.
32 'The Wanderings of Oisin', Ibid. p. 11.

THE SHAPE-CHANGERS

D. E. S. MAXWELL

(i)

The shape-changers are the artists: painters, sculptors, poets.
Their aim, in the Greek definition, is mimesis, imitation, a term
that can be variously understood. It can be taken to mean an
exact representation of reality, where fidelity to the original is
the criterion. Only God, we are told, can make a tree: the
realistic artist will try to make his imitation as close to the reality
as he can; and yet superior to it. In Yeats's words, to

> scorn aloud
> In glory of changeless metal
> Common bird or petal.[1]

Or imitation can undertake, in various degrees, modifications,
distortions of its subject. The subjects include, of course, not just
physical entities, but feelings, ideas, emotions, a situation, a set
of events. Their imitation in art is a process of selection and
emphasis. It imposes new shapes on its material. By doing so it
adopts a viewpoint, and at least alludes to comment and judgment. The new shape affects the way we see its counterparts in
the phenomenal world of objects and events. And it is often true
that events in life are not so credible as their depiction in art.
Life does not work upon a set of tricks designed to make us
suspend our disbelief, at least I don't think it does, and Sartre has
a comment to the effect that in order for an event to become real,
it must be told as a story.

There are various ways of talking about art and life and their
connections, often by analogy. Yeats's 'Among School Children',
for example, meditates upon schooling, education, but transforms
that into a metaphor of the imagination at work. Here is another
example, from Brian Friel's *Faith Healer*. Ostensibly this is a
play about, indeed, a faith healer, and his fickle, unreliable talent,

153

which will sometimes cure, sometimes not, all beyond his volition. The play is in four monologues. The third is by the faith-healer's manager, Teddy, in part about his ludicrous, seedy career in what he would call show-biz:

> Did you ever look back over all the great artists – old Freddy here, Lillie Langtry, Sir Laurence Olivier, Houdini, Charlie Chaplin, Gracie Fields – and did you ever ask yourself what makes them all top-liners, what have they all got in common? Okay, I'll tell you. Three things. Number one: they've got ambition this size. Okay? Number two: they've got a talent that is sensational and unique – there's only one Sir Laurence – right? Number three: not one of them has two brains to rub together. You think I'm joking? I promise you. They know they have something fantastic, sure, they're not that stupid. But what it is they have, how they do it, how it works, what that sensational talent is, what it all means – believe me, they don't know and they don't care and even if they did care they haven't the brains to analyse it.
> Let me tell you about two dogs I had once. Okay? One was a white poodle and she was so brilliant – I mean that dog she knew what you were thinking about before you even thought about it yourself. Before I'd come home at night d'you know what that dog would do? She'd switch on the electric fire, pull the curtains, and have my slippers and a bottle of beer sitting there beside my chair. But put her in front of an audience – fell apart – couldn't do nothing. Right. Now the other dog he was a whippet. Maybe you remember him, Rob Roy, The Piping Dog? (BRIEF PAUSE) Well, it was quite a few years ago. Anyway, you see that whippet – he was fantastic – I mean to say, just tell me how many times in your life has it been your privilege to hear a 3-year-old whippet dog play *COME INTO THE GARDEN, MAUD* on the bagpipes *and* follow for his encore with *PLAISIR D'AMOUR*. Okay? Agreed. Sensational talent. Ambition? I couldn't stop him rehearsing. Morning, noon and night he'd sit there blowing the bloody thing and working them bellows with his back leg – all night long if I'd let him. That's all he lived for – being on top of the heap. And brains? Had he brains, that whippet? Let me tell you. I had that dog four and a half years, until he expired from pulminary exhaustion. And in all that time that whippet

couldn't even learn his name! I mean it. I mean apart from his musical genius that whippet in human terms was education- ally subnormal. A retarded whippet in fact. I'd stub my toe against something and I'd say 'God!'; and who'd come running to me, wagging his tail? I tell you: a philosopher – that's what you became.

There we have a comic account of the performing arts, and, by extension, of the imagination setting itself tasks of expression. What is required? Intelligence? Industry? Philosophy? The context of Teddy's monologue is the much more sombre history of the faith-healer. He is, when it works, literally a shape- changer: of 'the crippled and the blind and the disfigured and the deaf and the barren.' His, he says, is 'a craft without an appren- ticeship, a ministry without responsibility, a vocation without a ministry,' and he asks about it, 'Was it all chance? or skill? or illusion? or delusion? Precisely what power did I possess? Could I summon it? When and how? Was I its servant?' Skill, illusion, control: the properties to which art addresses itself. The faith- healers's final test puts him at risk with death – literal death, but figuring the death of an imagination no longer certain of its 'shaping spirit.' In 'At Algeciras', Yeats asks what he 'Can with a fitting confidence reply' to the 'Great Questioner', and we may think of other poems on the treacheries, the misleadings, the uncertainties, and the loss of inspiration: Yeats's 'The Circus Animals' Desertion', Coleridge's 'Dejection':

> But oh! each visitation
> Suspends what nature gave me at my birth,
> My shaping spirit of Imagination.

Now out of that, the debate which concerns me at the moment is between, in its simplest form, those who argue that the shapes devised by the artist are autonomous, self-contained, insulating themselves from the world they draw upon; and on the other hand the belief that the art-object, the poem, say, impinges upon the world of reality and may give it new directions. As Yeats perhaps rather patronisingly enquires,

> Did that play of mine send out
> Certain men the English shot?[2]

155

In short, and rather crudely, art for art's sake versus art as propaganda. Oscar Wilde, professing art for art's sake, nevertheless remarked of the London fogs that they did not exist until impressionist painting imitated them. To put it more prosaically, the impressionists defined an essence, so to speak, of fogginess which had not been observed before.

Mimesis, then, imitation, can make large claims for itself. By imitating something you are in a way possessing it, appropriating it, seeking by an act of imagination to dominate the external world. The literary act might be seen as an act of aggression, imperialist in its designs, and like many imperialist designs, a kind of confidence trick, because if it doesn't make you believe in it, it won't work. If you are prepared to be a little far-fetched, as I am, the conduct of heroes in literature offers further analogies to the exercise of the literary imagination. Cuchulain, for example, was a shape-changer, as we know from the description in *The Táin* of his celebrated 'warp-spasm'. This was a kind of one-man military manoeuvre:

> His face and features became a red bowl: he sucked one eye so deep into his head that a wild crane couldn't probe it onto his cheek out of the depths of his skull; the other eye fell out along his cheek. His mouth weirdly distorted: his cheek peeled back from his jaws until the gullet appeared, his lungs and liver flapped in his mouth and throat, his lower jaw struck the upper a lion-killing blow, and fiery flakes large as a ram's fleece reached his mouth from his throat. His heart boomed loud in his breast like the baying of a watch-dog at its feed or the sound of a lion among bears. Malignant mists and spurts of fire – the torches of the Badb – flickered red in the vaporous clouds that rose boiling above his head, so fierce was his fury. The hair of his head twisted like the tangle of a red thornbush stuck in a gap; if a royal apple tree with all its kingly fruit were shaken above him, scarce an apple would reach the ground but each would be spiked on a bristle of his hair as it stood up on his scalp with rage. The hero-halo rose out of his brow, long and broad as a warrior's whetstone, long as a snout, and he went mad rattling his shields, urging on his charioteer and harassing the hosts. Then, tall and thick, steady and strong, high as the mast of a noble ship, rose up from the dead centre of his skull a straight spout of black blood darkly and magically

156

Those words open Ovid's *Metamorphoses*, which is of course full
of transformations. The transformations in Ovid extend and
refine upon the warriors' metaphor of art. The metamorphoses
narrated by Ovid, as you know, are often a tactic adopted by the
gods to have their way with mortal women. Leda, Europa, and
Danäe should have had more care of the swan, the bull, and the
shower of gold which were the causes of their respective down-
falls. However, it is the metamorphoses of the pursued, not the
pursuers, which allude most richly to parables of art.

We may see Niobe as an emblem of some correspondence
between life and art, turned to a statue of stone which still weeps
human tears: and her counterpart, Pygmalion's creation, where
ivory and the flesh which it becomes test discrimination, 'to try
whether it be flesh or ivory'. When Pan pursued Syrinx, the water
spirits turned her into marsh reeds, on which the breeze played
melodious airs: 'charmed by the sweet tones, the god exclaimed,
"This union, at least shall I have with thee." And so the pipes . . .
took and kept the name of the maiden.' Daphne prays for escape
from Apollo, whereupon,

> a down-dragging numbness seized her limbs, and her soft sides
> were begirt with thin bark. Her hair changed to leaves, her
> arms to branches. Her feet, but now so swift, grew fast in
> sluggish roots, and her head was now but a tree's top. Her
> gleaming beauty alone remained . . . And the god cried out,
> 'My hair, my lyre, my quiver, shall always be entwined with
> thee, O laurel.[6]

Alcyone finds her husband's body washed to shore, and flies to
it as a bird, embracing

> the dear limbs with her new-found wings and strove vainly to
> kiss the cold lips with her rough bill . . . but he did feel it. And
> at last, through the pity of the gods, both changed to birds.
> Though thus they suffered the same fate, still even thus their
> love remained . . . Still do they mate and rear their young; and
> for seven peaceful days in the winter season Alcyone broods
> upon her nest floating upon the surface of the waters . . . the
> waves of the sea are still.[7]

Halcyon days.
Juno punished the mother of Arcas by Jove:

> With bristling black hair, her hands were feet, tipped
> By their crooked nails; the lips that Jove once praised
> Became a pair of wide, misshapen jaws
> And to prevent her prayers from reaching heaven
> Her gift of speech was ripped away and from her throat
> Came gutteral noises horrible to hear.
>
> Though her emotions were of human kind . . .
>   she
> Could not say her thoughts.[8]

Finally reunited with Arcas, she and her son are translated by Jove to the skies:

>   as though his power
> Was of the invisible vortex of the wind,
> He swept up mother and son into the heavens
> And made them neighbouring companies of stars.[9]

It was a common enough apothesis, the destiny of Castor, Pollux, and of Ariadne's crown:

> And, that she might shine among the deathless stars,
> he sent the crown she wore up to the skies. Through
> the thin air it flew; and as it flew, it took its place
> between the Kneeler and the Serpent-Holder.[10]

By inheritance, *The Rape of the Lock* similarly resolves its delicate catastrophes:

> A sudden star it shot through liquid air,
> And drew behind a radiant trail of hair.
> Not Berenice's locks first rose so bright
> The heavens bespangling with dishevelled light.
> . . . .
> This Lock the Muse shall consecrate to fame,
> And midst the stars inscribe Belinda's name.

So much by way of Ovidian example. Ovid's narratives imply quite an elaborate iconography of aesthetics. They are not only stories of human passions discovered in the creatures of myth, of bodily transformations which represent conditions of mind and feeling. They are also fables of the metamorphoses in which art may engage. I do not intend to identify all these implications – for example, that Niobe and Pygmalion are figures of the art whose criterion is representational truth, the art which aspires to imitate the real world with faithful accuracy. That aim can lead to confusion. You will recall the misguided artist who was painting a river scene at dusk and rowed over to the other bank to have a closer look at the trees so that he could represent exactly the detail of their leaves.

Throughout the tales I've mentioned, Ovid is addressing more provocative possibilities for art. His metamorphoses are designed, in a literal sense, as a means of escape, of protection from danger, as with Syrinx; as a punishment which may be redeemed, as with Arcas's mother; as a transcendence of grief, a beauty come out of suffering, as with Alcyone; as an apothesis of mortal to immortal beauty, as with Ariadne – and indeed Belinda; as demonstrations of the frailty of beauty, which may be reduced to ugliness and may be restored, as with Io. They may entail, again as with Arcas's mother, the agony of losing the speech to articulate feeling, or as with Io, speech lost, then restored, and with it the assumption of divinity.

I do not think that one can extract any general aesthetic formula from that. The tales, however, are clearly moving among some of the claims of poetry, that, for example, its language, in literally an act of creation, calls into being secondary worlds. They are not reality, but in Dr Johnson's phrase, 'they bring realities to mind.' The metamorphoses of Ovid's heroines are tangible enactments of their changed condition: sorrowing mother to invulnerable star, speechless beast to goddess. The poet transforms the world of measured space and time to other designs, enhancing because they are other designs: designs of words which alter perspectives, speak to correspondences and reconciliations, or even find a language to denominate irresolution. Those of Yeats's poems, for example, which end in questions have converted mere irresolution into a statement of irresolution. Art is managing reality into determinations whose authority, whose rulings, whose re-alignments reside in verbal display.

'The Stolen Child', the early Yeats poem, is one illustration of one such process. The poem commends, or appears to commend, the life of fancy, of magic, of escape over the trials and anxieties of daily life. Language gives the fairies, who are the speakers, all their own way. Their 'Weaving olden dances/Mingling hands and mingling glances' wins over 'the world full of troubles'. Until the end, perhaps too late for the stolen child, the allure of a domestic charm has its say: 'calves on the warm hillside', 'the kettle on the hob/Sing peace into his breast'. The shape changes. The words give an alternative reality its voice, and subvert the poem's appeal for the glamour of the supernatural, the world of trance and vision, perhaps what Yeats later meant by 'the incon-querable delusion,/Magical shapes', in 'Ego Dominus Tuus'; or later again, in 'Meditations in Time of Civil War', 'The half-read wisdom of daemonic images'. 'The Stolen Child' is a good deal more complex than a casual reading of it might deliver .

Yeats speaks of shape-changers in *Explorations*. He is refer-ring, overtly to the 'communicators', spirit mediums, who con-verse with the dead. These spirits utter, through the medium, 'images not wholly different from themselves, figures in a galanty show not too strained or extravagant to speak their very thought.' Yeats goes on:

Yet we never long escape the phantasmagoria nor can long forget that we are among the shape-changers. Sometimes our own minds shape that mysterious substance, which may be life itself, according to desire or constrained by memory, and the dead no longer remembering their own names become the characters in the drama we ourselves have invented. John King, who has delighted melodramatic minds for hundreds of séances with his career on earth as Henry Morgan the Buccaneer, will tell more scientific visitors that he is merely a force, while some phantom long accustomed to a decent name, questioned by some pious Catholic, will admit very cheerfully that he is the Devil. Nor is it only present minds that perplex the shades with phantasy, for friends of Count Albert de Rochas once wrote out names and incidents but to discover that though the surname of the shade that spoke had been histori-cal, Christian name and incidents were from a romance run-ning at the time in some clerical newspaper no one there had ever opened.

Revenants are, to use the modern term, 'suggestible', and may be studied in the 'trance personalities' of hypnosis and in our dreams which are but hypnosis turned inside out, a modeller's clay for our suggestions, or, if we follow the *Spiritual Diary*, for those of invisible beings. Swedenborg has written that we are each in the midst of a group of associated spirits who sleep when we sleep and become the *dramatis personae* of our dreams, and are always the other will that wrestles with our thought, shaping it to our despite.[11]

The terms in which Yeats conducts the discussion are revealing of latent interests. He writes of the mind shaping life to the dictate of memory and desire; of an invented drama; of romance passed off as fact; of modeller's clay; of the *dramatis personae* of our dreams, actors in a struggle of wills which reshapes our conscious, voluntary thought. Yeats is providing parables of art, parables of the reflexes and intentions of the creative imagination. A later passage further clarifies his ideas:

Men of letters have sometimes said that the characters of a romance or of a play must be typical. They mean that the character must be typical of something which exists in all men because the writer has found it in his own mind. It is one of the most inexplicable things about human nature that a writer, with a strange temperament, an Edgar Allan Poe, let us say, made what he is by conditions that never existed before, can create personages and lyric emotions which startle us by being at once bizarre and an image of our own secret thoughts. Are we not face to face with the microcosm, mirroring everything in universal Nature? It is no more necessary for the characters created by a romance-writer, or a dramatist, to have existed before, than for his own personality to have done so; characters and personality alike, as is perhaps true in the instance of Poe, may draw half their life not from the solid earth but from some dreamy drug. This is true even of historical drama, for it was Goethe, the founder of the historical drama of Germany, who said, 'We do the people of history the honour of naming after them the creations of our own minds'. All that a dramatic writer need do is to persuade us, during the two hours' traffic of the stage, that the events of his play did really happen. He must know enough of the life of his country, or of history, to create this illusion, but no matter how much he knows, he will fail if his audience is not ready to give up something of the dead letter. If his mind is full of energy he will not be satisfied with little knowledge, but he will be far more likely to alter incidents and characters, wilfully even as it may seem, than to become a literal historian. It was one of the complaints against Shakespeare, in his own day, that he made Sir John Falstaff out of a praiseworthy old Lollard preacher. One day, as he sat over Holinshed's *History of England*, he persuaded himself that Richard II, with his French culture, 'his too great friendliness to his friends', his beauty of mind, and his fall before dry, repelling Bolingbroke, would be a good image for an accustomed mood of fanciful, impracticable lyricism in his own mind. The historical Richard has passed away for ever and the Richard of the play lives more intensely, it seems, than did every living man. Yet Richard II, as Shakespeare made him, could never have been born before the Renaissance, before the Italian influence, or even one hour before the innumberable streams that flowed in upon Shakespeare's mind, the innumerable experiences we can never know, brought Shakespeare to the making of him. He is typical not because he ever existed, but because he has made us know of something in our own minds we had never known of had he never been imagined.[12]

Whether Yeats is talking of the spirit medium, the spirit voice, the writer, the history or experience on which the writer's imagination seizes, it is the imagination which legislates access to reality. The artist does honour not only to the people of history but to all experiences by naming them after the creations of his own mind. Like the writer's, the reader's sense of what is real is quickened, as Yeats says in the *Memoirs*, by the artist's finding 'expression for a life that lacked it.'[13] The workings of art, again in Yeats's words, are 'to show us the reality that is within our minds, and the reality that our eyes look on.'[14] Yeats was in no doubt as to the relative value of the two realities. The inner controls the outer. The cartography of the outer world will come to reflect the shapes deployed upon it by a despotic imagination. According to the *Memoirs*, the writer because 'he reflects the world in a strange mirror . . . makes us also see' it.[15] The reader is surprised into recognising images both of his own secret thoughts; and of unsuspected contours in a malleable reality.

(iii)

Probably the clearest instance of Yeats's direct ambition to accommodate life to art is his prospectus for creating what 'The Municipal Gallery Revisited' calls 'an Ireland/The poets have imagined'. His early understanding of this was a simple one. In *The Celtic Twilight* he explains that Irish poets should 'create a little world out of the beautiful, pleasant, and significant things of this marred and clumsy world.' As Yeats, in *Beltaine*, saw in 1900, this literary celebration, and eventual metamorphosis, of Ireland, would recognise that, 'Our daily life has fallen among prosaic thing and unworthy things, but our dreams remember the enchanted valleys.'[16] The transforming dream was not to be of Ireland warts and all; and had at least to be indulgent of the sentimentalities and noisy rhetoric of Davis, Mangan, and the rest.

But these simplicities were in fact uncongenial to Yeats. The poets, whom he described as 'the secret transformers of the world,' needed 'a subtle, appropriate language',[17] and an 'impartial imagination, a furious impartiality . . . to say all that people did not want to have said.'[18] Mangan's Dark Rosaleen – 'my saint of saints', 'my virgin flower' – is not unlike Yeats's own Cathleen ni Houlihan – 'a young girl, and she had the walk of a queen.' Both are comfortable among the platitudes that people did want to have said. Neither would be comprehensible in Yeats's darker vision, where 'There is no laughter too bitter, no irony too harsh for utterance, no passion too terrible to be set before the minds of men.'[19] Neither Rosaleen nor Cathleen is at all kin to the implied and enigmatic Medusa of 'Easter 1916', who 'enchanted to a stone'. Nor could either play her part on the stage of *The Playboy of the Western World* or *The Plough and the Stars*, of which Yeats said that they were attacked 'because they contain what a belief, tamed down to a formula, shudders at, something wild and ancient.'[20]

Yeats thus abandoned 'the deliberate creation of a kind of Holy City in the imagination, a Holy Sepulchre, as it were, or Holy Grail for the Irish mind'.[21] Like Crazy Jane, he refused the stereotype of the 'heavenly mansion', or rather, he opened it to diabolic possession: 'Fair and foul are near of kin,/And fair needs foul'. 'September 1913', 'Easter 1916', 'Meditations in Time of Civil War', 'Parnell's Funeral', 'The Statues' are enabling

165

poems. They enable the facts, the historical facts, which are their genesis, to become interrogative not declarative. 'Parnell's Funeral' is interrogative. The poem 'The Death of Parnell', in Joyce's 'Ivy Day in the Committee Room' is declarative. Here is an exemplary stanza from Joyce:

> He would have had his Erin famed,
> The green flag gloriously unfurled,
> Her statesmen, bards and warriors raised
> Before the nations of the world.

After the audience's applause the immediate response, in Joyce's narrative, is that the cork in a bottle of Guinness goes derisively, 'Pok!' The sentiments of Yeats's 'Parnell's Funeral' are in fact not dissimilar. But Yeats's poem achieves, by its obliqueness, the elevation to which the popular ballad only aspires.

'Parnell's Funeral' moves from the briefest glimpse of a crowd of Dubliners under a stormy sky to a shooting star, to sacrificial death. It then concerns the deaths of Balder, of Apollo, gods slain to be re-born. Here, the cycle is interrupted. Parnell's death is without succession or renewal. The lonely god surrenders to 'the contagion of the throng'. The poem evokes a discouraging past – 'Swift's dark grove' – a dire present; and no future. 'Meditations in Time of Civil War', similarly distances its declared subject. It is, of course, a poem about the civil war in Ireland in the nineteen-twenties. More important, it is a poem about exits, entrances, passages: about terraces, doors, chambers, galleries, stairs, barricades, prospects. And in its ending, 'I turn away and shut the door'. The poem presents 'emblems of adversity' as well as 'marvellous accomplishment'. In poems such as these, Yeats's imitations alter the contours of Ireland by showing under their surface, images which are strange, but, once recognised, familiar. Like Ovid, he does not propose any simple therapy, solace or consolation. Any beauty or resolution that the poems arrive at undertakes, as a necessary part of it, loss, terror, desolation.

The poetic energy which changes the shapes of inert reality is in the images which Yeats invents. So it is throughout all his poems, early, middle, late, as for convenience we divide them, and not only in his poems about Ireland. Various shape-changers inhabit the early poems, not always persuasively. In 'He Mourns for the Change', 'I have been changed to a hound with one red ear'; in

'He Thinks of His Past Greatness', 'I have been a hazel tree';
Fergus tells us,

> I see my life go drifting like a river
> From change to change; I have been many things –
> A green drop in the surge, a gleam of light
> Upon a sword, a fir-tree on a hill,
> An old slave grinding at a heavy quern,
> A king sitting upon a throne of gold.

In 'Under the Moon' we hear of Fand, 'who could change to an otter or fawn'; Aengus sees a silver trout 'become a glimmering girl'; 'The White Birds' presents a lover who wishes that he and his beloved 'were changed to white birds' – not a proposition likely to appeal to Maud Gonne to whom it was addressed.

These shape changes have in common, it seems to me, that they represent an escape to a world of magic, enchantment, from a disheartening reality – the mundane, unrequited love – to which the poems do not give any solid presence. We have no lively awareness of the shapes to which the poems offer their alternatives. Yeats's intention is plain enough, and 'The Lover Tells of the Rose in His Heart' states it:

> The wrong of unshapely things is a wrong too
> > great to be told;
> I hunger to build them anew.

The poems I have mentioned, however, rather evade than contemplate without despair the 'unshapely things'.

As with his changing views on how to represent Ireland, so in these more general themes, Yeats arrived at 'the fascination of what's difficult', the necessary difficulty for any poetry which is not just a simpleminded celebration of the blatantly picturesque. His poems give body to the disquieting shape changes which life itself imposes: from youth to age, loss of beauty, mortality:

> What youthful mother, a shape upon her lap
> Honey of generation had betrayed,
> And that must sleep, shriek, struggle to escape
> As recollection of the drug decide,
> Would think her son, did she but see that shape

> With sixty or more winters on its head,
> A compensation for the pang of his birth,
> Or the uncertainty of his setting forth?

Yet the conclusion of 'Among School Children' triumphantly calls these disablements into its final incantation. 'Shriek', 'struggle', 'winters', 'pang' remain with us, but now set with blossoming, dancing, music. The poem's words invite us to re-envision the brutalities of growth and movement.

W. H. Auden said that 'Sailing to Byzantium' is a poem about a man who says he wants to become a golden bird, and 'I don't believe him.' There is more to the poem than that. Like 'Among School Children', it admits the heart 'sick with desire/And fastened to a dying animal'. But it is that heart which superbly commends the life it claims to deny: 'the salmon-falls, the mackerel-crowded seas'. Art colludes to sing 'Of what is past, or passing, or to come.'

It is not, I think, possible to pin Yeats down to a settled position. He dealt in truths and counter-truths. Essentially, however, he was a propagandist, in the most civilised meaning of the term. Art has its autonomy, and from its own kingdom re-enters and re-shapes life. 'Vacillation', from *The Winding Stair and Other poems*, poses and perhaps judges the duality in its question and answer:

> What's the meaning of all song?
> 'Let all things pass away.'

NOTES

1   W. B. Yeats, *Collected Poems*, London 1950, p. 281.
2   Ibid. p. 393.
3   *The Tain,* translated by Thomas Kinsella, Dolmen, Dublin, and Oxford University Press, London, 1970, pp. 150-3.
4   Alison Jolly, *The Evolution of Primate Behaviour,* New York 1972, p. 144. I am indebted to Dr Christopher Nichols, of the Department of Sociology, York University, Toronto, for his advice on these ethological matters.
5   Ovid, *Metamorphoses,* translated Horace Gregory, Mentor 1960, p. 31.
6   Ovid. *Metamorphoses,* Loeb translation, F. Miller, Harvard 1971, p. 41.
7   Ibid. Vol. II, pp. 172-3.
8   Ovid, Gregory translation. p. 70.

9 Ibid.
10 Ovid, Loeb translation, Vol. I, p. 419.
11 W. B. Yeats, *Explorations*, Macmillan, London 1962, pp. 55–6.
12 Ibid., pp. 144–5.
13 W. B. Yeats, *Memoirs*, ed. D. Donoghue, Macmillan, London 1972, p. 105.
14 *Explorations*, Macmillan, London 1962, p. 184.
15 *Memoirs*, p. 250.
16 *Beltaine* No. 2, p. 24.
17 *Uncollected Prose*, ed. John P. Frayne, Macmillan, London 1970, Vol. I, p. 361.
18 *Memoirs*, p. 223.
19 *Explorations*, p. 243.
20 *Uncollected Prose*, Vol. II, p. 485.
21 *Memoirs*, p. 184.

HOME LIFE AMONG THE YEATSES

WILLIAM M. MURPHY

For a half century students of William Butler Yeats have expressed fascinated interest in the nature and extent of his father's influence on him. With Joseph Hone's selection of John Butler Yeats's letters and Richard Ellmann's *Yeats: The Man and the Masks* the process was begun,[1] and since then there have been several studies which have attempted to satisfy that interest, among them the work of A. Norman Jeffares, Douglas N. Archibald, and, most recently, myself.[2]. In *Prodigal Father* I attempted a straightforward biography of John Butler Yeats, a simple story of a man's life, in which the unquestionable dependence of the son on the father became manifest as a matter of course. Yet, although the reception of that book has been almost wholly favourable (and most gratifying), I have detected in a few reviews a kind of counter-revolution against 'old JB', perhaps no more than a suggestion, a cloud now no bigger than a man's hand, an annoyance, subdued but present, that the father is getting too much of the limelight that ought to be reserved exclusively for the son. One way to suggest that the influence might be overstated is to present JBY as a worthless, inferior person by whom one so important as the godlike William Butler Yeats could not possibly have been influenced in any profound way. In a long and most detailed commentary on *Prodigal Father* in *The New Yorker*[3] Professor Helen Vendler, one of the most distinguished scholars and critics of our time, and one of the best writers as well, engages on such a diversionary assault on the father's character. Taking issue with my treatment of John Butler Yeats, she writes: 'a story quite other than the one [Murphy] tells could be made of the same facts and the same quotations.' To put it simply, and I hope correctly, where I found John Butler Yeats on the whole, making due allowance for his many faults and the severity thereof, to be altogether a good man, in many ways a great one, Professor Vendler on the whole, making due allowance for his many virtues and the

170

splendour thereof, finds him to be altogether a bad one, in many ways a downright wicked one. She warms to her denunciation slowly, choosing to judge that JBY was not 'a painter of notable genius' – a judgment to which I'll return later – that he was a conscious sponge and cadger, and, at the root of Dr Vendler's annoyance, that he was a distressingly irksome and inadequate husband and father. She speaks of 'the cost to his family of JBY's pursuit of a talent that has found no great place in the history of modern art. His insistence on the freedom of the individual – on which he rings changes throughout his long life – begins to seem a rather hollow boast: his way of life allowed no 'individual freedom' for his neglected wife, his confined daughters; and, in another place, 'he seems scarcely to have realized the damage he did to his daughters, who, unable to move freely in the world, lacked the social context that school might have provided, and lacked the money to appear in society, where they might have found husbands.' Although buried in the middle of her sprightly, readable essay, these passages constitute the core of her objection to John Butler Yeats. By them she judges him and his works. He was a bad man because he did not properly care for his wife and daughters, and all judgments about him radiate out from the same source. Where others find nothing reprehensible about JBY's accepting, at the age of seventy and beyond, gifts of money from his son and from John Quinn, Professor Vendler talks of his accepting 'dole', speaks of his 'selfishness', of his 'indolence, waywardness, childlikeness'.[4] In *Prodigal Father* I perhaps wrote as the optimist who saw that the glass was half full· Professor Vendler writes as the pessimist who sees the glass half empty.

To her opinion, of course, she is perfectly entitled, and she may dislike John Butler Yeats for any reason she wishes – I am concerned only that her evaluation – indeed, her description – of JBY as a husband and father may come to be accepted as the reality when, in my view, they are largely fantasy. Writing for *The New Yorker*, Professor Vendler has a readership of a quarter of a million to accept her pronouncements. I have no expectation that the readers of this article and of *Prodigal Father* itself will ever amount to more than a tiny fraction of that number, yet I feel that an objection to her view should be registered in print merely for the record. For the reductive portrait of JBY that emerges from her paragraphs is of a man so inferior that one could hardly imagine his having been an important influence on

171

so superior a son. She makes clear that she regards him as little more than a wastrel, if not merely a garrulous old duffer at least something very close to it.

Was he in fact a poor husband and father, as Professor Vendler asserts? Was he indifferent, selfish, uncaring? Was he, among the number of husbands and fathers whose careers have been laid open to public inspection, at the lower end of the scale of virtue? Clearly, the nature of life at Fitzroy Road, Edith Villas, Ashfield Terrace, Bedford Park, and elsewhere deserves looking into. If Professor Vendler, using the same material as I, can make out quite a different biography from the one I presented in *Prodigal Father*, then perhaps my book should be scrapped and another written to replace it. While I am hardly in a position to make a dispassionate judgment in the matter, I believe no such drastic step is called for at the moment. Perhaps I failed to make the circumstances of the Yeatses' family life clear enough, and if so a corrective is surely called for and I hope will be supplied here. Having spent many years gathering, sifting, and evaluating the evidence, I hoped I had described JBY and the members of his family in a way that would admit of no ambiguity, but clearly with Professor Vendler at least I have not succeeded.[5]

Yet a rereading of *Prodigal Father* and a reconsideration of the material on which it is based will I think show the impartial reader that despite whatever grains of meritorious opinion may lie in her assessment, the dram of reason rests with my more charitable interpretation. What in fact were the circumstances of JBY's life as a family man? Against him, to put the case strongly, can be weighed his improvidence, his inability to make his wife happy, his failure to provide for the formal education of his daughters – even, for that matter, of his sons. Where other Anglo-Irish families of his time swam in the waters of affluence and of social comfort – families such as Edward Dowden's, for example – the Yeatses seemed to live from day to day, were seldom out of debt, were never in the proper social swing; most important, the trapped mother, Susan Pollexfen Yeats, vegetated, grew ill, and died. (Mrs Vendler speaks of the daughters as 'burdened with the presence of their insane and feeble mother till her death.')

Having said that, one has said all, I believe, and perhaps more than all. Considering the extensive range and wide variation of family patterns, that of the Yeatses was in fact – considered without dismissive adjectives – not so wide of the 'average' or 'normal'. The members of the Yeats family – John Butler Yeats and his wife Susan Pollexfen Yeats, his sons Willie (WBY) and Jack, his daughters Lily and Lollie[6] – remained together as a stable unit during the entire thirty-seven years of the parents' marriage. Jack lived for eight years, from 1879 to 1887, with his grandparents in Sligo, not an uncommon feature in stable families, though the duration was certainly greater than the average. During the rare periods when JBY was not living with his family he was on the road seeking commissions or executing them, or working to improve his technique. The one extensive period of his absence from them was the twenty-eight months from mid-1872 until the fall of 1874, when he made his first serious attempts to make a living as a painter. Otherwise the family lived together as a unit, in London (at Fitzroy Road, Edith Villas, and Woodstock Road), in Dublin (at Howth and Terenure), in London again at Eardley Crescent and Blenheim Road. For a time in late 1876 and early 1877 he stayed, sometimes with his eldest son, at Farnham Common, but he returned on weekends to the family nest.[7] At no time during the long course of their marriage was there any suggestion – according to the records, at any rate – that JBY was a vagrant father who abandoned or thought of abandoning his wife and children. Judged for willingness to persevere as head of family, John Butler Yeats would have to score high, perhaps higher than we would score most husbands – higher certainly than other artists such as Gauguin, Augustus John, and Rockwell Kent.

Nor is there in the record any hint of marital infidelity, another of the derelictions of Victorian – and even more recent – moralists. JBY tells us of resisting the seductive blandishments of a highly-placed matron at Muckross Abbey,[8] but even if he should be guilty of a little black lie – and there is no reason to believe he is – a casual concealed fling is light years away from the keeping of a separate establishment. One would suspect that if his marriage to Susan was troubled by the presence of another woman we might have received some hint somewhere in the oceans of correspondence, memoirs, and diaries of himself, his children, and his friends. He seems rather to have been a staunch defender of the institution of marriage, and while his wife was alive appears to have remained faithful to her, even suppressing his strong feelings of attachment for Rosa Butt, daughter of Isaac Butt, father of Home Rule and a close friend of JBY's father.[9]

Nor, to close in on the other common cause of domestic infelicity, does JBY appear to have been the victim of drink. His daughter Lily hated people who drank and once showed displeasure openly when her father bought whiskey to serve to the members of the Calumet, a club of conversationalists scheduled to meet at his home. He himself wrote of the dangers of overdrinking, even though he believed a jigger or two was a great loosener of tongues and hence desirable at meetings of the club. He did not drink regularly. 'Perfect felicity is the second glass of Jameson stabilized forever,' he said, but he was seldom in a position to rise to even that modest eminence. John Sloan noted that at the Petitpas boarding house in New York as JBY grew older he tended to become argumentative and difficult after his second bottle of wine, but by that time he was well into his seventies, and Sloan's comment is sufficient indication that the condition was not a commonplace one.

In short, the more one looks at John Butler Yeats as a husband and father the more one sees that he was rigidly orthodox; the fact that he never discovered the secret either of making money or keeping it is a problem the analysis of which lies outside a study of his marital condition. Not only in practice but in theory he was relentlessly committed to marriage as an institution (a point noted many years ago by Professor Jeffares[10]) and proved the most undeviating of conformists. It seems to me that by any impartial judgment John Butler Yeats would have to be reckoned a considerate husband and father. He stayed with his wife through her long, troublesome illness of twelve years, and afterwards he remained with his two unmarried daughters until, regretfully aware that he was not carrying his share of the domestic burden, he left hearth and home at last, at the age of 68, to attempt to make his own way in New York. On a scale of one to ten, to make use of a common measure, it seems to me that he deserves a score of at least $7\frac{1}{2}$ or 8.

How account, then, for Professor Vendler's insistent assertion that JBY was a poor head of family? First, and chief, is the evidence of Susan Pollexfen's unhappiness, abundantly documented in *Prodigal Father*. There is no denying that from the moment in 1866 when her husband decided to throw away his career as a lawyer and go for a life of art in London until her death twenty-four years later she was a discontented woman. She suffered under the embarrassment of constant indebtedness to butcher and baker; she disliked her husband's friends and their arty talk; she wanted to breathe the salt air of Sligo, not the soft coal of London. If city life was required of her she wanted it to be spent in Dublin among the socially prominent and financially prosperous. She had on her side the undeniable fact that she had made her wishes clear from the beginning: when she married John Butler Yeats in 1863 she confidently looked forward to a life of ease among the professional people of Dublin. What she got was so far removed from her expectations that one can hardly accuse her of ingratitude. She entered upon a game with one set of rules only to find them changed almost as soon as the game began. From her point of view life was cruel and unfair,[11] and John Butler Yeats was responsible.

Of Lily and Lollie somewhat the same view might be taken, and indeed Professor Vendler has taken it. The two remained unmarried all their lives and from their early twenties worked hard to support first the household at Blenheim Road in Bedford Park and later the home shared with JBY, Gurteen Dhas, in Churchtown, County Dublin.[12] Perhaps their lack of a dowry drove prospective husbands away, and while the possibility of such a sordid bourgeois conclusion should not be dismissed, there is at least as much evidence, or suggestion of it, that their chances would not have been good even had their circumstances been different. Professor Vendler, incidentally, is in error in declaring that the sisters were not educated,[13] and in fact any man of intellect would have felt happy in their presence. Lily was also, as any reader of her letters can see, delightful, intelligent, affectionate, and maternal; but she was born prematurely and suffered from a chronic swelling of the throat that made breathing difficult, and she was never in really good health at any time in her life.[14] There is no hint in the voluminous family records that any man ever showed the slightest romantic interest in her, an unhappy comment on male perceptiveness but a fact nevertheless.[15] Lollie, on the other hand, was pursued relentlessly for more than twenty years by Louis Purser,[16] a suitor so dauntingly conservative and undaring that perhaps no woman could have brought him to the altar – as no woman ever did. In any event, it cannot be said that Lollie was without opportunity, and it may be that the difficulties of her own personality (discussed at length in *Prodigal Father*) were the cause of her spinsterhood rather than the result of it. John Butler Yeats can hardly be blamed, except remotely, tangentially, and on the whole doubtfully, for the romantic malnutrition of his daughters.

In fact, it is possible to overstate, as I believe Professor Vendler has overstated, JBY's failures as *pater familias*. If it is true that he never learned the importance of Mr Micawber's prescription about the sixpence more and the sixpence less, he was nevertheless not a deadbeat – if we define the term as one who contracts debts he knows he has no intention of paying. The record shows clearly that except for the sums given him in extreme old age by William Butler Yeats and John Quinn he paid off all his debts scrupulously if tardily. Terence de Vere White concludes that John Butler Yeats must be judged as we would judge Mr Micawber or Don Quixote,[17] – as one quite out of his natural environment in the practical world of 'getting on'. He was, as his daughter Lily said of him, 'headstrong, and no manager.' Yet neither he nor any member of his family was ever shipped to the workhouse. He seems also to have been genuinely troubled by his failure to provide and by the devastating effects on his wife. 'Had I had money your mother would never have been ill and would be alive now,' he wrote to Lily twelve years after his wife's death, ' – that is the thought always with me – *and I would have done anything to get it for her* – but had not the art.'[18] In a letter written late in life to John Quinn, JBY speaks of his 'pain and humiliation at seeing Lily and Lollie hard at work,' of his feeling that WBY did not respect him, and of his not respecting himself.[19] Professor Vendler quotes the passage but dismisses it as 'typically self-exculpating.'[19] The difference in our points of view could not be greater.

For in the Yeats household the relationships were quite different from those that readers of Professor Vendler's review might be led to expect. From it one might conclude that home life among the Yeatses was an unpleasant business, that a mutual hostility governed all, that the domestic seat of power was as often empty as not, and that when he sat in it JBY was the focus of family antagonisms, the centre of dissolution and controversy. Professor Vendler may feel called upon to rise to the defence of Susan Yeats as a wronged wife, but there is no evidence that she would be supported in her advocacy by the Yeats

children. William Butler Yeats is guarded in his comments about
his mother. We learn of her love of telling stories to her children
when the family was living in Howth, and of her sense of humour,
briefly but cryptically mentioned. We learn that she was 'un-
reasonable and habitual as the seasons.'[20] Like her husband and
her daughter Lily he speaks also of her worry about money, the
chief obvious source of her unhappiness. But he says nothing to
indicate any deeper feelings about her, certainly nothing to imply
affection. Lily wrote of her mother that she was 'always delicate,
no, delicate is not the word. She was very strong in constitution
but her nervous system was easily upset and her life was full of
anxiety over money affairs and the care of children, and worry
she could not stand.' She 'was quite unable for the care and
anxiety of life in London on an uncertain income.'[21] There
are only a few letters of Susan Yeats's extant, written to Matthew
Yeats, her husband's uncle and the agent for his estate. In one
of them (dated about 21 August 1880) she writes: 'I know that
you are doing all you can for us and I know we are very troublesome to you, but it can't be helped. I wish it could. We are in
this unsettled state.' She told Matt that JBY felt the only course
was to 'paint pictures and pay models, and that comes to a lot
of money.'

So there is no denying, and no one has ever denied, the funda-
mental truth that Susan Yeats was troubled by money and that
her husband failed to provide it in sufficient quantity. The issue
that needs to be raised is not merely JBY's improvidence but the
nature and appropriateness of her own response and, more important, the way in which she was viewed by others as a partner
in the marital enterprise. Whatever her husband's shortcomings,
it is clear that she made no attempt to adjust to them. As a young
housewife in London, while there was money flowing in from the
Thomastown estate, she was unapt at the simplest jobs. 'She was
not at all good at housekeeping, or child-minding,' Lily wrote.
'As a girl in Sligo her life had been very easy, enough money,
no cares.'[22] 'Susan could not have boiled an egg,' JBY told
his brother Isaac sixteen years after his wife's death, and he
hesitated to leave her at home with the children.[23] She took
no interest in his work as an artist,[24] except as it might bring
in funds, and made no attempt to familiarize herself with the
subject matter of her husband's conversations with the Dowdens,
John Todhunter, Edwin Ellis, and the rest.[25] Even the humane

and generous Todhunter darkly alluded to her as having a 'Philistine mind.'[26] It may be significant that in the correspondence of those outside the family Susan Yeats is seldom mentioned except as a mere presence; it is almost as if she were not regarded as a member in good standing. 'She was there as always,' JBY wrote to Willie in 1915, 'disliking everybody and everything, yet accepting everybody and everything. She liked green countries and sky and the sea. I never knew why or how she liked them.'[27] Yet there was some Pollexfen quality in her he admired. 'My father was always praising her to my sisters and to me,' WBY wrote in his *Reveries*, 'because she pretended to nothing that she did not feel.'[28]

Clearly, there was an intellectual incompatibility of spacious dimension separating husband and wife. It seems to me futile to explore the blame and unrewarding to assess it. In tragic life no villain need be. There was enough fault, undoubtedly, to spread among everyone involved. Use every man according to his desert, and who should 'scape whipping? I should suppose that the next-to-last word about the two is that they should never have got married – but that the last must be, 'Thank heaven they did'.

Whether fairly or not, the children make clear both by what they say and by what they leave unsaid that their father was the dominant force, and indeed almost the only force in the household.[29] When Susan Yeats is mentioned at all, it is seldom with affection and warmth. 'She was prim and austere, suffered all in silence,' wrote Lily. 'She asked no sympathy and gave none . . . When we were children and were ill she always said, "Grin and bear it," and so she did. She endured and made no moan.' In the fall of 1887 she suffered a stroke, which was followed shortly afterward by another. During the decade of the 'nineties she slowly grew worse, and she died during the first week of 1900. It is the common wisdom, I suppose, that the strokes were brought on by her worry,[30] yet they might as easily and mundanely – despite JBY's sense of guilt about them – have been the result of high blood pressure. What may be more significant is that during the last decade of her life she slowly lost touch with reality and may have been, indeed seems to have been, not merely a victim of stroke but a psychotic.

The change was slow. In Blenheim Road after her strokes she would allow no one to call her an invalid.[31] For many years she was able to move about, and she spent much time reading. Lollie's diary, covering the period from September 6, 1888, to May 24, 1889, says little about Susan. 'Mama seems better the last few days' (Sept 19). 'Mama is reading the story in the "Pall Mall"' (Sept 20). 'Mama is reading' (Sept 22). '[Mrs Walker] and Mama had a great chat all about Sligo people' (Sept 26). While Lollie was reading Dowden's biography of Shelley to Papa, 'Mama of course kept reading out scraps of the book she was reading' (Sept 30). She and Lily went to the theatre: 'Lily wanted to go in her old brown dress but was overruled by Mama so I lent her my red dress' (Oct 30). 'Mama has discovered how to cure the clock of its troubles at last by putting it standing upside down' (Nov 11). 'Had a battle royal with Mama over her way of going about the house half clothed. She sent off at me a fire of her delightful sarcasm' (Dec 4). 'Papa gone for a week, Mama reading The Star' (Jan 2). 'Mama better today' (Feb 4).

These constitute the references to 'Mama' in Lollie's diary. In the references to 'Papa' during the same period the tone is different. 'Wrote Papa's story to his dictation, a fine scene (Sept 8). 'I don't like an evening he dines out at all' (Sept 20). On two different days he played badminton with his daughters at the Bedford Park club even though it was not his ordinary recreation (Sept 24, 26), and one night he read to them about Daniel O'Connell and the Irish (Sept 29). On October 1st Lollie went for a walk with Papa in the evening, going down by the river and looking at the 'queer antique old houses,' and on the 13th accompanied him and Jack to the Irish Exhibition. She continued patiently copying short stories as her father composed and dictated them (Oct 19, 20, 28, Nov 1, 4, 5). She is distressed at Papa's 'very bad spirits' when he learns that the Irish Land Commission has awarded him much less than he expected for the inherited estate which he is selling to his tenants (Nov 5). She sympathises with his difficulties in selling his work: 'Cassells kept his drawing to look at, but that I suppose only means a freezingly polite letter in the course of a few days to say that 'The editor regrets he is unable to see his way to using it' – (Jan 21).[32]

By 1895, when Lily began a diary which she kept for a brief period, Mama had become withdrawn and needed constant attention. 'Mrs Llewellyn came in and fell on Mama's neck,' Lily wrote on August 1, 1895, 'and presented her with a bottle of scent, both impossible things to imagine Mama with, the embrace and the scent.' Then she added, in a phrase that becomes common in the diary, 'Put Mama to bed.' When Papa and Lollie and Jack are absent from home, she writes, 'Willy and I have the place to ourselves,' as if her mother didn't exist (Aug 17). One night she 'kept Mama up till 9 o'clock,' thinking the event worthy of notice in the diary (Aug 22). When she decides to go to Hyères she is happy to receive the approval of Rose Hodgins, one of the two servants, for 'on her will fall the care of Mama' (Oct 5). As with Lollie's diary, the entries are neutral, non-committal.

Her references to Papa, on the other hand, are full of feeling, of genuine affection, more so than those of Lollie. JBY fell ill in August, 1895, with rheumatism and other assorted ailments, perhaps psychosomatic ones brought on by the sense of failure he expressed in the 'typically self-exculpating memoir' to Quinn. Lily makes reference to her father's condition almost every day: 'Papa rather better (Aug 18); 'Papa better (Aug 19)· 'Papa much better' (Aug 22), and so on. Sometimes the description is more elaborate, and so is the expression of Lily's concern. 'Papa not well, never still a moment, sits down, then walks about, and repeats the same again, wish he was better,' she wrote on 23 August: 'Everything seems upside down when he is not well.' By the 27th she could express relief: 'The Good Man is better so things are beginning to feel comfortable again.' In October the difficulties returned: 'Papa not very well... Wish the Good Man was all right.' Clearly, Lily worshipped her father and found nothing in his character or behaviour to make her regard him as Professor Vendler does. A quarter century after the event she described to John Quinn a golden day at Blenheim Road in the 1890s. She had sent Quinn a pencil sketch of WBY done by his father:

I can remember so clearly the doing of it. It was a bank holiday, Good Friday or Easter Monday, I don't remember which. Anyway, I had a day of freedom from May Morris and was at home and had got myself into a happy state of mind by reading 'The Prisoner of Zenda'. I sat one side of the fire in Blenheim Road, Papa the other, and Willy between us. The talk was pleasant. We all had a holiday feeling and Papa did this beautiful sketch of Willy. If you ever get it reproduced I would be glad to have a copy in memory of that day of spring and holiday and youth.[33]

Mama was home that day but was clearly not a member of the club. She continued to deteriorate in physical health, suffering another stroke about 1895, and to grow more and more unaware of her surroundings, until 'she had found,' in the words of her eldest son, 'liberated at last from financial worry, perfect happiness feeding the birds at a London window.'[34] Toward the end, JBY wrote WBY, 'when in possession of only half her mind it was her daily task to write to me,' and she wrote of the sky, 'the only thing she ever wrote about, for everything else was only a worry.'[35] When she died her husband and eldest son were with her; she was not abandoned or alone. None of her children ever accused her husband of the kind of insouciance Professor Vendler finds in him. He felt keenly his own inability to make money, but his children appear to have accepted revolving credit as a fact of life without assigning their hapless father the blame for it. They would as soon have blamed their dog, Dan O'Connell, for barking.

Issues of personal conflict shouldn't be resolved by majority vote, and Susan Yeats may in some celestial Hall of Justice be awarded damages, but the fact is that all the available evidence suggests that she was regarded universally as an unfortunate and unhappy woman quite out of touch with the ideas and interests of the other members of the family, who nevertheless extended her every care and consideration. Those members felt quite differently about 'Papa' (the daughters' name for JBY), or 'Father' (as WBY called him). Professor Vendler suggests that JBY's 'devastating charm' was most effective on 'those who knew him outside the domestic circle' and that 'those who knew him best were least susceptible to it.'[36] Such an observation is generally true of most fascinating men, whose foibles are always more exasperating to those who know them intimately, like gentlemen and their valets. William Butler Yeats was annoyed and often infuriated by his father, as *Prodigal Father* shows, and he attributes his own quite different approach to practical life to his deliberate rebellion against JBY's 'infirmity of will', the 'family drifting, innocent and helpless',[37] yet he acknowledged his father's influence on him and continued to profit from it; and in the closing years of his own life he included as one of the 'Beautiful Lofty Things' in the poem of that title the picture of his father standing before the 'raging crowd' in the Abbey Theatre, 'his beautiful mischievous head thrown back.'[38] Lollie admired her father perhaps more than she was admired in return, and Lily as we have seen was utterly devoted to him, loving him, as she told John Quinn, not only 'as my father but as my greatest friend.' No, it was not only the outside companions who succumbed to his special qualities, to his 'astonishing intellectual vitality . . . and splendid intelligence' (as George Russell put it). 'He always left you with a feeling of exultation,' said Dolly Sloan. When he died, Oliver Elton felt that 'an illumination, a steady ray, has gone out.'[39]

I am troubled by another, indirect attack Professor Vendler makes on John Butler Yeats because it seems to inappropriate in so accurate a critic and writer. 'A reader might respond more warmly to this feckless man if he had been a painter of notable genius,' she says, and, while not wishing to make final pronouncements on a matter in which she claims no special insight,[40] she nevertheless brusquely asserts, 'One suspects that JBY does not rank very high as an artist.' But does she believe, as she implies, that if he had been a great artist what she regards as his maltreatment of his wife would have been excusable? Is genius sufficient expiation for evil? Her animus against JBY, induced by her wayward sympathy for an idealised Susan Yeats, transformed in her imagination from dull and commonplace housewife to martyr,[41] shows even more clearly in her mistaken denunciation of John Butler Yeats as one who willingly sponged off his own children – mistaken because the facts, all on the record, are against her. After quoting from JBY's 'typically self-exculpating memoir' to John Quinn – in which he expressed his own sense of depression and failure at the sight of his daughters working 'to keep *my* house' and calling it 'all my fault'· adding, 'And there behind all was my poor wife – *I knew perfectly well that it was this terrible struggle with want of means that had upset her mind*' – Mrs Vendler continues unforgivingly (the italics are mine):

At the time of which this memoir speaks, JBY was forty-seven – in relative youth for a man of his constitution. *Yet he had totally abandoned any thought of supporting his dependents.* A gentleman did not work; he lived on his rents. When the rents were gone, *he turned not to his profession but to his daughters.* It was a chilling logic.[42]

As the record makes clear – the contemporary record of Lollie's diary in 1888–1889 and of Lily's later diary – John Butler Yeats did nothing of the kind. He made what was for him a supreme sacrifice. What Professor Vendler calls his profession – that of portrait painter – had long since proved itself unprofitable. 'Turning to' his profession, or rather sticking with it, would have been futile. What John Butler Yeats did instead, against all his most deeply held principles – principles he urged his two sons never to abandon – was to turn to his craft, his skill, the techniques which were the foundation of his profession. For the sole purpose of making money he abandoned portrait painting and turned to drawing illustrations for religious tracts and for books, his illustrations for the Dent Defoe being the most noteworthy. As the diaries make clear, he was little more successful with these than with his portraits; and his attempts at selling short stories were equally unavailing, for he was too undisciplined a writer to make a good story-teller. Clearly, whether he achieved his ends or not, he had *not* 'totally abandoned any thought of supporting his dependents'. The picture Professor Vendler paints is of a John Butler Yeats who never existed.

She is so troubled by the unhappy life of Susan Yeats that she seems to suggest that it was an obligation on John Butler Yeats to have remained in Dublin practising at the bar. JBY often speculated on the subject himself: 'Had I been a man of the sort that weighs chances in the delicate scales of arithmetical anxiety I could never have left the bar in Ireland and taken my wife and children to London to face the uncertainty of the artist's career. I ought to have stayed in Dublin and worked hard for success, for that was the voice of prudence.'[43]

To the historian the question, 'What would have happened if . . . ?' is meaningless. What would American history have been if Lincoln had not been assassinated? What would have happened if the Nazis had won the Second World War? The answer to all such questions is that we don't know, and there is no possible way in which we can know. What we can say with some certainty is that things would have been different in some way. By examining the careers of well-born, conventional, Anglo-Irish Dubliners of the late nineteenth century we can suggest the probability that if John Butler Yeats had lived the kind of life that would have satisfied Susan Yeats his sons would not have become artists at all – and if by some chance WBY had wandered into poetry he would have written in a quite different way on quite different subjects, even if we don't know what the difference would have been. His daughters might or might not have married, but there is no certainty that they would have been happier. All in all, I think we should be grateful that things worked out as they did.

Professor Vendler ends her provocative essay by speaking of 'the long agon between a gifted father and a son of genius,' of the 'standstill' between them, of 'the tragicomic spectacle of family life.' Yet it was that very agon that gave us the poetry of which Helen Vendler herself is one of the most distinguished critics. In the family history we have to accept the bad along with the good – Susan's misery with Lily's joyous sense of life – and recognize that the relationship of WBY and his father was, like many such relationships, one that involved both influence and rebellion. As the beneficiaries we have to accept the good and the bad here also – though not all of us will agree on the distinction between the two. For my part, as *Prodigal Father* makes clear, I think WBY was wise to rebel against his father's 'drifting, innocent and helpless.' Where the older man refused to accept proper pay for his work, his son insisted on payment for virtually everything he did. Yet, like his father, WBY cared little for money in itself and refused to perform services hypocritically merely to gather gold. Where the father was a thorough-going rationalist – or was until Lily's visions made him skeptical of his own skepticism – the son reacted violently by haring off after the occult. Like a wise father concerned for his son's stability, JBY objected, yet WBY was able to convert the nonsense of occult speculation into the metaphors of great poetry. The one way in which WBY didn't escape his father's influence at all was in his insistence on the supremacy of art and the inferiority of the notion of 'getting on'.

Because of the father's ways we have the works of William Butler Yeats and the paintings and writings of Jack; we have the Dun Emer and Cuala Presses and Lily's letters; and we have the paintings and drawings of John Butler Yeats himself – which Robert Henri, differing from Professor Vendler's judgment, held in high esteem. How should the world be luckier if we had sacrificed all these for the sake of Susan Pollexfen's bourgeois aspirations? And what if all had been sacrificed and she had ended up unhappy anyhow, a fate to which her temperament seemed to consign her? All in all, with due sympathy for the unlucky Susan, I rather like the way things turned out.

NOTES

1 Joseph Hone, ed., *J. B. Yeats: Letters to His Son W. B. Yeats and Others, 1869–1922* (New York: E. P. Dutton, 1946). Richard Ellmann, *Yeats: The Man and The Masks* (London: Macmillan, 1949). In this paper I use the spellings (often varied even among the Yeatses) 'Willie' (William Butler Yeats), 'Lily' (Susan Mary Yeats), and 'Lollie' (Elizabeth Corbet Yeats). 'Susan Yeats' always refers to Susan Mary Pollexfen Yeats, wife of John Butler Yeats (JBY). When quoting I will use the spelling that appears in the original.

2 A. Norman Jeffares, 'John Butler Yeats,' *The Dublin Magazine* Summer, 1965), pp. 30–37; John Butler Yeats, Anglo-Irishman,' *The Circus Animals* (Stanford: Stanford University Press, 1970), pp. 117–146.

    Douglas N. Archibald, 'Father and Son: John Butler and William Butler Yeats,' *Massachusetts Review* (Summer, 1974); *John Butler Yeats* (Lewisburg: Bucknell University Press, 1974).

    William M. Murphy, 'Father and Son: The Early Education of William Butler Yeats', *A Review of English Literature* (London: Longmans, Green & Co., Ltd.), vol. VIII, No. 4 (October, 1967), pp. 75–96; *The Yeats Family and the Pollexfens of Sligo* (Dublin: Dolmen, 1971); *Prodigal Father: The Life of John Butler Yeats (1839–1922)* (Ithaca and London: Cornwall University Press, 1978).

3 Helen Vendler, 'J.B.Y.', *The New Yorker*, Jan. 8, 1979, pp. 66–77.

4 Pp. 73, 70.

5 Barbara W. Tuchman wrote a biography of General Joseph Stilwell, *Stilwell and the American Experience in China* (1971). After reading the reviews she wrote: 'The peculiar thing about him is that he left a different impression on different readers; some came away from the book admiring, and others rather disliking him, which only proves what every writer knows: that a certain number of readers will always find in one's book not what one has written, but what they bring to it' ('Biography as a Prism of History' in *Telling Lives: The Biographer's Art*, ed. Marc Pachter [Washington: New Republic Books/National Portrait Gallery, 1979], p. 141). I share Mrs Tuchman's sentiments.

6 Two other children, Robert Corbet and Jane Grace, died young.

7 Beech Villa, where JBY lodged, was in Farnham Common, not Farnham Royal, the address he used in his letters (and the one I used in *Prodigal Father*).

8 *Prodigal Father*, p. 96.

9 JBY's letters to Rosa Butt have just been released by the Bodleian Library from a restriction upon their use, imposed by their donor,

until 1979. I have just begun to transcribe these letters and cannot report on them fully until later. It can be said, however, that even a casual perusal reveals what some have long suspected, that JBY greatly admired Rosa Butt and would very much have liked to be married to her. His epistolary courtship did not begin, however, until almost a year after his wife's death – and despite the ardour of his prose he voluntarily abandoned Dublin for New York in late 1907 and never saw Miss Butt for the last fourteen years of his life. There is no evidence that he pursued her while Susan was living. See note 10 below.

10 *Dublin Magazine, op. cit.*, p. 32, and *The Circus Animals, op. cit.*, pp. 142–143. See also *Prodigal Father*, p. 216. Even when JBY was pressing his case with Rosa Butt, he wrote to her of his feelings about the American woman's attitude toward free love: 'America is full of these disturbing ideas, everyone in revolt against everything. It tires me even tho' it interests me. *I believe most profoundly in the marriage state, and in being faithful to it*' (JBY to Rosa Butt, ca. 1903, *fragment*, letter beginning 'More letters . . . '). The italics are JBY's.

11 Again, this conclusion is given in *Prodigal Father*, pp. 215–216.

12 Their life together was not happy. I have described it at length in *Prodigal Father*, pp. 267–268, 381, 425.

13 'The money that was to have gone for the schooling of Lily and Lollie went for old debts,' she writes (*New Yorker*, p. 69), but she is remembering only one occasion, when JBY had hoped to enrol his daughters in Alexandra College (*Prodigal Father*, p. 139). Although they, like their brothers, did not follow the customary course of Irish education, still Lily studied at the Notting Hill School, at the Metropolitan School of Art, and at Kelmscott House (*Prodigal Father*, pp. 120, 139, 156); and Lollie was certified in the Froebel System and also studied French with Lily and WBY at Kelmscott House and with her at the Metropolitan School of Art. Both were also subjected to a constant informal course in literature through their father's reading aloud of the classics. They were, in fact, two of the best informally educated women of their time.

14 'My breathing was never quite normal,' Lily wrote in her scrapbook ('Great Aunt Mary Yeats'). She notes that she was taken out of Notting Hill High School because 'I seemed always rather ill.' After falling ill in Hyères she was 'more or less an invalid for four years' (a period beginning when she was 31 and ending when she was 35). Not until 1930 did she discover the cause of her trouble: 'My thyroid gland is abnormally low down and has sent down a lobe for eight inches down behind my breast bone. It is pressing on my wind pipe and makes it difficult for me to breathe, and also presses on nerves and gives me incessant pain in my chest. The condition was I am told quite unknown till I produced it' (Lily Yeats's Scrapbook, 'Lily and May Morris').

15 Lollie's Diary (mostly unpublished) contains a number of suggestive references to the nature of the love life of the Yeats sisters. On December 29, 1888, they attended a dance at William Morris's house in Hammersmith. Lollie, with no self-consciousness, reports that other girls there danced with young men, but neither she nor Lily did.

Lollie herself danced with 'old Mr Morris' and with Lily. On the following February 26th, at a dance at the Art School, Lollie danced every number but two, noting that she had 'very nice partners, one Mr Turner who knew Maudie White'; but we hear no more of Mr Turner. 'Lily danced 8 times with Dr Hogg's eldest son, a boy of about 17, a nice shy boy'; Lily at the time was 22. Young Hogg never appears afterward in the Yeats family annals.

16 See *Prodigal Father*, entries in index under 'Yeats, Lollie, — Purser, Louis' (p. 677).

17 Terence de Vere White, 'A Great Man in his time', *The Irish Times*, July 15, 1978. He goes on to say that 'a censorious critic might add Harold Skimpole,' and he agrees with Mrs. Vendler when he writes: 'In the routine business of life he was a failure; the women in his family had their lives ruined by his incompetency.' So it is partly to his review that this essay is addressed, though it seems to me that Mr White puts the foibles in proper perspective against the merits.

18 JBY to Lily, 20 September 1912 (quoted in *The Yeats Family and the Pollexfens of Sligo*, p. 54. See also the passage in the note there (p. 87), from his letter to WBY of 10 May 1914, of his stressful dream about his father-in-law demanding to know how long JBY expected him to support him.

19 *Prodigal Father*, p. 494.

20 *Prodigal Father*, p. 86; WBY, *Autobiographies* (London: Macmillan, 1966), p. 167.

21 The first quotation is from Lily Yeats's Scrapbook, 'Mama's Health', the second from another section in the same scrapbook entitled 'Mama's Health and Other Things'.

22 'Mama's Health and Other Things'.

23 JBY to Isaac Yeats, 29 December 1915 (*Prodigal Father*, p. 56).

24 WBY, *Autobiographies*, 'Reveries', sec. XIII, pp. 61–62).

25 See *Prodigal Father*, pp. 60–71, for an account of the unpleasant relationship between her and Edwin Ellis. See also WBY, *Autobiographies*, 'Reveries', sec. XI (p. 58): 'I was asked to write an essay on "Men may rise on stepping-stones of their dead selves to higher things". My father read the subject to my mother, who had no interest in such matters.' Writing to Rosa Butt with unusual candour JBY said, 'Had my poor wife a little more intellect she would have been something very remarkable' (*ca.* 1903, *fragment*, letter beginning 'More letters . . .').

26 John Todhunter to Edward Dowden, 14 January 1870 (Trinity College Dublin); see *Prodigal Father*, p. 71.

27 JBY to WBY, 25 April 1915; quoted in *The Yeats Family and the Pollexfens of Sligo*, p. 87.

28 WBY, *Autobiographies*, 'Reveries', sec. XIII, p. 61.

29 By 'children' I mean chiefly, almost entirely, Willie, Lily, and Lollie. Jack destroyed his letters, diaries, and other papers. Little documentary material about him is available of the kind we have in abundance for other members of the family.

30 See Lily Yeats's Scrapbook, 'Mama's Health and Other Things': 'She

187

was not able for any strains – and in 1887 in the Autumn in London she had a stroke.'

31 *Ibid.*
32 Jack appears throughout Lollie's diary as a cheerful, affectionate, thoroughly likeable youth. From a reading of the family papers, it is clear that the members of the family were divided into two groups, those who immediately attracted the good will and liking of others, and those who were difficult and prickly and not likely to win friends easily. In the first group were JBY, Lily, and Jack, in the second Susan, Lollie, and WBY. To note this division in print is not of course to establish a list of 'heroes' and villains'.
33 Lily to John Quinn, 11 April 1921 (unpublished) (New York Public Library).
34 WBY, *Autobiographies*, 'Reveries', sec. XIII, p. 62.
35 JBY to WBY, 25 April 1915; *The Yeats Family and the Pollexfens of Sligo,* p. 87; *Prodigal Father,* p. 199.
36 *The New Yorker,* p. 73.
37 WBY to John Quinn, 30 September 1921 (quoted from B. L. Reid, *The Man from New York: John Quinn and His Friends* [New York: Oxford University Press, 1968], pp. 493–494);*Prodigal Father,* p. 532.
38 WBY, *Collected Poems* (London: Macmillan, 1965), p. 348.
39 Lily to John Quinn, 10 December 1917 (*Prodigal Father,* p. 474); George Russell to Lily, 4 February 1922; Dolly Sloan to Lily and Lollie, 8 February 1922; Oliver Elton to Lily, 4 February 1922. The last three of these letters, unpublished, are in the collection of Michael Yeats.
40 All quotations from Professor Vendler in this paragraph are from *The New Yorker,* p. 70. I claim no special insight as an art critic either, and in *Prodigal Father* left judgments of JBY's paintings to those better qualified to speak, scrupulously refraining from expressing my own opinions. I was not writing a book on art, as I made clear in the Preface, and I am not sure a critique in the jargon of the critics would have been illuminating.
41 I suspect that in real life Helen Vendler would have found Susan Yeats intolerable and JBY irresistibly attractive.
42 *The New Yorker,* p. 70.
43 JBY, *Memoirs,* I (unpublished).

YEATS, NATURE AND THE SELF

PATRICK RAFROIDI

To tackle the impossible subject I have chosen, *the best method is perhaps, at the start, the simplest: to consider Yeats's nature poems, for a moment, as if they were simple vignettes, methodised but fairly objective representations of what he actually perceived. And we can find help from Yeats himself here if we momentarily take at its face value and for the bulk of his production a statement concerning a particular period which he made to Katherine Tynan just after he had completed *The Wanderings of Oisin,* expressing his intention to give precedence to nature represented as coolly as possible, asserting, in other words, the superiority of nature over art and, to a certain extent, the superiority of nature over the self which is taken into account only in as much as a personal choice of scenery is allowed. Yeats carries on: 'We should make poems on the familiar landscapes we love', and, on many occasions – for instance in a letter to the same correspondent written in 1887 – he had made quite clear what the familiar landscapes he loved were:

It is a wonderfully beautiful day. The air is full of trembling light. The very feel of the familiar Sligo earth puts me in good spirits. I should like to live here always, not so much out of liking for the people as for the earth and the sky here.

adding, however – and this should pacify the citizens of Sligo! – 'though I like the people too'.[1]

I need not, I suppose, expatiate on this point, except perhaps in one passing and one longer remark. The passing remark is to recall that two of the greatest friends of the Summer School who have recently left us to sail into their rest had remarkably developed the subject, Sheelah Kirby in her book of 1962, *The*

---

* The text of a lecture given at the Sligo Summer School on Wednesday 13 August, 1975.

189

Yeats Country, and T. R. Henn in several writings and, among
others, the first chapter of *The Lonely Tower.*

Temporarily leaving us in sad or blissful ignorance of learned
and erudite discussions and keeping us from the dangerous pitfall
which Yeats himself once denounced:

> The fascination of what's difficult
> Has dried the sap out of my veins, and rent
> Spontaneous joy and natural content
> Out of my heart,[2]

my longer remark will allow us a short break in the Irish countryside, inviting us, before we become scholars again, shuffle there,
cough in ink and think what other people think, to listen – just
for the sound of it – to 'the flutter of the leaves that will not hush,
the beech leaves old',[3] to look – just for the beauty of it – at the
spots

> Where dips the rocky highland
> Of Sleuth Wood in the lake
> . . .
> Where the wave of moonlight glosses
> The dim grey sands with light,
> Far off by furthest Rosses
> . . .
> Where the wondering water gushes
> From the hills above Glen-Car,
> In pools among the rushes
> That scarce could bathe a star[4]

at 'the grass that grows on the weirs',[5] 'midnight's glimmer and
noon's purple glow' on the Lake Isle of Innisfree,[6] the 'cold and
vapour-turbaned steep' of Lugnagall,[7] the 'old brown thorn-trees'
high over Cummen Strand,[8] 'the light of evening' at Lissadell,[9]
'bare Ben Bulben's head'[10] or, leaving County Sligo for the Galway region, admire, at Coole, trees and woodland paths, 'water
mirroring a still sky'[11],

> Gregory's wood and one bare hill
> Whereby the haystack– and roof–levelling wind,
> Bred on the Atlantic, can be stayed[12]

190

or see, at Thoor Ballylee, where 'Tree, like a sooty finger, starts from the earth'[13].

This approach has a further advantage in compelling us to have another look at the early works as well, of which we have been told *ad nauseam* that they were inferior – Yeats himself had shown the way when he opposed his first and his late manners, 'the poetry of longing and complaint' and 'the poetry of insight and knowledge', but the critics were too swift in taking up his modest assessment.

The approach, then, has the further advantage of urging us to ask ourselves this question: is not Yeats's nature poetry – including his earliest examples – the least weighed down with insight and knowledge, the most external, the most reminiscent of Keats and Shelley and the Pre-Raphaelites with their too lovely compound adjectives, with the evanescent colours in which he delighted in *The Wanderings of Oisin* and in his first collections – is not even that type of poetry worth assessing as something different in texture from the then prevailing type? Whatever the excesses in decoration, the landscape which is described, or alluded to in the minor terms of similes and metaphors, has plainly been observed in its reality, not on some painting once removed from it. And this is one of the reasons why William Morris's remark, 'you write my sort of poetry', is not right, the other reason being, of course, that the mythical history of Ireland had more immediacy for an Irishman such as Yeats whose people had been deprived of their national tradition and who were recovering it with a vengeance, than the Arthurian past for an Englishman such as William Morris who, at best, looked back upon it in a nostalgic mood, as on the antidote to the Philistine present which he denounced, in the company of Matthew Arnold and a few others. In this respect, it might not be uninteresting to read *The Wanderings of Oisin* and *The Defence of Guinevere* side by side the better to establish the point.

The Irish – and more particularly the Sligo – landscape – was for Yeats the occasion and the instrument of becoming, like Synge, a 'rooted' man and, partly forgetting his self, of taking in the outside world.

* *
*

191

Yeats, however, as we all know, grew to think exactly the reverse of what he had written to Katherine Tynan. Far from encountering again statements implying the superiority of nature over art, the student of his work will soon enough come across pronouncements like that in the last stanza of 'Sailing to Byzantium':

> Once out of nature, I shall never take
> My bodily form from any natural thing,
> But such a form as Grecian goldsmiths make
> Of hammered gold and gold enamelling
> To keep a drowsy Emperor awake;
> Or set upon a golden bough to sing
> To lords and ladies of Byzantium
> Of what is past, or passing, or to come.[14]

But perhaps, although I see no ambiguity here, my example is ill chosen, for you will remember that William Empson, for one, refused to take the passage seriously, saying of Yeats 'Keeping his tongue in his cheek was one of his dearest pleasures' – something that never seemed evident to me from my reading of the works, but then I didn't know the man personally. Whatever the case may be, Empson carries on, coming to the form 'Grecian goldsmiths make':

One could see plenty of these mechanical singing birds in the Forbidden City of Peking. . . . No great reverence can be felt for them; what Yeats is saying is 'I tell you what I'll do; I'll turn myself into one of those clockwork dickey-birds, in a gild cage.'

Consider, few poets have cared to write down 'When I die I shall go to Heaven.' They would feel it bad luck as well as bad taste, and Yeats was not at all the man to feel otherwise. Then, as to symbolism, the more you think of birds as able to take messages up to Heaven, intensely spontaneous in their lyrics, and so forth, the more a clockwork bird with a built-in tweet-tweet is bound to seem pathetically ludicrous. Just the thing to please children, on the other hand, and there the poet does retain a firm contact with the world of the young which he must now school himself to leave. . . . Yeats, with his distaste for the machine age, cannot be supposed to give himself hearty praise in his incarnation as such a thing.'[15]

But this is irrelevant for, if the last stanza of 'Sailing to Byzantium' won't do, there are other passages that will, even in the same poem or in its sequel. Art is definitely considered as superior to nature, purer, because less of the material world, than the world of 'common bird or petal / And all complexities of mire or blood', an artifice, perhaps, but an 'artifice of eternity'. And Nature comes not only to become inferior but, in Robert O'Driscoll's excellent phrasing[16] the (mere) embodiment or expression of the inspired intuitions of the mind.

*   *
*

Looking back on Yeats's letter of 1887 to Katherine Tynan, one may wonder, however, whether Yeats ever managed, even for a while, to give up everything for the sake of outside reality. I am not the only one to believe that this never was among Yeats's achievements, any more, as Frank O'Connor remarked in *The Backward Look*[17], than it was within Yeats's reach to 'cast a cold eye' on anything.

The very same letter to Katherine Tynan contains a sentence which does not bear on nature, but – *mutatis mutandis* – can easily apply to it: 'I do not mean', Yeats says, 'that we should not go to old ballads and poems for inspiration, but we should search them for new methods of *expressing ourselves*' [my italics][18] and indeed it would be hard to find any natural spectacle, however realistically perceived by the poet, that was not, from the very start, coloured or discoloured by personal feelings:

No boughs have withered because of the wintry wind
The boughs have withered because I have told them my
    dreams.[19]

Yeats – and perhaps this is true of all poets – could not remain long with nature alone – for all true poets, and in fact all men, have only one quest: themselves and . . . the twin soul. Remember 'The Sorrow of Love'

The brawling of a sparrow in the eaves,
The brilliant moon and all the milky sky,
And all that famous harmony of leaves
Had blotted out man's image and his cry.

A girl arose that had red mournful lips
And seemed the greatness of the world in tears,
Doomed like Odysseus and the labouring ships
And proud as Priam murdered with his peers;

Arose, and on the instant clamorous eaves,
A climbing moon upon an empty sky,
And all that lamentation of the leaves,
Could but compose man's image and his cry.[20]

However, leaving the twin soul in order to concentrate on the omnipresent self, I would like, first of all, bravely to put forth the trite remark that, when studying a great poet, the 'self' we have to consider is bound to be something more than the simple sum of autobiographical experiences – or the mere reflection of individual traumas and complexes which, after all, exist in every one of us and, alas, do not make great poets of us all!

Among the items of Yeats's nature imagery on which we could concentrate, let us select, for instance, that of water – an important image with the author of *The Shadowy Waters* and the man who could write:

I am haunted by numberless islands, and many a Danaan
  shore,
Where Time would surely forget us, and Sorrow come near
  us no more;
Soon far from the rose and the lily and fret of the flames
  would we be,
Were we only white birds, my beloved, buoyed out on the
  foam of the sea.[21]

Well, if you go through, say, Brenda S. Webster's *Yeats, a Psychoanalytic Study,* one of the fairly recent books to come out of the United States on our poet[22], you will learn, if you haven't yet read Freud, that the island is a representation of the Oedipal drama, or of the female body (the alternative versions being the water

194

fall, or the broken boat, that is to say the boat without a mast –
leaving it to you to determine what the mast stands for.) I could
carry on if I had the time – except that it is not worth it if your
subject is literature and not psychoanalysis. It isn't so much that
psychoanalysts, as the saying goes, have sex on the brain, which
is the wrong place to have it; it isn't even that it is useless to
search for hidden sexual undertones in the works of a poet who
was quite capable of expressing himself very clearly on the subject. It is, more fundamentally, that the 'self' of a major writer
includes many other things beside what belongs to the man in the
street – let alone the most backward characters.

This 'self' includes the notion of moral duty which, in the case
of our particular theme, may be a hindrance rather than a help,
intruding so much that it puts a stop to the relationship with the
natural world:

> Although the summer sunlight gild
> Cloudy leafage of the sky,
> Or wintry moonlight sink the field
> In storm-scattered intricacy,
> I cannot look thereon,
> Responsibility so weighs me down.[23]

By and large, however, there is no such opposition with the self
in its entirety, which also includes the poet's idea of his racial
inheritance – and Yeats believed, after Ernest Renan and
Matthew Arnold, that 'The Celtic passion for Nature comes
almost more from a sense of her 'mystery' than of her beauty'[24],
which finally contains the poet's vision of the universe – the
symbolical vision, which Yeats might have adopted in any case
but which the French symbolist movement helped him to pursue
(in spite of what William York Tindall may have said on the
subject) after Blake had aided him in his discovery.

Yeats does not, any more than his master, only 'behold the
outward creation'[25] or how could he ask 'What's water but the
generated soul?'[26]. As he went along, he enriched his vision and
imagery with his intellectual findings, writing to Olivia
Shakespear[27] of the correspondence between the liquid element
and instinct or passion and placing it, in his system, just before
the fifteenth phase of the moon: still of this world, yet haunted
by eternity – 'That dolphin-torn, that gong-tormented sea'[28] – and

bearing the promise of the immortality towards which it carries the soul.

Yeats could not be a mere landscape photographer but he could never abandon natural emblems either. Not only had the Sligo countryside impressed itself on his mind for life, he also found what he had been desperately craving for: unity, in nature where 'Though leaves are many, the root is one'[29].

NOTES

1   13 August 1887, included in *The Letters of W. B. Yeats*, ed. Allan Wade, Hart Davis, London, 1954, p. 49.
2   'The Fascination of What's Difficult', *Collected Poems*, p. 104.
3   'The Madness of King Goll', *Collected Poems*, p. 17.
4   'The Stolen Child', *Collected Poems*, p. 20.
5   'Down by the Salley Gardens', *Collected Poems*, p. 23.
6   'The Lake Isle of Innisfree', *Collected Poems*, p. 44.
7   'The Man who Dreamed of Faeryland', *Collected Poems*, p. 50.
8   'Red Hanrahan's Song About Ireland', *Collected Poems*, p. 90.
9   'In Memory of Eva Gore-Booth . . .', *Collected Poems*, p. 263.
10   'Under Ben Bulben', *Collected Poems*, p. 400.
11   'The Wild Swans at Coole', *Collected Poems*, p. 147.
12   'A Prayer for My Daughter', *Collected Poems*, p. 211.
13   'The Tower', *Collected Poems*, p. 219.
14   'Sailing to Byzantium', *Collected Poems*, p. 218.
15   In *A Review of English Literature*, July 1960, pp. 51–6.
16   In *Yeats and The Theatre,* ed. Robert O'Driscoll and Lorna Reynolds, Macmillan of Canada and MacLean-Hunter, Toronto and Niagara Falls, 1975, p. 9.
17   London, 1967, p. 182.
18   21 December, 1888, *Letters*, p. 98.
19   'The Withering of the Boughs', *Collected Poems*, p. 87.
20   'The Sorrow of Love', *Collected Poems*, pp. 45–6.
21   'The White Bird', *Collected Poems*, p. 47.
22   Stanford, 1973; London, 1974.
23   'Vacillation', *Collected Poems*, p. 284.
24   *Mythologies*, p. 173.
25   See in Blake's M.S. book the passage concerning his picture of 'The Last Judgment'.
26   'Coole Park and Ballylee, 1931', *Collected Poems*, p. 275.
27   24 July, 1934, *Letters*, pp. 823–4.

THE 'DWARF—DRAMAS' OF THE EARLY ABBEY THEATRE

ANN SADDLEMYER

'No one act play, no dwarf-drama, can be a knockdown argument'.

With these words James Joyce dismissed *Riders to the Sea* and, by implication, the Irish dramatic movement, adding that Ireland needed 'less small talk and more irrefutable art'.[1] Yet when this discussion between Synge and Joyce took place in Paris early in 1903, W. G. Fay's small company of nationalist amateurs had already started to make its name with one-act plays in both Irish and English: Douglas Hyde's *Casadh an Tsugáin*, AE's *Deirdre*, Yeats's *Cathleen ni Houlihan*, *The Pot of Broth*, *The Hour-Glass*, James Cousins's *The Sleep of the King* and *The Racing Lug*, P. T. McGinley's *Eilis Agus an Bhean Déirce*, and Lady Gregory's *Twenty-Five*. Synge's *In the Shadow of the Glen* and Seamas MacManus's *The Townland of Tamney* would soon follow, as would Yeats's *The Shadowy Waters* and the offending *Riders to the Sea*. By the time the Abbey Theatre formally opened in December 1904 with yet two more one-act plays, Yeats's *On Baile's Strand* and Lady Gregory's *Spreading the News*, the tradition of 'dwarf-dramas' was firmly established as a staple of the Irish National Theatre Society.[2]

James Joyce notwithstanding, there were sound reasons for this rash of playlets. For the frankly political organisations such as Maud Gonne's Daughters of Erin (who had sponsored the first productions of *Deirdre* and *Cathleen ni Houlihan*,) brief *tableaux vivants* and other amateur theatricals had been effective propaganda, assuring attentive audiences and keen participation; for the Gaelic League, they provided additional encouragement for learning the Irish language, drawing as they did upon a long tradition of dramatic dialogues.[3] Actors from both these groups would join the Fay brothers to form the first national theatre company, and in turn seek out further plays to expand an evening's programme. In this way AE was urged to complete his

197

Deirdre, and Douglas Hyde was banished to his guest room at Coole with scenarios drafted by Yeats and his hostess; finally Lady Gregory also turned from passive secretarial duties to active play-making, churning out comedies 'to put beside the high poetic work' of her colleagues. Collaboration was inevitable, and Yeats and Lady Gregory have both left moving records in their autobiographies and prefaces of the interdependence inspired by these exciting early years of experiment and challenge. Co-operation extended not only into the Irish language, but out towards dramatic theory with Frank Fay's learned criticisms in *The United Irishman* and Yeats's responses to them not only in that journal but in the many other literary and nationalist magazines of the period.[4] It would continue with Florence Farr's erratic brilliance as a speaker of verse and Miss Horniman's magnificent gift of a theatre building.

But even before the founding of the Irish Literary Theatre by Yeats, Martyn and Lady Gregory, and while Willie and Frank Fay were still preparing traditional farces for Dublin coffee-houses, Yeats had taken up the challenges of the dramatic form. Early in 1889 he was writing enthusiastically to Katharine Tynan about his 'new poem,' *The Countess Cathleen*: 'I shall try and get it acted by amateurs (if possible in Dublin) and afterwards try it perhaps on some stage manager or actor. It is in five scenes and full of action and very Irish.' Several weeks later he admitted that Maud Gonne 'felt inclined to help, indeed suggested the attempt herself if I remember rightly.'[5] Yeats's determination to study his play in performance bore fruit when *The Countess Cathleen* received its first production in Dublin by the Irish Literary Theatre in 1889, but with Lady Gregory's help, not Maud Gonne's, and by an English cast supervised by George Moore. Perhaps more appropriately still, he had by then seen his one-act play *The Land of Heart's Desire* produced by Florence Farr at the Avenue Theatre in London in 1894, with funds provided anonymously by Miss Horniman.

Yeats confided to his unpublished autobiography that he had put into this second play 'my own despair. I could not tell why Maud Gonne had turned from me unless she had done so from some vague desire for some impossible life, for some unvarying excitement like that of the heroine of my play.'[6] But whatever the original impulse (and the published play is dedicated to

198

Florence Farr), *The Land of Heart's Desire* established not only a form but subject, argument, mood, setting and even characters which would recur again and again in the plays of Yeats and his collaborators. It is a simple telling of folk matter which he had already celebrated in 'The Stolen Child' – the seduction of a soul seeking a completion not possible in the domestic life of the fireside with its arranged marriages, stockings of gold, and circumscription by aged parents, police and priest; the call by a melodious stranger, frequently glorified further by song or ballad, conjures up another world which may be glimpsed through the open door or window of the scrupulously realistic cottage setting. And although an apparent resolution occurs on the plane of action, the play itself ends on a question mark. This strange, yet familiar, wooing evokes distant memories in all who hear it; and the audience leaves the theatre disturbed, roused from a 'base of realism' to touch 'the apex of beauty' which according to Lady Gregory was the playwrights' ambition.[7] It is the universal dream of escape from the commonplaces of every day, that 'vague desire for some impossible life'; yet it remains specifically Irish also in its rejection of poverty, political oppression, and authoritarian strictures.

The Land of Heart's Desire was written in verse Yeats later believed too ornate, 'mere ornament with dramatic value', he did not allow a production, and then much revised, at the Abbey until 1911.[8] Perhaps (though given his theatre's tempestuous determination to remain free of censorship it seems unlikely) he feared that the Priest's indulgent putting aside of the crucifix would rouse the ire of his Catholic audience; more likely he realized the risks involved in placing an all-too-human actress as fleet-footed Faery Child in a well-lighted traditional cottage interior. Whatever the reason, this one-act play does not appear to have been taken seriously by the early theatre movement, and so it was *Cathleen ni Houlihan* that Yeats offered to Willie Fay in 1902. Written once again with Maud Gonne in mind, this play avoided these pitfalls while following the same basic pattern. Where his earlier play was, he explained to *The United Irishman,* 'in a sense, the call of the heart, the heart seeking its own dream; this play is the call of country, and I have a plan of following it up with a little play about the call of religion.'[9] And this time he had Maud herself, carefully prepared under his own tutelage, to perform 'with creepy realism'[10] the half-mad old crone who calls Ireland's young manhood from fireside and bride, new clothes and old coins, to accompany her to battle. He also had a popular theme:

My subject is Ireland and its struggle for independence. The scene is laid in the West of Ireland at the time of the French landing. I have described a household preparing for the wedding of the son of the house. Everyone expects some good thing from the wedding. The bridegroom is thinking of his bride, the father of the fortune which will make them all more prosperous, and the mother of a plan of turning this prosperity to account by making her youngest son a priest, and the youngest son of a greyhound pup the bride promised to give him when she marries. Into this household comes Kathleen Ni Houlihan herself, and the bridegroom leaves his bride, and all the hopes come to nothing. It is the perpetual struggle of the cause of Ireland and every other ideal cause against private hopes and dreams, against all that we mean when we say the world.[11]

Two years later in a memorandum submitted for the Abbey Theatre's application for a patent, he was to play down this strident political voice: 'It may be said that it is a political play of a propagandist kind. This I deny. I took a piece of human life, thoughts that men had felt, hopes they had died for, and I put this into what I believe to be a sincere dramatic form.'[12] But by then Maire nic Shiubhlaigh had replaced Maud Gonne as Cathleen with 'weird beauty and intense pathos'; with the performances by her and Sara Allgood (whose photograph with upraised arm, standing in the cottage doorway before a kneeling Michael became the postcard advertisement for the play), and even later on the occasion when Lady Gregory stepped into the role, Ireland's Joan of Arc had given way to Eire's Mother of Sorrow.[13]

But whether with the statuesque Maud Gonne's aura of 'a divine being fallen into our mortal infirmity'[14] or the more measured tones of later actresses, the language retained its hypnotic power, brought down with Lady Gregory's help 'from that high window of dramatic verse' which had framed Yeats's earlier plays. During his lifetime Yeats eloquently acknowledged

Lady Gregory's share in the making of *Cathleen ni Houlihan,*
especially her responsibility in dialogue: 'I had not the country
speech. . . . We turned my dream into the little play, "Cathleen
ni Houlihan", and when we gave it to the little theatre in Dublin
and found that the working people liked it, you helped me to put
my other dramatic fables into speech.'[15] It has even been
suggested that to her goes the credit for perhaps the most famous
line of all, 'They shall be remembered for ever'.[16] It is likely, also,
that she encouraged a stronger contrast between 'the matter-of-
fact ways of the household and the weird, uncanny conduct of
the strange visitor' noted by Joseph Holloway.[17] Certainly, in
comparison with Yeats's two earlier plays, the cottage kitchen is
more realistic, the elder Gillanes more country shrewd and penny
wise, gold coins are ostentatiously fingered at the kitchen table,
and young Peter's ambition, a greyhound pup, is similarly rooted.
Later Yeats was to think the language, though true in temper,
lacked richness and abundance.[18] Yet the very prosaic nature of
this life confined to the comforts of home and hearth, its cosy
vulgarisms and awkward appeal, is in the graspable present, while
the lonely road seen from the doorway promises evanescent glory,
the romance of time past and a place in future mythology. The
intruder's magic is further preserved by having transformation
take place offstage, where sentiment has no place and the ending
is once again disturbingly ambivalent. Momentarily wrapped in
the nobility of the chosen, with no opportunity for weighing the
scales, we realize only later that Kathleen's pathway leads to
death. It is the parodox of the heroic fool, where reasoned
argument has no place by the instinct for gesture.

The playwrights had some difficulty adjusting these various
contrasting elements. On opening night the audience received
with delighted laughter the mild humour of the opening movement; Yeats reported to Lady Gregory, 'it took them some little
while to realize the tragic meaning of Kathleen's part, though
Maud Gonne played it magnificently, and with weird power.' He
contemplated striking a tragic note at the start, but when after
a second performance there appeared to be 'no difficulty in
getting from humour to tragedy,' he wisely refrained from
tampering.[19] This shock of making the familiar strange depended
much also on acting style, and Yeats praised 'the illusion of daily
life' Fay's company provided for his play, while admiring the

'decorative acting' they had achieved for AE's *Deirdre* on the same programme.[20] When George Moore urged that Maud Gonne 'walk up and down all the time in front of the footlights,' Yeats countered that 'she was as it were wandering in a dream, made restless as it were by the coming rebellion, but with no more fixed intention than a dreamer has.' 'She looks far ahead and far backward and cannot be excited in that sense, or rather she will be a less poetical personage if she is.'[21] He now knew what he wanted, and was at last able to distinguish between 'the essentially modern,' 'natural school' admired by Edward Martyn, and 'Irish-trained Irish actors who are likely to be extravagant, romantic, oratorical, and traditional, like Irish poetry and legend themselves.'[22]

The Pot of Broth, written probably during the same summer as *Cathleen ni Houlihan,* was an even closer collaboration between Yeats and Lady Gregory, and very much dependent upon the crude simplicity of Willie Fay's small company of amateurs. Again setting and subject are familiar: a wandering Tramp invades country kitchen with an audacious blending of folk-tale (a variation on the goose that lays the golden eggs) and folk-song. The situation has something in common with McGinley's *Eilis Agus an Bhean Déirce,* which Yeats and Lady Gregory had come up from Coole to see when produced by the Fays' Ormonde Dramatic Society for the Daughters of Erin in August 1901; but the comedy of the Irish play depends mainly on a young son's tricking his mother with Maeve the beggar woman unwittingly supporting him, the ending a grand crescendo of cursing as Maeve flounces out. We are given little beyond the clever device, although that similarity may well have influenced Yeats to alter his original title, *The Beggarman. The Pot of Broth* extends plot situation and develops characterisation, first by the use of folk airs (one, 'There's Broth in the Pot,' taken down by Lady Gregory herself from Cracked Mary, later to be immortalized by Yeats in his Crazy Jane poems), second by the wide reference to folk tradition, with which the cunning Tramp lulls the young wife out of her usual shrewish suspicion into a jovial, more generous mood. The play ends with the elderly husband John accompanying the Tramp, 'a very gifted man,' up the boreen with his prizes, as the priest appears above, innocently expecting his dinner. Later Yeats would disparage the dialect for not having the 'right

temper, being gay, mercurial, and suggestive of rapid speech'
rather than 'the slow-moving country dialect,' perhaps unconsciously comparing it with Synge's country comedies.[23] What
remained in his memory was William Fay as tramp, who 'played
it not only with great humour but with great delicacy and charm.'
'That trivial, unambitious retelling of an old folk-tale showed
William Fay for the first time as a most lovable comedian. He
could play dirty tramp, stupid countryman, legendary fool, insist
on dirt and imbecility, yet play – paradox of the stage – with
indescribable personal distinction.'[24]

The style of this little play, 'the first comedy in dialect of our
movement,' won other admirers. Arthur Griffith, editor of *The
United Irishman* and soon to become the noisiest objector to
In the Shadow of the Glen, praised *The Pot of Broth* on its first
production as 'the first Irish piece which is not a caricature.'[25]
And two years later in an unsigned review of a production of
Dion Boucicault's *The Shaughraun,* J. M. Synge commented, 'It
is fortunate for the Irish National Theatre Society that it has
preserved – in plays like *The Pot of Broth* – a great deal of
what was best in the traditional comedy of the Irish stage, and still
has contrived by its care and taste to put an end to the reaction
against the careless Irish humour of which everyone has had too
much.'[26] Synge remained fond of the play, recommending it
(against Lady Gregory's wishes) as a curtain-raiser to his longer
country comedy, *The Playboy of the Western World,* where the
same features recur though circumstances differ – a dirty tramper
woos the women, carries off the prizes and the admiration of the
audience – and where again performance by Willie Fay required
the apparently opposing qualities of poetry and farce. However,
the trickster who remained most clearly in Synge's mind was that
of Hanrahan, played by Douglas Hyde, in *Casadh an Tsugáin.*
Later he was to describe this 'charming little playlet' as 'in some
ways the most important of all those produced by the Irish
Literary Theatre, as it alone has had an influence [on] the plays
that have been written since and have built up the present
movement.'[27] On the occasion of its first production alongside
Yeats and Moore's *Diarmuid and Grania* in October 1901, he
summarized most accurately the various elements mingled not
only in the one-act plays we have already noticed, but in the
audience for whom they were written:

It was the first time that a play in Irish had ever been acted in a theatre, and the enthusiastic members of the Gaelic League stormed the cheaper seats. In spite of the importance of the League, when it organizes a demonstration one always senses (as in all deep-seated popular movements) the ridiculous rubbing shoulders with feelings of profound emotion. Thus, at the beginning of the play one could not help but smile at seeing all around the room the beautiful girls of the Gaelic League, who were chattering away in very bad Irish with palely enthusiastic young clerks. But during an intermission of *Diarmuid and Grania* it happened that the people in the galleries began to sing, as is the custom in this theatre. They sang the old songs of the people. Until then I had never heard these songs sung in the ancient Irish tongue by so many voices. The auditorium shook. In these lingering notes, of incomparable sadness, there was something like the death-rattle of a nation. I saw one head bend down behind a program, and then another. People were weeping.

Then the curtain rose and the play was resumed in the midst of lively emotion. One sensed that the spirit of a nation had hovered for an instant in the room.[28]

Douglas Hyde's play, written at Coole one summer from a scenario provided by Yeats, finds its comedy in a trickster tricked: Hanrahan, a wheedling rogue who is spell-binding with his talk and poetry, arrives at a farmhouse in Munster during the celebration of a marriage arranged for the widow's daughter and proceeds to woo her in front of the entire company. Alarmed at the stranger's skills as dancer and poet, her fiancé is encouraged by the woman of the house and her neighbours to oust Hanrahan by persuading him to make a hay-rope; as the need for a hay-rope is enlarged upon, so Hanrahan's pride as a Connacht man increases, until finally he agrees to twist the hay-rope and is manoeuvred out through the door. The comedy ends with the Munster folk congratulating the widow and her daughter on a narrow escape as the fiddler strikes up for another dance, while the poet Hanrahan hammers on door and windows, his mighty oaths rendered powerless. Hyde himself, moustaches bristling, played Hanrahan with verve. 'A born actor,' declared *The Freeman's Journal:* 'His eloquent tenderness to Una threw into strong

relief the fierce savagery and scorching contempt with which he
turned on Sheamus and his friends when they attempted to
interrupt him, and his soft, weird crooning of his passionate
verses was inimitable.'[29] Looking back from the distance of his
autobiographies, Yeats marvelled at the facility and style of
Hyde's plays, almost all of them written speedily from scenarios
provided by Yeats or Lady Gregory, and saw there one of the
keys to his own concern with style and dialect and to his ambitions for the dramatic movement of which he was a part:

> His Gaelic, like the dialect of his *Love Songs of Connacht,*
> written a couple of years earlier, had charm, seemed all spon-
> taneous, all joyous, every speech born out of itself. Had he
> shared our modern preoccupation with the mystery of life,
> learnt our modern construction, he might have grown into
> another and happier Synge . . . . He had the folk mind as no
> modern man has had it, its qualities and its defects, and for
> a few days in the year Lady Gregory and I shared his absorption
> in that mind . . . . He wrote in joy and at great speed because
> emotion brought the appropriate word. Nothing in that
> language of his was abstract, nothing worn-out . . . . I read
> him, translated by Lady Gregory or by himself into that
> dialect which gets from Gaelic its syntax and keeps its
> still partly Tudor vocabulary; little was, I think, lost I
> began to test my poetical inventions by translating them into
> like speech. Lady Gregory had already, I think, without
> knowing it, begun a transformation of her whole mind into
> the mind of the people, begun 'to think like a wise man' but
> to express herself like 'the common people.'[30]

Not only did Lady Gregory provide Hyde with scenarios, she
translated his plays into English, using the dialect later perfected
as 'Kiltartanese.' For her, as for Synge, Hyde's work heralded
the beginning of modern Irish drama,[31] but simultaneously she
too was determining the direction of that movement. Not
surprisingly given her contribution to the plays already discussed,
A Losing Game, her first independent attempt, bears all the
hallmarks already noted: a cottage kitchen in the west, an
arranged marriage, the uninvited stranger who speaks eloquently

and allegorically of a great loss, references to folk songs, much
discussion of hard times and the counting out of money, concluding with the rejection of material comforts for a dream of
another world. When it was rejected by the Fays because it 'might
encourage emigration,' she re-wrote it as *Twenty-Five*, but the
basic plot remained the same: a young man returns from America
to seek his promised bride, 'looking for a treasure I had a dream
about,' only to find that in despair she had married someone
else – an older man – the previous year; learning that the couple
are about to be evicted, the stranger challenges the farmer to a
game of cards, and despite the young wife's objections, refuses
to take back the money that he has lost. Yeats wrote encourag-
ingly to Lady Gregory after its 1903 performance, 'I thought your
play went very well. Fay was charming as Christie. The game of
cards is still the weak place, but with all defects the little play
has a real charm. If we could amend the cards it would be a
strong play too.'[32] But the playwright disliked the sentimentalism
and the fact that it ended weakly 'as did for the most part the
Gaelic plays that began to be written, in a piper and a dance.'[33]
She tried to lay the ghost of sentiment by writing the farcical
Jackdaw (1907), and parodying the main theme by turning the
setting from country into town, the benefactor into a suspicious
curmudgeon who is caught up in the trick he originally suggested.
Dissatisfied, twenty years later she provided a further commentary
on the emotions and theme of her first play in *On the Racecourse*
(1926), abolishing community altogether, making all three characters penurious rogues, the stranger cheated by the cheating
husband, and songs highlighted.

   The ruthlessness with which she covered her self-admitted
'leaning towards sentimentality' in part explains why Lady
Gregory's next play, *Spreading the News* (1904), was a striking
departure from the one-act plays already in the theatre's reper-
toire. Like her comedy *Hyacinth Halvey* (1906), cottage interior
and family cosiness are eschewed for the brilliant sunlight of the
Cloon Fair Green and Town Square; all members of this cracked
community live their separate lives and dreams, and laughter
arises out of their lack of communication; Don Quixote and
Sancho Panza are one and the same, and the plot spirals unbroken
as each Cloonite helpfully contributes his message to the over-
burdened narrative. 'The talk is all,' and as quickly as disaster

threatens, it and its meaning are dispersed in nonsense. Carefully crafted to keep sentiment out and invite laughter in, the plays, though redolent of the language of western Ireland, are set in no man's land. The door of wonder is indeed ajar, but everyone enters.

All the more puzzling, therefore, that her moving little nationalist drama, *The Rising of the Moon*, although accepted by the company as early as February 1904 and published the same year, was not produced until March 1907. For here we have a striking development of, and commentary on, *Cathleen ni Houlihan*. Once again the setting is the west of Ireland, but the time is the present,[34] and the site is the Galway quays by moonlight. Three policemen enter in search of a runaway rebel; the sergeant is left on guard alone, and a ballad-singer joins him. He is the escaped prisoner in disguise, and in a brief twenty minutes or so, with only his eloquence and his patriotic ballads to aid him, the stranger has won over the Sergeant to the friendship of 'Granuaile' and the time when 'the small rise up and the big fall down . . . when we all change places at the Rising of the Moon.' Emphasising – and thereby escaping into the objectivity of comedy – the duality of moonlit patriotism and sunlit reason at the end of the play, in a peculiarly Gregorian twist to Yeats's blending of humour and tragedy, the Sergeant's last words spoken directly to the audience are, 'A hundred pounds reward! A hundred pounds! I wonder now, am I as great a fool as I think I am?' The question called forth opposing answers: Lady Gregory reports that 'the play was considered offensive to some extreme Nationalists before it was acted, because it showed the police in too favourable a light, and a Unionist paper attacked it after it was acted because the policeman was represented "as a coward and a traitor"; but after the Belfast police strike that same paper praised its "insight into Irish character".'[35] Heroic folly has been reduced to the paradox of patriotism.

Although*The Shadow of the Glen*, like *Riders to the Sea* and the first draft of *The Tinker's Wedding*, was written before Synge attended a performance of Fay's company in December 1902, he had already joined forces with Yeats and Lady Gregory and described his mixed feelings during the performance of *Casadh an Tsugáin*. He had also rejected the autobiographical *When the*

Moon Has Set, but not before his colleagues had noticed the striking difference between the dialect of his country people and the journalism written for the towns – the same anomaly Yeats had observed in Douglas Hyde.[36] Now, shortly after the appearance of *Kathleen ni Houlihan,* Synge presented *his* play of cottage life. Again the seductive stranger sings of a life beyond the cottage door; we see the effects of an arranged marriage between May and January, and the fruits of that security, a stocking of money, counted over, then rejected; the cottage setting itself is scrupulously copied from life (Synge knew well the cottage and glen he had chosen); again a trick is played, catching the trickster. And once more the moods of comedy and romance are mingled, leaving the audience disturbed and shocked into another reality. But where *Kathleen ni Houlihan* raised a shudder of presentiment, and *The Pot of Broth* ended with comfortable laughter, *The Shadow of the Glen* catches the observer midway, swinging between the comedy of resolution as Dan Burke and his erstwhile rival settle down for a quiet drink, and the dangerous world of the shadows themselves, into which Nora and the sweetly singing Tramp are banished. Throughout the play Nora has come to terms with and overcome her need for fireside, 'the half of a dry bed, and good food in your mouth'. The greater need, protection from the shadows which devoured Patch Darcy and threaten her own sanity, can be outfaced only by something more powerful than material comforts, even more powerful than her own strong urge to sexuality and motherhood. (We are given an indication by Synge's own change in stage directions from one published draft to another: first the Tramp makes his final most lyrical speech in defiance of Dan; then he pulls her eagerly by the sleeve; finally he stands quietly at the door.) By joining the Tramp she enters into a further reality beyond his lyricism: 'I'm thinking it's myself will be wheezing that time with lying down under the Heavens when the night is cold, but you've a fine bit of talk, stranger, and it's with yourself I'll go.' Only with someone whose imaginative perceptions encompass the threat and intense beauty of nature can she find refuge from the loneliness haunting her of time passing her by.

The Shadow of the Glen (Synge dropped the initial word *In* after its first production) created the first serious split in the audience's response to the Irish National Theatre Company.

Ann Saddlemyer

Shortly after Synge's death Yeats was to identify the qualities which were partly responsible for that rejection:

> . . . always throughout his plays you will find this, the grotesque reality beside the vision. Every one of his plays comes down to that when you analyse it. [In *The Well of the Saints*] you have two old blind people, for instance, who are awakened, brought back to sight by a saint, and what they see with their eyes is merely the grotesque reality compared with their vision, and they go back into their blindness, and when the saint wishes to cure them again they refuse with indignation. Then you have "The Shadow of the Glen," where you have a passionate woman with desire, of every kind of splendour life has to give, who spends her life between a young milksop, a man who goes mad on the mountains, and a half-drunken dirty tramp! [37]

Just as bluntly, Synge explained the audience's reaction to his close friend Stephen MacKenna: 'On [the] French stage you get sex without its balancing elements: on [the] Irish stage you [get] the other elements without sex. I restored sex and the people were so surprised they saw the sex only.'[38] But to emphasize Nora's sensuality (played by Maire nic Shiubhlaigh with innocent intensity[39]) is, in turn, to see only one aspect, the romance, at the expense of the equally important comic element in the play; indeed, to isolate the sexual passion suggested in this lonely woman of the hills is to do injustice to the other kinds of romance Synge borrowed, while heightening, from the earlier plays of the movement. And each element is, in turn, commented upon through the devices of comedy.

The first movement of the play builds on the audience's expectations from earlier cottage dramas: a stranger appears out of the darkness and almost immediately establishes a sympathetic alliance with the woman of the house. This is familiar, but different: instead of the enclosed harmony of the family we are offered a man who 'was always queer' both in life and now in death, cold 'every day . . . and every night'; instead of the uninvited visitor taking command of action and subject, he is at first relegated to the secondary role of observer and comic chorus, bringing messages from the heroic dead.[40] The mood intensifies as Patch Darcy's spirit is evoked, then lightened by the first of

209

Dan's 'resurrections.' During the second movement, when the audience is now aware of two eavesdroppers, thus creating a parody of the romantic theme developed on stage, once again the intensity of Nora's feeling is heightened only to be punctured by Dan's second comic resurrection. The final movement holds the opposing moods in balance, with the Tramp embodying both the heroic folly of the dead Patch Darcy and the promise of romantic nature Nora sought unsuccessfully in Michael Dara. Here the call from the fireside to another world is achieved without either sentiment or patriotism, for the world evoked by the Tramp is present day Wicklow brushed with the folly and dreams of the folksong.

Synge would borrow again from *Cathleen ni Houlihan* and *The Twisting of the Rope* in his comedy *The Tinker's Wedding* and even in *The Playboy*; he would further develop his aesthetic concerning the tension of 'the dreamer . . . leaning out to reality', 'the timber of poetry that has . . . strong roots among the clay and worms'. In his next one-act play, *On Baile's Strand,* Yeats too continued to elaborate on the base of realism while reaching out to an apex of poetry drawn from Irish poetry and legend:

> I am doing a play – with the following central idea – that the politic far seeing mind represented in my play of Conachar is in reality blind because the plans it makes are opposed to the plans of nature. It is always following some artificial idea. In Conchubar the idea is the greatness and prosperity of Ireland. This idea as is always the way with the artificial idea, is all but undistinguishable from mere egotism. In contrast to Conchubar is Cuchulain. He is in tune with nature. This is represented by the Sidhe being his friends.[41]

By the time his play was ready for production, the idea Yeats had enthusiastically outlined in this scenario had altered considerably, the framework of Fool and Blind Man taking on greater individuality than as mere foils to Conchubar and Cuchulain. The folk figures of this comic framework threaten to drown, instead of contrast with, the 'pure aimless joy' of Cuchulain's fight with 'the ungovernable sea'; irony and cross-reference intellectualise the tragic folly of Cuchulain. And so, after *The Golden Helmet* (1908)[42] Yeats left comedy to his two colleagues, content to provide the tragedy which 'heightens their comedy and tragi-comedy, and grows itself more moving and intelligible from being mixed into the circumstances of the world by the circumstantial art of comedy'.[43] By then, too, tradition and experiment combined to lead him away from the narrow Abbey stage – its very restrictions ideal for Irish cottage scenes –[44] to the high lonely art of allusion and dance. When he next tackled the Cuchulain saga, hero and fool became one; but even *At the Hawk's Well* ends on ambiguity, 'who but an idiot would praise/Dry stones in a well?'

Of the three collaborators, Lady Gregory alone retained the original one-act pattern of the 'dwarf-dramas' so contemptuously dismissed by Joyce. Yet Synge's three-act plays continued to celebrate the contrasting elements inherent in the earlier form while expanding and elaborating theme and personality; and with few exceptions Yeats strove to perfect and simplify in his struggle to capture 'a moment of intense life'. But the concept of a mysterious crooning stranger urgently beckoning from cottage doorway towards a dangerous pathway into another world remained one of the haunting images of Irish theatre. While that theatre's audience, helplessly pinned between reality and wonder, would continue to swing uneasily, sometimes angrily, between laughter and tears. 'Small talk' did indeed become 'knockdown argument.'

NOTES

1 Quoted from Herbert Gorman's notes in Richard Ellmann, *James Joyce*, Oxford University Press, New York, 1959, p. 129. Later, however, Joyce translated *Riders to the Sea* into Italian, and arranged for its production in Zurich.

2 See Robert Hogan and James Kilroy, *Laying the Foundations: 1902–1904*, Dolmen, Dublin, 1976 for the dates and casts of these plays; Robert Hogan and James Kilroy, eds., *Lost Plays of the Irish Renaissance*, Proscenium Press, 1970, for *Lizzie and the Tinker*, a translation of McGinley's *Eilis agus an Bhean Déirce*; Lady Gregory, *Poets and Dreamers* (1903), Colin Smythe, Gerrards Cross, 1974, for *The Twisting of the Rope*, her translation of *Casadh an Tsugáin*.

3 As Lady Gregory points out in '*An Craoibhin*'s Plays,' *Poets and Dreamers*, p. 136.

4 Frank Fay's articles are collected and edited by Robert Hogan in *Towards a National Theatre*, Dolmen, Dublin, 1970; see Yeats's letters and the early articles of *Beltaine* and *Samhain* for the development of his theories on staging and performance.

5 *The Letters of William Yeats,* ed. Allan Wade, Macmillan, New York, 1955, pp. 114 and 117.

6 See his 'Autobiography – First Draft' in *Memoirs,* ed. Denis Donoghue, Macmillan, London, 1972, pp. 72–73.

7 'What we wanted was to create for Ireland a theatre with a base of realism, with an apex of beauty', Lady Gregory's notes to *Damer's Gold* quoted in *Collected Plays,* vol. I, ed. Ann Saddlemyer, Colin Smythe, Gerrards Cross, 1971, p. 262.

8 Preface to *The Land of Heart's Desire,* in W. B. Yeats, *Plays and Controversies,* Macmillan, London, 1923, p. 299.

9 5 April 1902, p. 5, quoted in *The Uncollected Prose of W. B. Yeats, II,* ed. John P. Frayne and Colton Johnson, Macmillan, London, 1975, p. 284.

10 Joseph Holloway described her performance in his journal after the first production on April 3rd: 'a part realised with creepy realism by the tall and willowy Miss Maud Gonne, who chanted her lines with rare musical effect, and crooned fascinatingly, if somewhat indistinctly, some lyrics', printed in *Joseph Holloway's Abbey Theatre,* ed. Robert Hogan and Michael J. O'Neill, Southern Illinois University Press, Carbondale and Edwardsville, 1967, p. 17. In 'Yeats and Ireland', *Scattering Branches,* ed. Stephen Gwynn, Macmillan, London, 1940, pp. 29–30, Maud Gonne describes Yeats's rehearsals with the company.

11 *The United Irishman,* 5 May 1902, quoted in full in A. Norman Jeffares and A. S. Knowland, *A Commentary on The Collected Plays of W. B. Yeats,* Macmillan, London, 1975, pp. 27–28.

12 Quoted by Richard Ellmann in *The Identity of Yeats,* Macmillan, London, 1954, pp. 295–96.

13 Holloway describes Maire nic Shiubhlaigh's performance on 27 December 1904: 'Anything more strangely pathetic than her chanting as she leaves the cottage I have never heard. Her words sunk into one's very soul! . . . . Of all the "Cathleens" I have seen, this was the truest embodiment. The sorrows of centuries were on her brow and in her eye, and her words pierced the heart with grief at her woe!' (*Joseph Holloway's Abbey Theatre,* p. 51). A photograph of Sara Allgood is reproduced in Lady Gregory, *Our Irish Theatre,* Colin Smythe, Gerrards Cross, 1972, illus. no. 18 and of Lady Gregory, illus. no. 9; a further photograph of Lady Gregory with Arthur Shields as Michael Gillane is reproduced on the dust jacket of Lady Gregory's *Journals Volums I Books* 1–29, Colin Smythe, Gerrards Cross, 1978. A photograph of Maud Gonne and the first cast is reproduced in Frank Tuohy, *Yeats,* Macmillan, London, 1976, p. 101; a different photograph of the same production appears in James Flannery, *W. B. Yeats and the Idea of a Theatre,* Macmillan, Toronto, 1976, plate 6.

14 Quoted in *A Commentary on the Collected Plays of W. B. Yeats,* p. 36.

15 Yeats's dedication to Lady Gregory of volumes One and Two of *Plays for an Irish Theatre,* February 1903, quoted in *A Commentary on the Collected Plays of W. B. Yeats,* pp. 28–29.

16 Donald T. Torchiana, *W. B. Yeats and Georgian Ireland,* Northwestern University Press, Evanston, 1966, pp. 78–79.

Ann Saddlemyer

17 *Joseph Holloway's Abbey Theatre*, p. 17.

18 Note to *The Pot of Broth, Plays in Prose and Verse,* Macmillan, London, 1922, p. 421.

19 *Letters,* pp. 367–368.

20 'The Acting at St. Teresa's Hall', *The United Irishman,* 12 April 1902, reprinted in *Uncollected Prose, II,* pp. 285–86.

21 *Letters,* p. 441 and 367.

22 'The Acting at St. Teresa's Hall', *The United Irishman,* 19 April 1902, reprinted in *Uncollected Prose, II,* pp. 291–292. See also Yeats's letter to F. J. Fay in *Laying the Foundations,* 1902–1904, pp. 17–18.

23 Although it is *Riders to the Sea* and *Spreading the News* he points to in his notes to the play in *Plays in Prose and Verse,* p. 421. In a letter to a Californian School, published in 1924 and reprinted from the original typescript in "Two Lectures on the Irish Theatre by W. B. Yeats', *Theatre and Nationalism in 20th Century Ireland,* ed. Robert O'Driscoll, University of Toronto Press, Toronto, 1971, p. 83, Yeats attributed their deliberate choice of dialect to the qualities of the company: 'I soon saw that their greatest success would be in comedy, or in observed tragedy; not in poetical drama, which needs considerable poetical and general culture. I had found an old Dublin pamphlet about the blind beggar, "Zozimus", and noticed that whereas the parts written in ordinary English are badly written, certain long passages in dialect are terse and vivid. I pointed this out to Lady Gregory, and said if we could persuade our writers to use dialect, no longer able to copy the newspapers, or some second-rate English author, they would become original and vigorous. Perhaps no one reason ever drives one to anything. Perhaps I do not remember clearly after so many years; but I believe it was that thought that made me write, with Lady Gregory's help, *The Pot of Broth,* and *Cathleen ni Houlihan.* The dialect in those two plays is neither rich nor supple, for I had not the right ear, and Lady Gregory had not as yet taken down among the cottages two hundred thousand words of folklore. But they began the long series of plays in dialect that have given our theatre the greater portion of its fame'.

24 Note to *Plays in Prose and Verse,* 1922, and W. B. Yeats, *Autobiographies,* Macmillan, London, 1955, pp. 451–52.

25 'Cuguan', *The United Irishman,* 8 November 1902, p. 3.

26 Unsigned note in *The Academy and Literature,* June 1904, reprinted in J. M. Synge, *Prose,* ed. Alan Price, Oxford University Press, London, 1966, pp. 397–98.

27 Notes written in 1906, quoted in J. M. Synge, *Plays: Book I,* ed. Ann Saddlemyer, Oxford University Press, London, 1968, p. xxviii.

28 'Le Mouvement Intellectuel Irlandais', *L'Européen,* 31 May 1902, translated as 'The Irish Literary Movement' and published in John M. Synge, *The Aran Islands and Other Writings,* ed. Robert Tracy, Vintage, New York, 1962, pp. 364–65. In the same article, pp. 363–64, Synge notes the contrasting emotions evoked by Edward Martyn's *The Heather Field:* 'The playwright has made of this dreamer, who

213

comforts himself with great and chimerical hopes, a truly attractive character. He wins all our sympathy beside his brutally realistic wife.'

29 22 October 1901, reprinted in Robert Hogan and James Kilroy, *The Irish Literary Theatre: 1899–1901,* Dolmen, Dublin, 1975, p. 103.

30 *Autobiographies,* pp. 439–440.

31 *'An Craoibhin's Plays', Poets and Dreamers,* 1903; *The Twisting of the Rope* and other translations of Douglas Hyde's work were first published by her in this volume, and reprinted with further plays by Hyde in the Coole Edition, Colin Smythe, Gerrards Cross, 1974.

32 *Letters,* p. 400.

33 Lady Gregory, *Our Irish Theatre* 1913, Colin Smythe, Gerrards Cross, 1972, p. 57.

34 In *Our Irish Theatre,* p. 60, Lady Gregory describes *The Rising of the Moon* as 'an historical play, as my history goes, for the scene is laid in the historical time of the rising of the Fenians in the sixties. But the real fight in the play goes on in the sergeant's own mind, and so its human side makes it go as well in Oxford or London or Chicago as in Ireland itself.' There is nothing in the text or stage directions concerning time or rebellion, but the Castle authorities considered it sufficiently incendiary to forbid the borrowing of uniforms.

35 Notes to *The Rising of the Moon,* quoted in *Collected Plays I,* p. 257.

36 *When the Moon Has Set,* first rejected by Yeats and Lady Gregory in 1901, remained among Synge's papers and in revised form was rejected again after his death; it was first published in Synge, *Plays Book I* in 1968.

37 Yeats's lecture on 'Contemporary Irish Theatre', edited by Robert O'Driscoll, *Yeats and the Theatre,* ed. Robert O'Driscoll and Lorna Reynolds, Macmillan, Toronto, 1975, p. 49.

38 'Synge to MacKenna: The Mature Years', ed. Ann Saddlemyer, *Irish Renaissance,* ed. Robin Skelton and David R. Clark, Dolmen, Dublin, 1965, p. 67.

39 'I found the part a difficult one to master for it was completely unlike anything that I or anybody else in the company had ever played previously'. Maire nic Shiubhlaigh, *The Splendid Years,* Duffy, Dublin, 1955, p. 42.

40 Synge wrote to Frank Fay after the London production in 1904, 'Miss W[alker, Maire nic Shiubhlaigh] is clever and charming in the part, but your brother is so strong he dominates the play – unconsciously and inevitably – and of course the woman should dominate'. Quoted in Synge Plays *Book I,* p. xx.

41 Undated statement by Yeats in Lady Gregory's hand, probably prepared in 1904 for the patent application, in the possession of the Berg Collection, New York Public Library.

42 Later revised as *The Green Helmet: an Heroic Farce* 1910. *The Player Queen,* originally intended for Mrs Patrick Campbell, was not completed until 1919 when it was produced by the Stage Society in London.

43 Introduction to *Fighting the Waves, Wheels and Butterflies,* Macmillan, London, 1934, p. 71.

44 The Abbey stage measured fourteen feet high, twenty-one feet wide, and fifteen feet deep. Willie Fay reports, 'All our cottage scenes were the exact dimensions of an Irish cottage – 12 feet high in front, sloping down to 8 feet at the back wall, 20 feet long and 12 feet wide.' W. G. Fay and Catherine Carswell, *The Fays of the Abbey Theatre*, Harcourt Brace, New York, 1935, p. 200.

FOUR ELEGIES

HELEN VENDLER

Like all great poets, Yeats re-invented every traditional form he
touched – the sonnet, the love-poem, the ode, the patriotic poem,
the country-house poem, and so on. He was immensely learned
in poetry; when he touched any genre he knew its lineaments. His
own reformation of form is best seen when classic generic
examples are kept in mind, and so I should like to examine
four of his elegies in the light of departures they exhibit from
our received notions of the elegiac genre. The poems I will
look at are unusual in that they are group-elegies, that is, elegies
for several persons – 'Easter 1916', 'In Memory of Eva Gore-
Booth and Con Markiewicz', 'Beautiful Lofty Things', and 'The
Municipal Gallery Revisited'. Elegies about several persons are
not unprecedented (Hopkins, for instance, wrote *The Wreck of
the Deutschland* about the death of five nuns) but they are rare,
especially in the Yeatsian form which attempts to mark distinctions among the persons. In each of these cases, I will be asking,
essentially, what makes this poem beautiful, original, or striking,
and I will be recalling our expectations of the genre.

'Easter 1916' is so well known that it takes an effort to see it
freshly. Today we find in it a certain creaky formality; it is much
less free-wheeling than poems written later. Of its four carefully
delineated parts – the picture of the quotidian encounters between
poet and patriots before the Easter Rising; the gallery of sketches
of the revolutionaries; the meditation on the heart of stone in the
midst of the living stream; and the final elegiac conclusion, the
most original is the second, with its four brief unnamed portraits,
which are eighteenth-century in their worldliness and in their willingness to be unheroic, even uncomplimentary. The dead in this
poem are like any group of people – ignorant, arguing, shrill in
one case; sensitive, daring, and sweet in another; drunken and
vainglorious in a third. Earlier elegies demanded *a priori* a personal worth in the person celebrated; Yeats will prescind from
personal worth and praise instead corporate action. Conven-
tionally, change plays the rôle of the villain in elegy ('But O the

216

heavy change, now thou art gone! '); Yeats will make change the philosopher's stone which can transform even base metal into gold: 'All changed, changed utterly: . . . / He, too, has been changed in his turn,/ Transformed utterly: / A terrible beauty is born.' But to have been changed is not to change, and the metaphysical heart of the elegy is a meditation on changing and unchangingness, and, implicitly, on being changed. Yeats has been changed, along with the patriots. Elder poets depended on a convention of a golden past shared by the dead and their mourners: 'For we were nursed upon the selfsame hill,' but Yeats has repudiated this convention in the opening of the poem, where the shared past is represented merely as an uncomprehending existence side-by-side, in which the poet committed the one sin forbidden to poets, to utter 'polite meaningless words'. For all the 'vivid faces' of the patriots, their fixed focus on a single aim seemed to the poet repellent and unnatural. The old Biblical opposition between hearts of flesh and hearts of stone is here crossed with the fairy-tale punishment of a living creature's being turned to stone, and the final indictment made by the elegy against those it laments is that 'hearts with one purpose alone . . . seem enchanted to a stone/ To trouble the living stream.'

In every elegy a moment comes in which the deadness of the corpse has to be confronted and exposed to the full: this moment comes, in 'Easter 1916', in the picture of the stone; and to draw the immobility and lifelessness even more firmly, Yeats does something entirely traditional in elegy, which is to place the corpse in a setting brilliant with natural life. In *Lycidas*, the surmised bier is imagined covered with all the flowers of the spring; here, the stone is placed obdurately in the midst of all the active life over, around, beside, and in the living stream.

> The horse that comes from the road,
> The rider, the birds that range
> From cloud to tumbling cloud,
> Minute by minute they change;
> A shadow of cloud on the stream
> Changes minute by minute;
> A horse-hoof slides on the brim,
> And a horse plashes within it;
> The long-legged moor-hens dive,
> And hens to moor-cocks call;

Minute by minute they live:
The stone's in the midst of all.

This rapid scherzo, written in the most beautiful verse in the poem, establishes the fluidity of nature stubbornly opposed by the concentrated purposiveness of one kind of human will.

Once he has arrived at this point, Yeats must find a way to end his elegy. Can he approve of the stone? Can he find a perspective in which his personal disapproval of revolutionary fixity will not matter? Can he find an unstony, but still accurate, image for driven activity? Can he salve his own guilt for having relegated the revolutionaries and himself to motley-wearers until their intransigence changed Irish history? Can he address them now with other than meaningless and polite words, as he could not in their life? What is he to say of their battle in the General Post Office and their subsequent execution (with the exception of Con Markiewicz) by the British?

Yeats solved these aesthetic and moral problems in different ways. His most extraordinary decision was to say precisely nothing at all about the Rising itself or about the executions. Where we might have expected from another poet a narrative of heroic valour and imprecations against England – a Miltonic 'Avenge, O Lord, thy slaughtered saints' – we find total silence. This elegy – like any other poem – serves as a self-definition for the elegist. Yeats did not believe in the wisdom of the street-battle, and he is not about to undertake a recantation in practical terms. His remorse is a spiritual one. In a striking re-adjustment of his earlier view of the revolutionaries, he decides that far from being stony-hearted, they were led astray by an excess of love – as knights-errant have immemorially been led away by some Belle Dame Sans Merci, some *ignis fatuus* that bewildered them till they died. In 'September 1913', Yeats had written that the 'delirium of the brave' looked like the delirium of love; that if Edward Fitzgerald, Robert Emmet, and Wolfe Tone were to return, the people would cry 'Some woman's yellow hair/Has maddened every mother's son.' Remembering this comparison, he can now see the patriots as among those who, like himself and Hanrahan his creation, display the 'horrible splendour of desire', and so he can join them in spirit. He sees their death as freely chosen – love bewildered them, not till they were killed, but till they died, stumbling into death in pursuit of their hearts' desire.

218

Yeats indulges, in his concluding stanza, that classic impulse of elegy to deny some portion of the cold truth of death. As Milton attempts to interpose a little ease by imagining that Lycidas's corpse is present, and can be placed on a bier decked with flowers, while in reality the corpse is at sea, weltering to the parching wind, so Yeats too dallies with false surmise as he lightly suggests that the patriots are only sleeping. At first, he had appointed himself their judge; knowing that 'Too long a sacrifice/Can make a stone of the heart,' he had asked, 'O when may it suffice?' But he then declines the rôle of judge, remembering how the ghost had told Hamlet not to judge his mother, but rather to 'leave her to Heaven.' If he like Hamlet is not to judge ('That is Heaven's part'), perhaps he is to brood over the dead as a mother would over heedless children:

> To murmur name upon name,
> As a mother names her child
> When sleep at last has come
> On limbs that had run wild.
> What is it but nightfall?

This eddy toward patronising sentiment and frailty of thought is coldly checked: 'No, no, not night but death.' A brief and uncertain hope ('England may keep faith') is also discarded, at least as a justification for the deaths. Instead, the patriots are transformed into something quite like Yeatsian heroes, beset by a dream, enchanted, bewildered by an excess of love, their wits led astray by an imaginative yearning. The pun on 'wild' limbs and 'bewildered' death associates revolutionary activity with a confounding of reason by the enchanted heart:

> We know their dream; enough
> To know they dreamed and are dead;
> And what if excess of love
> Bewildered them till they died?

What if they are dead, like all heroes? Yeats has found by the end his proper rôle, which is not judicial, not magisterial, not even elegiac, but rather epic. He speaks no longer in the private 'I' ('I have met them at close of day') but rather in the public 'we': 'Our part' is to memoralise them; 'We' know their dream. He

219

works as the chartered bard, doing what his fellow-citizens cannot: he will call the roll of heroes, doing it as his public duty –
'I write it out in a verse –/ MacDonagh and McBride/ And
Connolly and Pearse.' He here reverses the convention of naming
the elegiac subject early in the poem: the leaders, nameless till
now, are enrolled in that small number of men whose names alone
evoke history. In this way, without denying their physical death
('they dreamed and are dead') Yeats finds a device of style – the
epic catalogue of heroes – which implies immortality. The wearing of the green becomes, in this context, something like the
wearing of a lady's colours by her knight, and the 'terrible beauty'
of Revolution (borrowed from Blake's 'fearful symmetry'), has
at last been endorsed in a way genuine to Yeats.

'Easter 1916' is by no means the greatest of Yeats's elegies –
he reserved his best elegiac powers for the poems on his own
death. But it does demonstrate how easily he solved a problem –
how to write about an unwieldy group of sixteen people engaged
in an action of which he had disapproved, and to say something
true both as critic and as mourner, while at the same time writing
a poem of remorse for his own dismissal of their desire, which he
discovers to have no small affinity with his own.

The terms are tightened in the elegy on the Gore-Booth sisters:
there are only two dead people to be mourned, and the occasion is
a private, not a public, one. 'In Memory of Eva Gore-Booth and
Con Markiewicz' is a more brilliant poem than 'Easter
1916', more daring and showy, less formal, more violent.
The strokes are hurried – a sketch here, a violent slash
across the canvas there. Yeats writes as if in shorthand: for all
the vanished past a few light notations, stage directions for a
Chekhov play:

> The light of evening, Lissadell,
> Great windows open to the south,
> Two girls in silk kimonos, both
> Beautiful, one a gazelle.

Then, remembering Milton's 'blind Fury with th'abhorred shears,'
Yeats takes Keats's benevolent autumn who spares the next swath
and all its twined flowers and turns her into Atropos: 'A raving
autumn shears/ Blossoms from the summer's wreath.' The two
young girls are aged instantly into skeletal figures, which forecast

the corpses they will become: the older drags out lonely years, and the younger, says Yeats cruelly, is 'withered old and skeleton-gaunt.' The sexual taunt is combined with an intellectual one: she is an image of her equally withered politics, that 'vague Utopia' she dreams of. To endanger an elegy to this degree is a thing unheard of before Yeats. Though Yeats has seen the sisters nostalgically in their youth, he sees them contemptuously in their old age. Yeats at first attempts to save the elegy by a fantasy – that he and the sisters, though long estranged, could meet and together recall Lissadell; and in this circling-back, the first stanza ends as it had begun, with the recollection of 'two girls in silk kimonos, both/ Beautiful, one a gazelle.'

Then the poem pauses. In that pause, as we realise when we read the first words following it, 'Dear shadows,' the sisters have died. Before the pause, the poet could think to 'seek/One or the other out and speak/ Of that old Georgian mansion,' but now that possibility is forever closed. He can address the sisters only as they live in his shadowy thought as shades of memory. Yeats did not invent this striking moment in which the sisters disappear in the mid-course of the poem; he learned it, I suppose, from Wordsworth's 'A slumber did my spirit seal', where a death takes place between the two stanzas. Nor did he invent the wonderful change from the third person ('two girls') to the second ('Dear shadows, now you know it all') with its suddent tenderness – he could have seen a comparable change in Bishop's King s 'Exequy'. Nonetheless, both the silent death, within an ellipsis, of the sisters and the sudden turn to direct address serve to heal the wounds of estrangement recalled from life. Impatient and irritated consciousness of political difference seems to have kept Yeats from visiting the sisters while they were still alive; but now they join the pantheon of his permanent images, and are suffused with the heartbreak of the forever dead.

As he now finds both nostalgia and contempt impossible as tones to adopt *vis-à-vis* the Gore-Booths, Yeats tries a lofty kindness, saying that they have now learned, in their posthumous life, what he has always known – 'the folly of a fight/ With a common wrong or right.' The poem reaches its metaphysical heart in the lines later imitated by Auden:

> The innocent and beautiful
> Have no enemy but time.

In succession, Yeats the mourner has been Yeats the judge, Yeats the scorner, Yeats the pitying voice. But now, in a striking reversal of attitude, Yeats becomes a supplicant. The poem turns Blakean in its desire to consume time, but its earthly protagonist suddenly realises that he is helpless to act alone, being the merest novice in activism. He has never been a fighter; it is the sisters who took up arms. Now, in the fight against the only true enemy, time, the poet cannot move till the sisters take command in his mind and impel his spirit. 'Arise and bid me strike a match/ And strike another till time catch.' The sisters, in his mind, are young again; if the great bonfire of the temporal world lights up, they should 'run till all the sages know.' Finally, the poet, first separated in life and then separated even in memory from the dear shadows he addresses, finds a broader frame of reference that encompasses both their political life and his artistic one. All of their separate endeavours, he sees, went to form the great fanci-ful structure-in-time of moral activity, all of it equally con-taminated. Though he had convicted the sisters of folly earlier, both he and they stand convicted of mortal guilt by the sages who see the corruption of all earthly work. It is a triumph of the poem that the Yeats who had first said 'They', with respect to the sisters, and then had been able to say 'You', can now finally, of himself and the sisters, say 'We':

> We the great gazebo built,
> They convicted us of guilt;
> Bid me strike a match and blow.

The sages are the resurrected forms here, as they are in other late poems, ghostly monitors of the changeless and immortal. They watch the poet-turned-incendiary as they had watched the girls-turned-revolutionaries; they watch the gazebo-folly ignited as they watched the Post Office occupied. In the last fight, Con and Eva are the commanders and Yeats their inexperienced lieutenant, waiting for his moment of initiation – 'Bid me strike a match and blow.' If this is not Yeats's most authentic stance – he was not, after all, Blake with his love of 'mental fight' – it is still a wrenched tribute to the power of the Irish activists in his memory, that to join them in thought he is willing to conceive of himself as putting the torch to all their common civilisation.

I turn next to a late elegy, more unmixed in its feeling. The activist patriots as a group were never wholly congenial to Yeats. In 'Beautiful Lofty Things', free from historical occasion, he can choose his own group, and the only activists he includes are O'Leary, who said there were some things a man must not do to save his country, and Maud Gonne, remembered here only for her physical beauty. This is the most modern of Yeats's group elegies, the most stripped, the most self-effacing. Yeats here borrows from his own earlier work; the poem contains brief portraits comparable to those in 'Easter 1916', and, in using, like that poem, a roll call of names instantly recognizable for their part in the history of modern Ireland, shares a bardic ambition. On the other hand, patriotism as such is no longer in question here: the title speaks only of the sublime and the beautiful. Many things are beautiful; others are lofty; but only a very few – six or seven in a lifetime – can be said to be both at once, to be beautiful lofty things. Yeats's elegiac tone has loosened so as to admit humour, drunkenness, the nonsensical; the line is long enough, being an Alexandrine, to permit a small dramatic vignette here, a quotation there. The beautiful lofty 'things' are, we discover, people and their human looks and actions: to call them 'things' is to make oneself the curator of a museum of the best things human beings can be and do and show.

Two images recur in the poem—heads (O'Leary's noble head, John Butler Yeats's mischievous head, Maud Gonne's arrogant head) and plebeian or unworthy settings for these heads – a raging crowd at the Abbey riots, a drunken audience for Standish O'Grady, a cowardly potential attacker of Augusta Gregory, a common train station for Maud Gonne. This array of Olympian busts is not found in a pagan heaven; if Olympus is anywhere, it is where these Olympians are. This elegy presupposes no transfiguration, transmutation, or resurrection; it does not even insist on historical memory like 'Easter 1916'. If Maud Gonne is remembered by conventional history, it is not for her straight back and arrogant head. The only worth of Yeats's gallery is that conferred by the poet who makes his select list. By it he defends himself. He loved nobility in John O'Leary; freethinking, daring, and humour in his father; grand visionariness in the drunken O'Grady; imperturbable courage in Augusta Gregory; and arrogant beauty in Maud Gonne. The last beautiful lofty thing is the appearance of this race of divinities in one place at one time – 'All the Olympians'. This last is 'a thing never known again.' It is only the closing phrase which transforms this poem from a eulogy into an elegy; it is as though the colours changed before our eyes and all these heroes, caught in moments of characteristic and memorable selfhood, turn to ghosts. If we turn back to the beginning and reread the poem, they live, radiantly, again. The mourner here appears as magician, doing portraits not like those conclusive memorials-for-the-dead in 'Easter 1916') ('He might have won fame in the end,'...), not even like the nostalgic sketch of 'that old Georgian mansion' in the elegy of the Gore-Booths, but rather snapshots uninvaded by an elegiac tone. Yeats creates his snapshots by abolishing any temporal frame. There is never in the poem, until the end, any mention of 'now' or 'then', there are simply actions and people – Maud Gonne waiting a train, Augusta Gregory seated at a table, O'Grady speaking high nonsensical words, J. B. Yeats upon the Abbey stage. The theatre of the mind throws up these scenes immortalised, floating free of time or extinction. When the pantheon is complete, the mourner allows himself his one adjective and two adverbs for elegy – 'never known again'. The corpses and the brimmingly alive people are in this poem one and the same, and the beautiful and lofty, as categories, are able to accommodate the widest range of human types, behaviour, and language. What this elegy regrets is all of life as it is lived by people like Yeats's Olympians. It is assumed by the poem that the beauty and loftiness which it celebrates will be perceived as such by all observers. There is no tone of personal taste, no 'I', no concession that such sights might not be to everyone's liking – on the contrary. In 'The Municipal Gallery Revisited', for instance, Yeats makes it clear that he can be satisfied by no new sorts of excellence, no matter how worthy – he wants the excellence he himself has loved:

> And I am in despair that time may bring
> Approved patterns of women or of men
> But not that selfsame excellence again.

But 'Beautiful Lofty Things' suppresses the personal voice, and chooses the dramatic as its mode of lyric. It offers no conceptual basis for its list, but flaunts instead an intuition which it assumes universal – that anyone could recognise these flashes of human life as beautiful and lofty, that such things need not be conceptualised. By its refusal of a metaphysical core such as those

224

present in 'Easter 1916' and 'In Memory of Eva Gore-Booth and Con Markiewicz', by its isolating of moments rather than of whole lives, by its impartial inclusion of the humorous and the drunken along with the splendid and the noble, by its abandon of any notion of afterlife, the poem is quintessentially modern. The elegiac conventions of the mourner, the corpse, the prolonged lament, the questioning of the justice of the gods, the moral emphasis, the apotheosis, have so vanished or been changed that the poem belongs only tenuously, formally speaking, to the genre of elegy as we know it. And yet it is unmistakably an elegy, recognisable even in its new guise.

I come finally to Yeats's last group elegy, 'The Municipal Gallery Revisited'. It is reminiscent in many ways of 'In Memory of Major Robert Gregory' (1918) and 'All Souls' Night' (1920) in which Yeats memoralised Lionel Johnson, Synge, George Pollexfen, Robert Gregory, William Thomas Horton, Florence Farr Emery, and MacGregor Mathers. Now, seventeen years after 'All Souls' Night' and little more than a year before his own death, Yeats visits the Dublin Municipal Gallery. He made a speech about the visit to the Irish Academy of Letters:

> For a long time I had not visited the Municipal Gallery. I went there a week ago and was restored to many friends. I sat down after a few minutes, overwhelmed with emotion. There were pictures painted by men, now dead, who were once my intimate friends. There were the portraits of my fellow-workers; there was that portrait of Lady Gregory, by Mancini, which John Synge thought the greatest portrait since Rembrandt; there was John Synge himself; there, too, were portraits of our States-men; the events of the last thirty years in fine pictures: a peasant ambush, the trial of Roger Casement, a pilgrimage to Lough Derg, event after event: Ireland not as she is displayed in guide book or history, but Ireland seen because of the magni-ficent vitality of her painters, in the glory of her passions.*

When Yeats made this material into a poem, 'a little over a verse a day,' he set us as readers a difficult task. The poem is courtly, remote, lofty, and formal. By comparison with the

---

* A Norman Jeffares, *A Commentary on the Collected Poems of W. B. Yeats*, Macmillan, London, 1968, pp 482-3, quoted from *A Speech and Two Poems* [1937].

deliberate violence and plain-speaking of some of the late poetry, and the tones of pain, loss, outcry, and protest Yeats there permitted himself, this last look at his friends seems almost cold. Emotion is narrated rather than enacted. 'Heart-smitten with emotion I sink down', he says, or 'I am in despair that time may bring/ Approved patterns of women or of men/ But not that selfsame excellence again.' Yet no one would call this language heart-smitten or despairing. This is a distinction difficult to make, but one has only to read 'John Kinsella's Lament' or 'Why Should Not Old Men Be Mad? or 'Crazy Jane on the Mountain' or 'The Circus Animals' Desertion' – all poems contemporary with this one – to feel the difference in diction and tone. Readers of this reticent poem must bring to it not only knowledge of the generation it wishes to hallow, but also a lively sense of how it draws upon and rethinks generic elegiac principles.

A poem can enter its genre, so to speak, at any point along a formal continuum. A lyric – though always written by an adult – may enter the speaking voice of lyric in babyhood ('I am but three days old', says one of Blake's speakers) or after death 'Love bade me welcome', says Herbert, speaking as a soul who has just died and is knocking at heaven's gate). One famous love poem, 'Since there's no help, come let us kiss and part' enters its genre at the latest possible moment – when the lovers have apparently acknowledged that their affair is over. When we look at 'The Municipal Gallery Revisited' we can see that it too enters its generic form, the elegy, at the latest possible moment. The conventional beginnings – the announcement of death, the grouping of mourners, the lament, the indignation at loss – are all missing. Those stages have passed. We enter the genre at the last stage – that of apotheosis. The dead have been apotheosised by having been made into icons, painted images: the gallery is a frieze of forms as transfixed as those marble men and maidens on the Grecian Urn. Arland Ussher did not understand this when he regretted that Sarah Purser's portrait of Maud Gonne did not yet hang in the gallery at the time of Yeats's visit – 'an accident,' he wrote, 'which has no doubt deprived us of a burning stanza.' On the contrary, since Maud Gonne outlived Yeats, she could not have appeared in this enumeration of the dead. Nor would such 'a burning stanza' be containable within the ceremonial tone of this poem – as we can see by a glance at Yeats's poem about a portrait-bust of Maud Gonne, 'A Bronze Head', which rages

against 'this foul world in its decline and fall . . ./ Ancestral
pearls all pitched into a sty.'

'The Municipal Gallery Revisited' avoids all such fiery language.
It avoids even the mention of death. But because all in the poem
are dead, it is for us to pronounce, *sotto voce,* the roll call of
deaths as Yeats glances from picture to picture: Casement,
hanged; Griffith, dead at fifty; O'Higgins, assassinated; Robert
Gregory, shot down in the War; Hugh Lane, who endowed the
Gallery, drowned at sea; Lady Gregory, dead five years earlier;
John Synge, dead at thirty-eight of Hodgkin's disease; and,
secretly present, Yeats's father, the painter of Synge, dead for
fifteen years.

The poem, written in the present tense, wonderfully traces the
stages of Yeats's entry, physical and spiritual, into the gallery.
He enters, and is at first the tourist:

> Around me the images of thirty years:
> An ambush; pilgrims at the water side.

Then he becomes the curious contemporary of public men, seeing
their pictures:

> Casement upon trial, half hidden by the bars,
> Guarded; Griffith staring in hysterical pride;
> Kevin O'Higgins' countenance.

He reverts to the tourist stance, seeing,

> A revolutionary soldier kneeling to be blessed;

> An Abbot or Archbishop with an upraised hand
> Blessing the Tricolour.

These 'short takes,' as film language would name them, are compared in the poet's mind with the dreary and hopeless realities of
nineteenth-century Ireland as he remembers them, and the dis-
crepancy between the deadness of life and the vigour of art, one
of Yeats's great subjects, is brought into play:

> 'This is not,' I say,
> 'The dead Ireland of my youth, but an Ireland
> The poets have imagined, terrible and gay.'

At this point, the disjunction between art and life seems complete. But by the end of the poem, art and life will be conjoined, even inseparable: the task of that conjunction occupies the rest of the stanzas.

The fulcrum on which the poem turns is an anonymous one. Yeats suddenly stands before a woman's portrait and recognises her as someone he met 'all but fifty years ago/ For twenty minutes in some studio'. A single fugitive moment – twenty minutes of Yeats's long-ago life – has been entered by this portrait into the register of art. That moment, and that woman, are (we must assume) forever dead. Yeats sinks down, overwhelmed, and covers his eyes, unable for a moment to look further, shaken by the thought that wherever he has looked he has looked upon his permanent or impermanent images. He assumes that some images are impermanent, and may in time wane or die. But for the moment, permanent or impermanent, they are present and visible. The list of the living who are now dead accelerates in the poem until a whole life and death can take place in three short words, in the description of the two pictures Sir John Lavery painted of his young wife:

> Augusta Gregory's son; her sister's son,
> Hugh Lane, 'onlie begetter' of all these;
> Hazel Lavery living and dying.

So summarily named, all these lives seem a 'tale/ As though some ballad-singer had sung it all,' a recital simplified into formulaic terms. At this point, however, Yeats represents himself coming to the portrait of one of the persons he knew best in all the world, and the pace of the poem – that pace so finely-geared to the events taking place in Yeats's mind – slows to a halt. Art, which had seemed to so transfigure life in inventing an Ireland 'terrible and gay,' suddenly seems wholly inadequate to life. One can't object, Yeats feels, to Mancini's portrait of Lady Gregory; after all, Synge had pronounced it the greatest portrait since Rembrandt, and it is a 'great ebullient portrait, certainly.' Yet Yeats experiences a sharp disappointment in contemplating it, and asserts that no artist, however great, could possibly show in a portrait all the qualities of a remarkable person. Art is, after all, a poor mimic – and nothing makes Yeats so feel the absolute loss of Augusta Gregory as this portrait, however well done it may be. For all the

portraits that survive them, the dead are gone for good, and it is
no comfort to be told that other worthy people will take their
place. It is not excellence alone that Yeats loves, but rather the
particular excellence he has known, identified himself with, and
been attached to. At this point, this elegy touches that definitive
knowledge of loss, the confrontation with the deadness of the
dead, present in all such poems: Yeats is 'in despair that time
may bring/ Approved patters of women or of men/ But not that
selfsame excellence again.' The richness of the word 'selfsame'
includes, I think, a reference to Yeats's own self and its adherence
to this excellence, which became to him the same as his self. However, even in this moment recognising irremediable loss, the
language of the poem remains chaste, formal, and measured:
'approved patterns' is not the usual diction of despair. And Yeats
tells us that he refuses here the elegiac lament: 'And now that
end has come I have not wept.' The permanence of virtue is
asserted through Spenser's proverb used in the elegy for the Earl
of Leicester: 'No fox can foul the lair the badger swept.'

The elegy had halted in homage to Lady Gregory, but the halt
is prolonged by Yeats's own meditation on his long links to her
and to her house. The poem turns, for the first time, wholly lyric,
as its subject becomes the poet and his final view of himself. At
first, he thinks to conceive of himself as an artist, united with
Lady Gregory and John Synge in a conviction that all good action,
speech, and art must come 'from contact with the soil.' If the
poem were an elegy of the self-as-artist, it would end here, with
the poet's boast:

> We three alone in modern times had brought
> Everything down to that sole test again,
> Dream of the noble and the beggar-man . . .

The poem would then resemble 'Coole Park and Ballylee, 1931,
which ends with the self-epitaph 'we were the last romantics.'
But, as we know, 'The Municipal Gallery Revisited' adds another
stanza, which makes explicit much that has hitherto lain latent in
the poem. The stanza continues the fictive narrative (we can see,
by comparison with the speech Yeats made on the same experience, how carefully he arranged in the poem the steps in his walk
through the gallery for the purposes of increased closeness of
focus, increased autobiographical import, and moral climax).

229

Yeats now takes one final look at the gallery of portraits and sees, last of all, his father's painting of Synge – 'And here's John Synge himself' – as if by confirmation of his having mentioned him a moment earlier, in the stanza on art – 'John Synge, I, and Augusta Gregory,' he had said. We have seen Augusta Gregory, we now see John Synge. Between them, if the gallery and the elegy are to coincide, should hang one other other portrait – the portrait, we realise, that this whole poem, in another medium, has been drawing – the self-portrait of William Butler Yeats. And immediately that effigy is before us, and we, his readers, have replaced the poet as the gazers in the gallery. From his portrait, so to speak, Yeats speaks to us, asking to be grouped not with his books but with his friends. To judge him as an artist, we need only read his works; and we have just seen him, in the penultimate stanza, as an artist. But we also know, from his reaction to the portrait of Augusta Gregory, his dissatisfaction with art – at least with the conventional solo portrait – as a representation of life. He refuses, then, a solo portrait of himself, and requests instead that we set him, as this poem sets him, in the context wherein his life was lived. We are to see this poem, finally, as something called 'Self-Portrait with Friends':

> You that would judge me, do not judge alone
> This book or that, come to this hallowed place
> Where my friends' portraits hang and look thereon;
> Ireland's history in their lineaments trace.

We recognize the vocabulary of elegiac apotheosis: judgment, a hallowed place, Blakean lineaments. Yeats saves the word that for him symbolises heavenly presences, and which is also a technical word for apotheosis – 'glory' – for his closing couplet:

> Think where man's glory most begins and ends,
> And say my glory was I had such friends.

We, Yeats's readers, speak of him, in the indirect discourse he attributes to us in his close, in the past tense: we are to say, after his death, in judging him, that Yeats's glory was he had such friends. By giving us an epitaph to speak over him, he effectively makes himself a corpse by the end of the poem, but a corpse apotheosised by the glorious company he keeps. Yeats's greatest group elegy is finally an elegy for himself.

In the successive exploratory treatments of group elegy that we find in the *Collected Poems,* Yeats comes very far from the relatively conventional elegiac terms of 'Easter 1916', and finds truthful ways to treat what Stevens called 'the mythology of modern death.' He leaves behind the invocation of a rather forced apotheosis – 'a terrible beauty is born' – and a somewhat forced apocalypse in which he strikes matches to burn up time, forsaking these for a wholly human apotheosis of characteristic individual appearances and actions in 'Beautiful Lofty Things' and, in 'The Municipal Gallery Revisited', for a group of virtues exemplified by a beautiful and gentle woman, Major Gregory, Hugh Lane, Hazel and John Lavery, Augusta Gregory, Mancini, John Synge, John Butler Yeats, and the poet himself. Those virtues, as we think of the personages who inhabit the poem, are easily named – beauty, bravery in war, philanthropy, connoisseurship, care for the poor, and the creation of art. Because in this poem life, for Yeats, is over – he is dead by the end – he can speak of his own associations and emotions with the measured voice of a historian. It is not the most immediately moving voice in Yeats – but it is one that grows more moving with time. In declaring, 'I have not wept', Yeats recalls the Wordsworth who told us that there exist 'thoughts that do often lie too deep for tears.' Yeats here, like Whitman in another poem, is as one disembodied, triumphant, dead.

These are not Yeats's greatest elegies. His most profound use of the form comes in the poems he wrote for his own death: 'The Tower', 'The Man and the Echo', 'The Circus Animals' Desertion,' 'Cuchulain Comforted,' 'Under Ben Bulben,' 'The Black Tower'. He also wrote great elegies for the fall of civilisations – 'Lapis Lazuli,' 'Meru,' 'The Gyres.' By comparison with such poems, the four I have taken up may seem minor works. And yet they reveal Yeats's constant inquiry into the renewal of genre, and record a brilliant and forcible modernisation of one of the oldest of literary forms.

BOOKS AND NUMBERLESS DREAMS: YEATS'S RELATIONS WITH HIS EARLY PUBLISHERS

JOHN S. KELLY

> I have gone about the house, gone up and down
> As a man does who has published a new book . . .

So Yeats describes his efforts in later life to hear praise of Maud Gonne. The simile is one rooted in his personal experience, for he had known not only the excitement of publishing new books but also the difficulties of bringing his early volumes to the point of publication: the delays and uncertainties that made their ultimate appearance occasions of keen anticipation in which the delight of seeing his poetry in appropriate book form was tempered by apprehensions about its reception in the large world. In this essay I want to follow, with the aid of letters, contemporary reviews and account books, Yeats's relationship with the first two publishers of his verse, Charles Kegan Paul and T. Fisher Unwin.

Yeats had some difficulty in getting himself launched as a professional poet. His earliest verse he contributed to English and American periodicals of limited circulation, which paid little, and to Irish publications, with even smaller circulations, which paid nothing. His first book was in fact an off-print from one of the latter, an edition of the play, *Mosada*, reprinted from the *Dublin University Review* of June 1886 by Sealy, Bryers and Walker, a Dublin printing firm. The edition was of 100 copies, had hardly any distribution outside family friends, and attracted only one review. A bare start then, but it was at least a start, and not long afterwards the young poet, eager to put his name more assuredly before the public, began to prepare a full collection of poems and to look for a real publisher. In due course he found one, a rather reluctant one as it turned out, but this man, Kegan Paul, gave his poetry the backing of an established firm. And when relations between the two became strained he was in a stronger position, especially backed by the characteristically shrewd Edward Garnett, to transfer to T. Fisher Unwin. Between them Paul and Unwin looked after Yeats's books of verse in his first decade as a published poet, at the end of which period he was an established name with a growing reputation.

It was in the autumn of 1887 that Yeats started to think seriously of a substantial edition of his work, the centre-piece of which would be a long Irish poem that he had already commenced telling of the adventures of Oisin in Tir na nOg. There were a number of reasons why his thoughts should have turned to Kegan Paul as a possible publisher. In the first place, Paul handled Katherine Tynan's poems and at this time was doing reasonably well out of them. He had taken her first book, *Louise de la Vallière* at her father's expense but, no doubt to his surprise, the first edition quickly sold out and a further edition of 500 copies was printed. This may have disposed Paul to look more favourably on young Irish poets (he had brought out Tynan's second book, *Shamrocks*, in an edition of 1000 in the spring of 1887) and the firm did have some connections with Ireland. The Kegan in Paul's name (which Yeats consistently misspelled 'Keegan') came from an Irish forbear on the maternal side and one of the partners in the firm, Alfred Trench, was the son of Archbishop Trench of Dublin. Even more to the point, John Todhunter, Yeats's friend and neighbour in Bedford Park, published with Paul and knew him fairly well, as did George Coffey, the Dublin antiquarian and archaeologist, who was another family friend. Both were to put in a good word for Yeats at an opportune moment.

Useful though such friendly support was, Yeats knew that no publisher would risk any considerable amount of money on an unknown poet and that if he wanted to see his name on a volume of poems he would have either to defray the costs himself or guarantee a readership that would allow the book at least to break even. Unhappily, his father was not a 'strong farmer', like Katherine Tynan's, but an impecunious painter more prone to borrow from his son than to subsidise him. The publication of *Mosada*, which J. B. Yeats had paid for, was one thing: a more substantial and consequently more expensive volume quite another. Yeats could have no hope of a direct financial subvention from either family or friends. There was, however, another way of issuing the book. Yeats, together with John

O'Leary, T. W. Rolleston and Katherine Tynan, had taken a large hand in publishing *Poems and Ballads of Young Ireland*, an anthology of new Irish verse that had appeared in May 1888 and which had been financed by subscription. Encouraged by the success of this venture and strongly backed by John O'Leary, Yeats now thought of finding subscribers for a book of his own. By the autumn of 1887 he had had the forms printed (probably by Sealy, Bryers and Walker who thus had a part in his second book of poetry as well as issuing his first) and he and, more successfully John O'Leary, were sending them out to prospective customers, well before the book was completed and long before a publisher had been secured. As Yeats was later to acknowledge, O'Leary was the moving force in the enterprise and found 'almost all the subscribers'. The old Fenian had a wide acquaintanceship and a directness of approach in seeking subscriptions which proved remarkably effective. The twenty-two year old Yeats, shy and diffident, was less happy in selling himself directly. He was, in addition, sequestered in Sligo and overwhelmed with the fatigues of composition: his long poem, 'The Wanderings of Oisin,' upon which he pinned many hopes, was draining him emotionally,

'never has any poem given me such a trouble – making me sleepless a good deal, it has kept me out of spirits and nervous – the thing always on my mind. . . .'[1]

But he persevered and, as subscriptions began to mount up, he finished the poem. By mid-December he was back in Dublin and copying it out, and felt able to give Stephen Gwynn, the Irish M.P. and man of letters who had generously signed up for four copies, a provisional outline of what he might expect for his money. 'The Wanderings of Oisin,' 'an Irish poem of some length and about my best' was to be the most important part of the book, the rest of which would be made up of short lyrics and ballads. Meanwhile, he was just starting for London where he would 'begin sorting things' and might 'modify it indefinitely'.[2] This process of sorting and modifying continued for the rest of the winter (inded, had he but known it, it was to continue for many years after publication) and in February he could tell Katherine Tynan that he had 'copied out most of the poems for the book' and a short while later that, as a result of O'Leary's unremitting efforts, he had promises for at least ninety copies. Armed with these names and flourishing a manuscript that he estimated would make a book of 140 pages, he began to make overtures to publishers – naïvely hoping even as late as March to be in time to catch the spring season. For reasons already mentioned, Kegan Paul seemed a likely choice and he got Todhunter and Coffey to prepare the way for him. They did their job well and Paul asked to see Yeats in person.

The meeting between the over-eager but touchy young poet and the ageing publisher who had few illusions about literature and even less about new talent, was not an unqualified success. Yeats was impatient to push on to immediate publication but Paul, although courteous in manner, was more circumspect in his business arrangements. He accepted the manuscript but would not undertake definitely to publish the book until there were at least 180 or, better still, 200 subscribers. Although Yeats, who now had 130 promises, was confident of finding a further fifty, he was clearly disappointed at the inevitable delays that this would cause and his disappointment no doubt deepened his suspicion of Paul's temperate blandness. The resulting hostility is apparent in a report of the meeting that he sent to Katherine Tynan:

'Coffey and Todhunter had spoken of me, so he professed much interest in all my doings. I gave, I fear, very mono-syllabic answers, not much liking his particular compound of the superciliousness of the man of letters with the oiliness of a tradesman.'[3]

This final scratch, demonstrating that snobbery which, if not habitual with Yeats, was always tempting as a defence mechanism, was perhaps prompted by some haggling over the price of the book. Paul had suggested that it should be published at 3/6d rather than the more princely 5/- advertised to the subscribers, an alteration that would not only involve tiresome re-arrangements but which Yeats thought not altogether compatible with his dignity.

Oleaginous or not, Paul was, in fact, something more than a tradesman. He, like Yeats's father, was the son of a clergyman and he had been educated at Eton and later Oxford, where he had come under the influence of Charles Kingsley. He went on to take holy orders himself and, through his friendship with Kingsley, met F. D. Maurice, Tom Hughes and other leaders of

235

the Christian socialist movement. As Curate of Tew in Oxford-shire, then Chaplain and master at Eton, and finally Vicar of Sturminster in Dorset, his doctrine became increasingly High Church and ritualistic while his politics became more radical. His contributions to the series, *Tracts for Priests and People*, edited by Maurice and Hughes, brought him into conflict with some sections of the Anglican hierarchy, and in 1874 he gave up his living and moved to London where he took a post in the publish-ing business of Samuel King. He continued to write, and in 1876 brought out his most important work, a two-volume biography of William Godwin. The following year, King decided to sell his publishing interests and Paul bought the firm, thus becoming for a time Tennyson's publisher. He went on to handle books by Hardy, Meredith, Robert Louis Stevenson and Wilfrid Scawen Blunt. In 1881 Alfred Trench joined him as a partner and shortly after the publication of Yeats's book they amalgamated with Trubner and Co. At the time when Yeats was dealing with it the firm was fairly prosperous, but in 1895 it began to lose a lot of money and it was eventually taken over by Routledge.

A sixty-year-old semi-public man and evidently smiling when Yeats met him first, Paul was of a different generation and a different way of thinking. Even by nineteenth-century standards he had embraced an impressive variety of theological and philo-sophical positions: socialism, positivism, Anglicanism, Unitarian-ism, Mesmerism and, in the late eighties, Catholicism. He had published Tennyson, seen Browning plain at a number of London dinner-parties, and had arrived at definite views on the state of literature and publishing. Under the shadow of the great literary men of the mid-century the younger generation appeared not so much dwarfed as non-existent:

'Since Browning, Mrs Browning and Tennyson were all stars of the literary firmament at the same time, no one has appeared whose verses . . . could move me in any degree.'[4]

and, in a comment written some time after he had published Yeats, he found 'no one now worthy of being a poet' – although he was prepared to countenance the claims of Blunt, William Morris and Coventry Patmore. While he did not believe that literature could in itself be a profession, he prided himself on his willingness to encourage promise:

'For good or evil our firm always preferred to be literary and scholarly, and nothing was so great a delight . . . . as to lend a helping hand to any young authors in whom we saw promise rather than immediate profit.'[5]

On the other hand, his views on the possibility of promise realising itself in genuine achievement fell somewhat short of enthusiasm since he judged that 'at any given time the real men of letters can be counted by twos and threes, and . . . the literary clique is invariably composed of very second- or third-rate people. . . .'[6] There was no reason for a man holding such opinions to suppose that the tongue-tied and sullen young Irishman seated before him on 12 March 1888 and clutching a manuscript which, although copied out carefully, would still have been barely legible and full of misspellings, would prove to be even third-rate.

As it happens, Yeats's promise or potential rating seems to have worried Paul a good deal less than the commercial risk he entailed. Although Todhunter found him leafing through the manuscript on the day following Yeats's visit, he didn't bother to read the book thoroughly until the middle of the summer when publication had become more of a possibility. This took until the summer because the remaining fifty subscribers were proving to be more elusive than Yeats had anticipated. In his enthusiasm he had evidently overlooked the fact that as O'Leary had used up his most likely contacts in the initial stages of compiling the list, new subscribers would be increasingly difficult to muster. Given this, the question of whether the book should be sold for 3/6d or 5/- became crucial and caused the poet much unease. Todhunter suggested that each subscriber should be sent two copies for 5/- instead of one, 'in that way turning 200 copies at 5/- into 400 at 2/6, 2/6 being about the ordinary price of a 3/6 book when you take the discount off.'[7] But, as with the 3/6 suggestion, this involved questions of propriety as well as economics since Yeats found it 'somewhat unceremonious as well as a losing arrangement, exhausting my whole edition but 100.' This last remark reveals the hopes he had that the book would sell appreciably in the open market, hopes that were hardly to be fulfilled.

Another possibility that he took seriously was that he should cut costs, and thereby the number of subscribers required, by cutting the book and he began to debate what he might 'throw overboard'. This debate, like the earlier letter to Gwynn, shows how far the Irish dimension of his work was becoming essential to his character as a poet. He thought of dropping 'The Seeker' and 'How Ferencz Renyi Kept Silent,' the first having a vaguely pastoral setting, the other set in Hungary during the 1848 rebellion, but he was adamant that 'the Irish poems must all be kept, making the personality of the book'.[8] Since there was no longer any question of catching the spring tide he had ample occasion for reflection, especially since Paul had still not undertaken definitely to publish him.

Indeed, it seems clear that Paul was playing a waiting game, putting Yeats off from month to month until the subscriptions were sufficient to make the financial risk negligible. Todhunter had first raised the question of publication on 6 March and Yeats, hoping for the swift appearance of his book, had delivered the manuscript on the 12th of the same month. Yet in April Paul thought 'June time enough to be out'. In May it was still not decided how much the book should cost, and consequently how many subscribers would be needed, because Paul was being 'very dilatory' about presenting his final estimate of the costs. Later in the month Yeats reported with chagrin 'that through a mistake of Kegan Paul's my book will have to wait till Autumn, worse luck.' Not until 25 August could he announce that Paul had at last decided to 'go on with my book now'.[9]

Paul's first estimate was that the book would be 144 pages, so that composing, paper and printing for 500 copies would come to £27. In the event, the book made 162 pages all told and the proportionate estimate was £30-7-6d, but even the lower estimate was high enough to ensure that it would have to be priced at 5/- and that the number of subscribers would need to be 200.[10] This left Yeats with some delicate tasks of diplomacy, for during the months of uncertainty some subscribers had signed up for copies at 3/6d and now had to be asked to raise their stake by eighteen pence. In need of the extra money but loath to break faith in getting it, he called upon the tact of his friends, admonishing Katherine Tynan to be circumspect with those she approached: 'anybody you do not think would mind would you ask?' He planned, in the case of those who would mind, to pay the difference himself.

A book deferred, no less than hope, maketh the heart sick. As the proofs came in during the autumn Yeats, after over seven months of labour in negotiations, fell into a sort of pre-natal depression. 'All seems confused, incoherent, inarticulate,' he lamented to Katherine Tynan and confessed to having no great hopes for the work. But this was a passing phase. Correcting 'The Wanderings of Oisin' he found the second part 'much more coherent' than he had supposed and he awaited proofs of the third part with keen anticipation. He also decided to add the last scene of 'TheIsland of Statues' to the book since he thought it 'good of its kind'. As his excitement mounted he sent out spare proofs to York Powell and Katherine Tynan and was impatient for their opinions.

Five hundred copies of *The Wanderings of Oisin and Other Poems* were duly printed by 12 December 1888 and of these three hundred were bound. The publication costs, including the fee, advertisements, postage and booksellers' discount, amounted to £59-15-2d and Paul's prudence turned out to be justified: he did not recover his expenses until Yeats bought back the remainder of the edition over three years later.

The book was actually issued in January 1889 and by June Paul had disposed of 270 copies. Unfortunately, only 174 of these had actually been sold. Of the rest, Yeats himself took thirty-five (although some of these went to subscribers whose contributions he had diverted to his own chronically empty pocket on their way to Kegan Paul) and one he sent to a friend. Five went to the copyright libraries and fifty-five were earmarked as review copies, although it seems that only fifty-one of these were sent out. At the final count Yeats and O'Leary had enlisted 208 subscribers but while 146 of these honoured their pledges at once, the others were less punctilious and there were still nineteen subscriptions unpaid by the beginning of 1892. Following the initial sales in January, fifty more quires were bound on 1 February and a further fifty on 15 July, accounting for the slight variations in binding noted in Wade's *Bibliography*. By the end of its first year the book had sold 204 copies but only thirty-five of these were bought on the open market. This hardly constituted a roaring success and for the next two years sales settled down to a steady but extremely modest thirty a year. In 1890 the majority of these (19) went, as one might have expected, to laggardly subscribers but by the following year the book was reaching, relatively speaking, a wider audience, nearly all the copies being sold through booksellers.

239

There can be no doubt that these sales fell well short of what Yeats hoped and he realised both that he, like other poets before him, would have to create the taste by which he was to be relished and that Irish writers needed some organization or institution that would provide them with an adequate bookbuying public. To accomplish the first aim he began to increase his output of articles and reviews and through his journalism he gradually formulated the aesthetic that was to underpin his creative work in the nineties. It was now, too, that he and O'Leary discussed plans for amalgamating various Young Ireland Societies into a cohesive body that would provide an active and informed readership for Irish writers. By the time that his next book of poetry was published these plans had helped to bring into being the prestigious National Literary Society and had embroiled him in controversial schemes to establish a 'New Library of Ireland,' a series of cheap but imaginative books that would have a guaranteed sale in the new association of Irish literary societies.

If *The Wanderings of Oisin* failed to sell generally this was hardly the fault of the reviewers for it was widely noticed (partly as the result of vigorous propaganda work by Yeats and O'Leary) and most of the notices were reasonably enthusiastic. By June 1888 Paul had sent out fifty-one review copies and he was rewarded with at least thirty-seven reviews. The majority of these, twenty-one, were in British newspapers and periodicals, ten were Irish and four appeared in America – although three of these were by cisatlantic critics. Yeats awaited his reviews eagerly and professed himself happy with them on the whole. Yet in at least two respects they must have disappointed him. In the first place, the title poem, which had cost him such nervous exhaustion and which he regarded as the best in the book, was not generally liked. Even friends like Todhunter and Father Mathew Russell were qualified in their praise of it and clearly preferred the shorter pieces. George Coffey in the Dublin *Evening Telegraph* found the poem 'the least satisfactory' and 'looked for a more bardic treatment'.[11] He thought the second part 'too unsubstantial to be readily acceptable' and in this he was echoed by other critics. The Dublin *Evening Mail* also considered that the long poem did 'not reach the heights which much less assuming work attains'[12] and *United Ireland* was not inclined to rank the poem as best.[13] In fact, the most popular poems were 'Jealousy,' (later retitled 'Anashuya and Vijaya') and another non-Irish poem, 'How

240

Ferencz Renyi Kept Silent,' which, as we have seen, Yeats had contemplated leaving out. The reviewers, especially the Irish ones, had failed to notice the Irish 'personality' of the book as fully as the author could have wished.

Indeed, and this must have been the second disturbing feature of the reviews, some of the Irish commentators seemed unnecessarily carping in their notices. Robert Donovan in an article in the *Nation* that still stung Yeats as late as 1908, found little 'promise of better things' in the book. Yeats had, he said, indulged his imagination 'at the expense of his other faculties . . . we think his imagination will never be brighter or more active in the future'.[14] It is a hard thing to be consigned so smugly to limbo at the age of twenty-three. The review in the *Freeman's Journal*, the leading nationalist paper, was more cuttingly hostile. It began with one of those sentences that strike chill into an author's heart: 'Many readers will take up Mr W. B. Yeats' volume with pleasure and lay it down with a sense of disappointment.' While acknowledging the musicality of the verse it warned that 'more, much more, than a knack of easy versification goes to the making of a poet'. What the reviewer objected to principally was what he described as Yeats's 'obscurity'

> 'Mr Yeats has yet to rid his mind of the delusion that obscurity is an acceptable substitute for strenuous thought and sound judgement. People who desire to occupy their time in solving riddles and similar exercises can buy riddle books or mechanical puzzles; Mr Yeats does justice neither to himself nor his readers when he hides a jumble of confused ideas in a maze of verbiage and calls it all "The Wanderings of Oisin".'[15]

Other Irish reviewers mentioned his obscurity in passing but complained more of the remoteness of the poems from real life; it was 'this sense of unreality, of remoteness from living interests which makes the general effect of Mr Yeats's poetry pall'.[16] The *Evening Mail*, in a friendlier comment, hoped that the poet would devote his undoubted powers 'to the creation of works of imagination which will have exclusively for subject the joys and sorrows, hopes and fears, of humanity; for man alone . . . is interesting to man'.[17]

English notices were less concerned with this unworldliness, which was regarded as part of the Celtic element in the book; they concentrated more on the rhythms, over the correctness of

241

which there was some disagreement, and on Yeats's originality of subject and style. This originality (Henley and Todhunter were particularly warm in their praise of it) was generally thought to be strongly coloured by the Romantic tradition and reviewers variously detected the influence of Shelley, Keats, Swinburne and, in ballads such as 'Moll Magee,' Wordsworth.

Both author and publisher must have grieved that this critical reception did not stimulate greater sales. Yeats, his initial optimism checked, learned to be philosophical: 'I shall sell but not yet,' he predicted to Katherine Tynan, 'Many things of my own and other folks' have to grow first.' He had himself anticipated some of the critics' objections to his obscurity and unreality before the book was published and, under the added impetus of their objections, 'deliberately reshaped my style . . . (and) . . . became as emotional as possible but with an emotion which I described to myself as cold.' In his next collection he was to attempt to overcome the sense of remoteness by grounding his poems in traditional symbols, such as the Rose, or in Irish mythology, and in 'Apologia addressed to Ireland in the coming days' explained that his apparent obscurity and unworldliness did not make him any the less an Irish poet. He was, then, sensitive but not hypersensitive to criticism, and his comments on his reviews, to Tynan and others, indicate a balanced recognition that his development as a poet will be double-pronged: he must develop his technique and mastery of theme, but the responses of his readers must also be educated and broadened. Nor was he unduly cast down by the luke-warm reaction to his poem about Oisin. Few of the book's readers had praised it, but two of those few were the most distinguished critics he had, William Morris and Edward Dowden, and he was pleased to be able to add their approbation to his own conviction that it was his best poem to date.

Yeats was confident that he would 'sell but not yet'. Paul, with a business to run and bills to pay, could not afford the luxury of such a long-term view. Far from making any profit, it now seemed uncertain that he would even cover his costs. He obviously took little pains to hide his dissatisfaction from Yeats who began, from an early stage in the book's career, to search for another publisher to take over the unsold copies. At first it seemed that the recently established Mathews might oblige and in October 1889 he wrote 'asking for an experimental dozen of *Oisin*, sale or return of course, and promising to advertise me – with press opinions – in his catalogue'.[18] Mathews was apparently pleased with what he saw and negotiations about his republication of the work continued fitfully until he discovered that Yeats intended to publish his next book of poetry with T. Fisher Unwin, at which point he let the matter drop.

Yeats was introduced to Unwin by Edward Garnett who had recently become the firm's reader and who was to go on to become one of the greatest talent-spotters in the history of modern publishing. The two men probably met through the Rhymers' Club and Yeats lost no time in showing his new friend the manuscript of a novel that he was writing, at his father's suggestion, to make money after the financial disappointment of *The Wanderings of Oisin*. Garnett was 'quite enthusiastic' about what he read and by March 1891 the book, *John Sherman*, had been accepted for Unwin's very successful 'Pseudonym Library'. Garnett also signed Yeats up to edit an anthology of Irish adventurers that was to contain sections on Fighting Fitzgerald, Tiger Roche, Brian Maguire, Freeney the Robber and Michael Dwyer.[19] In the course of arranging this, the friendship between them grew and it became clear that Garnett was a judicious admirer of Yeats's verse. Yeats was already writing *The Countess Kathleen* for Maud Gonne and, since he was eager to keep his name 'well in evidence' before what public he had, he was planning a new book of poems with this play as its focal piece. He went to stay with Garnett for a couple of days in the summer of 1891 and no doubt spoke of this project. Garnett was encouraging and thought the book might do for Unwin's 'Cameo' series 'if he likes the Countess as well as he does the rest of my poems'. Yeats was confident that he would since 'Dr Todhunter says "the Countess" is my best work so far and I dare say the reader will think the same. I shall submit to him the 3 acts I have finished and do the rest in Ireland'.[20]

The book now became his top priority and, in the hope that it would follow *John Sherman* (which was to be published in November) 'almost immediately', he laid aside his editorial work on Blake and the *Irish Fairy Tales* and *Irish Adventurers* anthologies. He toiled away at the play throughout the summer and by October he had finished it and 'was now doing stray lyrics and other things'. The success of *John Sherman* disposed Unwin well towards Yeats and the sentiment was enforced by Garnett's shrewdly commendatory reader's report on the proposed new book:

> 'The *Countess Kathleen*, with the lyrics, will we think make a most charming volume. The *Countess* will be appreciated in the proper quarter, if not by critics generally. It is not an ambitious piece of work, but for genuine poetry it is the best thing Yeats has done. It is also *"sui generis"* – & worth in reality a dozen Watsons.'[21]

Since William Watson gave the book its most scathing review one wonders whether this last remark somehow reached his ears.

Unwin was no doubt glad to be assured of the book's artistic merit, but he was also known as one of the more parsimonious of London publishers and Garnett was careful to spell out the financial arrangements that he had made:

> 'Mr Yeats of course does not expect to get anything from the sale of the book, but in the event of its attracting attention, a clause should be added giving so much percent, on all copies sold after so and so.'[22]

He also revealed that Yeats was unwilling to surrender the copyright absolutely 'though of course there need be no question of the property changing hands'. These conditions satisfied Unwin and the manuscript of the play and some of the poems was handed to him on 26 November. It was, however, impossible to publish the book before April because Elkin Mathews insisted on keeping the copyright on the six poems that he was including in *The Book of the Rhymers' Club* until the end of March and, since Yeats thought that among these were 'some of my best lyrics', he felt that he 'must wait until April to reprint them'. In the event, *The Countess Kathleen and Various Legends and Lyrics* did not appear until September.

With the publication of the new book of poems thus delayed, Yeats had time to consider the fate of his first volume. Indeed, even had he lacked time, the issue would have been thrust upon his attention, for Kegan Paul's patience was now exhausted to the point that he was calling in lawyers. Faced with this, Yeats wrote to John O'Leary in January 1892 asking if he could help him out of 'a difficulty'

'There is still £2-3-10 owing to Kegan Paul on Oisin & they threaten me with lawyers. I want to take the remaining 100 copies out of their hands and get Fisher Unwin to sell them which he will do with ease. There is as it is, some slight sale and a steadily increasing one. The new book will sell the rest of the copies. I want you to lend me £2-10-0 so that I can make the transfer at once.'[23]

O'Leary obliged as usual and Yeats was able to settle with Paul, a great relief one imagines to both parties. This done, he wrote on 31 January to Unwin, offering him the book:

'I have between 90 & 100 copies (in sheets) of my book of poems "The Wanderings of Oisin" . . . I am taking these 90 copies from Kegan Paul & shall have them here in a few days. I want to know would you be so kind as to take them over & bind them & put a new title page. My friend Edwin Ellis has drawn & printed a charming frontispiece. He has a lithographic press & proposes to strike off a hundred copies of the frontis·piece to be bound into this volume.'[24]

He went on to suggest that the book, which had 'a slow but latterly an increasing sale', would 'sell off' if advertised inside *The Countess Kathleen*. Unwin agreed to take over the property and the second issue of the book appeared in May 1892 in green paper boards and with the Ellis frontispiece depicting Niam, Oisin and St. Patrick. Wade's *Bibliography*, citing the letter to O'Leary quoted above, suggests that this version ran to a hundred copies. In fact, it seems to have been a little smaller. Paul held 98 unbound copies at the beginning of 1892 but, presumably at Yeats's instigation, he bound a further 25 copies in cloth on 31 March. It may have been this binding that Roth recorded:

'the cloth is smoother and slightly darker; there is no publishers' monogram on the back; and T H E on the spine is more widely spaced'.[25]

One imagines that Yeats used these volumes as presentation copies, so that the Unwin issue could only have consisted of the remaining 73 quires, together with the sheets for the nineteen still unpaid subscription copies, that is to say a total of at most 92 volumes.

The play, *The Countess Kathleen,* was meanwhile being printed in advance of the rest of the book and Yeats spent late February and early March correcting it for the press 'and getting a quantity of lyrics and ballads to go with it'. The doubts that had assailed him at the proof stage of *The Wanderings of Oisin* were completely absent. 'It will,' he claimed, 'be infinitely my best book' – an extravagant boast given that this was only his second volume of poetry. The publication of a play involved Yeats in the problems of securing performing rights. He had to have the play read or performed in a public theatre to make sure of these and he asked Unwin for extra proof sheets 'one for the manager, the other for the licenser of plays' so that the play could be read at the Athenaeum in Shepherd's Bush early in May.

Since the new book had no subscribers to smooth its financial path into the world, Yeats was assiduous in exploiting any opportunity for publicity. His journalism in London had given him access to a number of editors and reviewers there, while in Ireland the fall and subsequent death of Parnell had produced a political shock that had cultural consequences. Literature now seemed a surer means of expressing national identity and national aspirations than a political movement suddenly divided against itself. Newspapers began to pay far more attention to books published by Irish writers and, in the case of the Parnellite weekly, *United Ireland,* to actually push them. Yeats, who wrote for the paper, was not slow to make use of the new facilities it offered and throughout the spring of 1892 dashed off letters to the literary editor, John McGrath, and his assistant, D. J. O'Donoghue, detailing the progress of his various literary schemes and publications. If not exactly creating the taste by which he was to be relished, these short notes did at least whet the appetite. At the same time, his own plans for a series of Irish books and a central Irish literary society seemed to be coming to fruition and he moved to Dublin in May to act as midwife to a National Society that he hoped would 'focus the scattered energies of lovers of Irish literature'. Such institutions obviously had significance for Irish literature in general. But they also had a more precise value to Yeats himself, a fact that was never far from his mind. As the moment for the inaugural meeting of the new society drew near he grew increasingly impatient with the delays over the publication of his book, for, as he wrote to Garnett,

> 'It would be an advantage if it came soon as the reviews, here in Ireland, would help the society, and the sale would in its turn be helped probably by the coming meetings at which my name will of necessity be rather prominent.'[26]

Happily, the book was ready by early September and thus caught the publicity connected with the Society. It was well and, on the whole, more intelligently received than *The Wanderings of Oisin,* although critics picked out similar features for comment. The rhythms again attracted attention and, in the case of an immoderate and foolish notice by William Watson, abuse.[27] Watson also attacked the want of 'life or life likeness' in Yeats's verse, a point taken up by more temperate reviewers who were thus echoing the charge of 'remoteness' brought against the earlier volume. The *Spectator* found that 'his verse wants human interest'[28] and his drama was 'too remote' for the *National Observer*.[29] The *Irish Daily Independent* made the same criticism but in a sympathetically avuncular manner. Yeats had, the reviewer said, 'fine and worthy reverence for his art' but 'he should not set it up in high and remote places, but should bring it among the things of everyday life, and inform it with the sympathy for humanity, which . . . would give it its highest development.'[30]

The most valuable reviews were those written by Richard Le Gallienne, then at the height of his popularity, in the *Star* and by Lionel Johnson in the *Academy*.[31] The Le Gallienne piece gave Yeats 'the best lift I have yet had – with this or any book', while Johnson tried to 'place' Yeats's importance in a more serious way than had yet been attempted. Many critics of *Oisin* had, as we have seen, noted Yeats's 'Celticism'. They had formed their views on what constituted 'Celticism' from Matthew Arnold's famous lectures on 'The Study of Celtic Literature'. Here Arnold had praised Celtic poetry for its sentiment, its delicacy, its melancholy, its feelings for style and its ability to render 'natural magic'. But he had complained that the Celts lacked the shaping power of the Greeks, the *architectonice* without which a great work of art was impossible. Johnson clearly had Arnold's distinctions and qualifications in mind when writing of Yeats and, read in this light, his article makes large claims. For he maintains that Yeats's poetry

247

John Kelly

shows all the qualities that Arnold associated with the 'Celtic note' but that it also has a classical organization that gives it a sustaining power well beyond that of a typical Celtic poet:

> 'The distinction of Mr Yeats . . . is his ability to write Celtic poetry, with all the Celtic notes of style and imagination, in a classical manner. Like all men of the true poetical spirit, he is not overcome by the apparent antagonism of the classical and the romantic in art. Like the fine Greeks or Romans, he treats his subject according to its nature. . . . When he takes a Celtic theme, some vast and epic legend, or some sad and lyrical fancy, he does not reflect the mere confused vastness of the one, the mere flying vagueness of the other; his art is full of reason.'[32]

There was to be much derivative nonsense written in the nineties about supposed 'Celtic notes' in Irish poetry. Johnson's review, although still enmeshed in a racially inspired terminology that we find unhelpful today, is an attempt to examine and transcend categories that were all too glibly accepted by his contemporaries.

Not all the favourable reviews managed Johnson's judicious tone and considered argument. The unlikely enthusiasm of the up-market and Ascendancy *Irish Society* became, as Yeats wryly noted, 'wildly laudatory'. According to this reviewer Yeats had succeeded 'skilfully and brilliantly . . . Mr Yeats has no equal . . . as a poet of abnormal powers, Mr Yeats stands alone' and he concluded with a prophesy that should give the Yeats Summer School in Sligo an agreeable confidence in its long-term prospects:

> 'I have no hesitation in saying that Mr Yeats' poems will live and will find innumerable commentators and would-be interpreters, as long as the world lasts.'[33]

Since the Fisher Unwin archives were destroyed in the Second World War, we cannot be certain of the terms that he made with Yeats over *The Countess Kathleen,* nor of the speed at which the book sold. It is evident from Garnett's report that Yeats was to receive a royalty at some point and this may have been set at $12\frac{1}{2}\%$ after the first 250 in an edition of 500, for at this number Unwin should have covered his costs. It seems from odd remarks in letters that the book sold reasonably well and certainly within two years plans were in hand for a new collection of Yeats's poems.

It is in the arrangements, both literary and commercial, for this third collection, *Poems* (1895), that the experience Yeats had gained in publishing his first two books of verse begins to bear fruit. His growing confidence as a poet is matched by his growing confidence as a man of affairs. He no longer works through the intermediate offices of Garnett, but meets Unwin face to face to negotiate his own terms from a position of strength. And in dealing with Unwin he needed both confidence and strength of purpose for, as Stanley Unwin, a nephew and sometime employee of the firm, has written:

'Of the many peculiar characters to be found in the British book publishing world of the 'nineties, T. Fisher Unwin was in some ways the strangest. Tall, handsome, bearded, with a floppy yellow tie, physically as straight as a dart, a keen mountaineer, he was wonderfully good company out of office hours. But in business he was a different person.'[34]

Descended from printers on both sides, Fisher Unwin had branched out into publishing when he bought the firm of Marshall Japp & Co. in 1882 and then made it pay for itself within six months. He was a shy man who, perhaps because of his nervousness, ran his office autocratically. He had the happy knack of finding able and decisive lieutenants, such as Garnett and Stanley Unwin, but in the course of time these fell away from him, disgruntled by his stinginess over money and his oppressively authoritarian business methods. Yet, in spite of his insistence upon his authority as head of the firm, he was, as one of his managers recalled, in a constant state of vacillation:

'He could never understand how he antagonised people yet he was doing it all the time . . . a highly nervous disposition . . . in business his ability to avoid decision was considerable. . . .'[35]

Joseph Conrad was only narrowly restrained on one occasion from throwing him out of a window. Yeats's methods were less physical but effective in their way – at least until the relationship broke up in 1906. He saw that it was essential to get things down in writing as quickly as possible, so he would see Unwin, state his terms, and then follow up the meeting with a business-like recapitulation of the arrangement as he understood it. He wrote such a letter following a visit to Unwin on 8 October 1894 at which the new volume had been discussed. Elkin Mathews had been fishing for the book and so he could open with a strong card, graciously played: he mentioned that he had received 'a good offer' for the poems 'but as our relations have always been friendly and pleasant I would would just as soon go on with you if we can come to terms.' The terms they did come to show the confidence with which Yeats was planning for the future. He insisted upon one point above others, that the new volume should be published 'in such a way that I can make all my future books of verse resemble .it in size and printing'. Other stipulations followed from this:

> 'I would therefore ask first that it be of a certain height and breadth, second that it be printed by either Clarke or Constable, third that I be consulted about an artist to do the title page. . . .'[36]

Yeats was always to take a keen interest in the appearance as well as the contents of his books. Until now he had had little power to bargain over this matter, but his insistence upon a uniform size at this early opportunity in his career indicates the assurance he had in his continuing productivity as a poet. And, indeed, the size of the 1895 edition of *Poems*, $7\frac{1}{2} \times 5$, did set the pattern for the majority of his commercially produced books.

Although he had lost on his first book of poems and did 'not expect to get anything' from his second, he felt established enough now to ask for a reasonable scale of royalties. Unwin was only to have the copyright of the book for four years and Yeats demanded 'that my royalty for this period be *$12\frac{1}{2}$% from the first copy* instead of 10% for the first 500 as you suggest & $12\frac{1}{2}$% for the next 100 & so on'.[37] Such terms were not going to make his fortune, but they signalled that he was at last a fully professional poet and they laid the basis for future negotiations, not merely with Unwin but also with other publishers.

This growing professionalism was not just a matter of haggling over terms, of course, but, more profoundly, involved his taking stock of what he had done and what he intended to do. He was now able to acknowledge the uncertainty of his setting forth as a poet by gathering up a selection of the poems from *The Wanderings of Oisin* into a section in the new book which he entitled 'Crossways' 'because in them he tried many pathways'. The poems from *The Countess Kathleen* he brought together as 'The Rose', a title which represented his attempt to make his poetry less remote and unworldly by rooting it in symbols that he hoped would have traditional significance. All the poems were carefully selected and many were rigorously reworked for, as he tells us in his Preface, this book was to contain

> '. . . all the writer cares to preserve out of his previous volumes of verse. He has revised and to a large extent re-written. *The Wanderings of Usheen* and the lyrics and ballads from the same volume and has expanded and, he hopes, strengthened *The Countess Kathleen'*.[38]

Something achieved, then, but much still left to do, for he had 'been compelled to leave unchanged many lines he would have gladly re-written, because his present skill is not great enough. . . .' He was to go on re-writing and the history of the various editions of this volume is the history of his developing command of technique.

The subdued determination and self-awareness registered in this Preface was paralleled by a more sober attitude towards his audience. If he went up and down the house on the publication of this new book his step, as befitted an older and wiser poet, was more measured, his anticipation tempered by the experience of his previous receptions:

> 'My new book is in the press . . . I wonder how they will receive it in Ireland. Patronize it I expect and give it faint praise and yet I feel it is good, that whether the coming generations in England accept me or reject me, the coming generations in Ireland cannot but value what I have done.'[39]

Throughout his career, and especially in the nineties, Yeats was intensely preoccupied with the relationship of the poet to his society. In Ireland he hoped to find an audience that because of an oral tradition, a shared mythology, and an idealist mode of thought, would respond most fully to the kind of poetry he wished

251

John Kelly

to write. In the actual production and distribution of his books these hopes and theories came into collision with the hard facts of contemporary literary life and few of them survived unmodified. Yeats's growing realisation that the interrelation between him and his readers was far more complex than he had at first understood had a crucial influence on his development as a poet. There was still a long way to go in this process by 1895 and the way would be more bitter than he could possibly have imagined at that stage. But his first three books started him on that occupation of making and remaking himself, that complicated movement of response to and reaction from his critics, especially his Irish critics, that was to transform him from an excitable and sometimes careless young romantic poet into a more exact, self-conscious and accomplished craftsman.

NOTES

1 *The Letters of W. B. Yeats*, ed. Alan Wade, Hart-Davis, London, p. 54.
2 Unpublished letter.
3 *Letters*, p. 63.
4 C. Kegan Paul, *Memories*, p. 278.
5 Ibid, p. 294.
6 Ibid, p. 279.
7 *Letters*. p. 66.
8 Ibid.
9 Ibid. p. 82.
10 All facts and figures relating to the publication of *The Wanderings of Oisin* are taken from the relevant account books of the Kegan Paul, Trench & Co. unless otherwise stated.
11 Dublin *Evening Telegraph*, 6 February 1889.
12 Dublin *Evening Mail*. 13 February 1889.
13 *United Ireland*. 23 March 1889.
14 The *Nation*. 25 May 1889.
15 *Freeman's Journal*. 1 February 1889.
16 The *Nation*. 25 May 1889.
17 Dublin *Evening Mail*. 13 February 1889.
18 *Letters*. p. 138.
19 Unpublished letter.
20 *Letters*. p. 173.
21 Unpublished reader's report.
22 Ibid.
23 *Letters*. p. 198.
24 Unpublished letter.
25 Allan Wade. *A Bibliography of the Writings of W. B. Yeats*, Hart-Davis. London, 1951, p. 21.

26 *Letters*, p. 208.
27 *Illustrated London News*, 10 September 1892.
28 *Spectator*, 29 July 1893.
29 *National Observer*, 3 September 1892.
30 *Irish Daily Independent*, 2 September 1892.
31 The *Star*, 1 September 1892; *Academy*, 1 October 1892.
32 *Academy*, 1 October 1891.
33 *Irish Society*, 22 October 1892.
34 Sir Stanley Unwin, *The Truth About A Publisher*, 1960, p. 79.
35 Ibid, p. 111.
36 Unpublished letter.
37 Ibid
38 *Variorum Poems*, p. 845.
39 *Letters*, pp. 254–5.

CONTRIBUTORS

LESTER CONNER was Assistant Director of the Yeats International Summer School for seven of the more than twelve years that he has been associated with the school. Frequently a Visiting Professor in Trinity College Dublin, Professor Conner, who took his Ph.D degree at Columbia University, is Professor of English in Chestnut Hill College, Philadelphia. He is currently at work, in collaboration with D. E. S. Maxwell. on a critical history of Irish Drama, for the Cambridge University Press.

DENIS DONOGHUE holds the Henry James Chair of Letters at New York University. He was formerly Professor of Modern English and American Literature at University College, Dublin; and, before that, University Lecturer in English, and Fellow of King's College, Cambridge. He has written *The Third Voice* (1959), *Connoisseurs of Chaos* (1964), *The Ordinary Universe* (1968). *Jonathan Swift* (1969), *Emily Dickinson* (1969), *Yeats* (1971), *Thieves of Fire* (1974) and *The Sovereign Ghost* (1976). His new book is *Ferocious Alphabets* (1980). He has also edited Yeats's *Memoirs* (1972), *An Honoured Guest: New Essays on Yeats* (1965), and the *Swift* volume in the Penguin Critical Anthologies series. He directed the Yeats International Summer School in its first year.

BARBARA HARDY was educated in Swansea, and subsequently at University College, London. She was a lecturer in English at Birkbeck College before becoming Professor at Royal Holloway College, University of London and then at Birkbeck College, University of London. Her publications include: *The Novels of George Eliot, A Study in Form; The Appropriate Form: an Essay on the Novel*; The Penguin English Library Edition of *Daniel Deronda; Middlemarch; Critical Approaches to the Novel; Critical Essays on George Eliot; The Moral Art of Dickens; The Exposure of Luxury: radical themes in Thackery*; the New Wessex Edition of *The Trumpet Major* and *A Laodicean; A Reading of Jane Austen; Tellers and Listeners; the Narrative Imagination*; and *The Advantage of Lyric*.

SEAMUS HEANEY was born in Co. Derry; he was educated at St Columb's College, Derry and Queen's University. Belfast. He taught at Queen's University from 1966 to 1972. He moved to Co. Wicklow in 1972 to write full-time; at present he is Head of the English Department, Carysfort College, Blackrock. He has published five volumes of poetry, most recently *Field Work* (1979). Later this year Faber will publish his *Selected Poems 1965–1975* and a volume of selected lectures, essays and reviews, including 'Yeats as an Example', to be entitled *Preoccupations*.

T. R. HENN (1901–1974) was a Fellow of St Catharine's College and a University teacher at Cambridge for 45 years, except for five years' distinguished war service, and was President before he retired. For many years Director of the Yeats International Summer School at Sligo. he was a pre-eminent figure among scholars of Anglo-Irish Literature. His published work includes *The Lonely Tower, The Harvest of Tragedy, The Apple and the Spectroscope, The Bible as Literature, Shooting a Bat, Last Essays,* and his autobiography, *Five Arches* which is published this year as a double volume with *'Philoctetes' and other poems.*

JOHN HOLLOWAY. poet, critic, academic, was born in London, educated locally and at Oxford, with war service in artillery and intelligence. He was a Fellow of All Souls (1946-60) and has lectured in Philosophy at the Universities of Oxford and Aberdeen, and at the University of Cambridge since 1954 where he was appointed Professor of Modern English in 1972. He was Byron Professor at the University of Athens from 1961-63. He has travelled widely in the Indian sub-continent, the Middle East, the Mediterranean, Europe, and America; and he has spent part of each year since 1966 in the West of Ireland. His published verse includes *New Poems* (New York, 1970) and *Planet of Winds* (1977). His latest prose work is *The Proud Knowledge* (1977); he has also written on Victorian prose. Shakespeare, Blake and the twentieth century, and collaborated in extensive publishing of Victorian street-ballads.

A. NORMAN JEFFARES is Hon. Life President and founding chairman of the International Association for the Study of Anglo-Irish Literature. He was educated at Trinity College, Dublin, of which he is an Honorary Fellow, and at Oriel College, Oxford. He taught classics at Trinity College, Dublin, and English at the Universities of Groningen and Edinburgh before becoming Professor at the Universities of Adelaide, Leeds and Stirling, his present University. He is the author of several books on Yeats, including *Yeats: man and poet* and *Yeats: the Critical Heritage* as well as commentaries on his *Collected Poems,* and. with A. S. Knowland, on his *Collected Plays.* He is completing a *History of Anglo-Irish Literature* and is Deputy Chairman of the Scottish Arts Council.

JOHN S. KELLY, M.A.. D.Phil., was educated at Trinity College Dublin, and was a lecturer at the University of Kent at Canterbury. He is now Fellow and Tutor in English at St. John's College, Oxford, and editor of the *Collected Letters of W. B. Yeats.* which will be published in several volumes. He has also contributed a number of essays and articles on nineteenth and twentieth century literature to various books and periodicals. He was Director of the Yeats International Summer School from 1972 to 1976. Besides the Yeats *Letters,* he is currently working on a critical history of twentieth century English poetry, and a book on literature and society in Ireland.

BRENDAN KENNELLY was born in Ballylongford, Co. Kerry, and educated at St Ita's College, Tarbert, Trinity College, Dublin, and Leeds University. He was appointed as Lecturer in the Department of English, Trinity College, in 1963, and appointed Professor of Modern Literature there in

Contributors

1973. He is a Fellow of Trinity College. He was awarded the AE Memorial Prize for Poetry in 1967, and has published several books of poetry including *Dream of a Black Fox* (1968), *Salvation, the Stranger* (1972), *A Kind of Trust* (1975), *New and Selected Poems* (1976), *Islandman* (1977), *A Small Light* (1979). He is the author of two novels, *The Crooked Cross* (1963) and *The Florentines* (1967). He is Editor of *The Penguin Book of Irish Verse*, first published in 1970, second edition due in 1981.

F. S. L. Lyons, Provost of Trinity College, Dublin, and formerly Professor of History at the University of Kent at Canterbury, has written widely on Irish themes. Among his books are *Ireland Since the Famine* (1971), *Charles Stewart Parnell* (1977) and most recently (1979) *Culture and Anarchy in Ireland, 1890–1939* the text of the Ford Lectures delivered at the University of Oxford in 1978. Dr Lyons is at present engaged upon the authorised life of W. B. Yeats.

Augustine Martin was born in Co. Leitrim, 1935, and educated at Cistercian College, Roscrea, and University College, Dublin (where he took the degrees of M.A. and Ph.D.) where he has been teaching since 1965. Among his publications are *James Stephens, a Critical Study* (1977), *Anglo-Irish Literature, A History* (1980), an edition of *Winter's Tales from Ireland* (1971) and of *The Charwoman's Daughter* (1972), articles on Yeats, Joyce, Synge, Behan, Mary Lavin, and Sean O'Casey. He was elected by the graduates of the National University to the Irish Senate in 1973 and 1977. He was Visiting Professor to Hofstra University (1974) and Scholar in Residence at Miami, Ohio (1980) and has been Professor of Anglo-Irish Literature and Drama at University College, Dublin, since 1979. He is engaged on a history of the Irish Short Story and a book on the politics of W. B. Yeats. He was Associate Director of the Yeats Summer School in 1977, and Director in 1979 and 1980.

D. E. S. Maxwell was educated at Foyle College, Derry, and Trinity College, Dublin, where he took his B.A. and Ph.D. He has been a Lecturer at the University of Ghana; Assistant Director of Examinations, Civil Service Commission, London; Professor of English, University of Ibadan; and is now Professor of English, York University, where he was Master of Winters College (1969–79). He is a Visiting Professor at Trinity College, Dublin (1979–80). His publications include: *The Poetry of T. S. Eliot; American Fiction; Cozzens;* (as co-editor) *W. B. Yeats Centenary Essays; Poets of the Thirties;* and *Brian Friel.* His work in progress is a critical history of Irish drama.

William M. Murphy is Thomas Lamont Professor of Ancient and Modern Literature, and Professor of English, at Union College in Schenectady, New York. He holds B.A., M.A., and Ph.D. degrees from Harvard. His biography, *Prodigal Father: The Life of John Butler Yeats (1839–1922)* was published in 1978 by Cornell University Press. He is also the author of *The Yeats Family and the Pollexfens of Sligo* (Dublin: 1971), editor of the Cuala Press volume, *Letters from Bedford Park* (1972), and co-

256

editor of the Macmillan volume of *Letters to W. B. Yeats* (1977), and he has published a number of articles on Yeatsian subjects. He is presently working on editions of the letters and other writings of John Butler Yeats, Lily Yeats, and Elizabeth Corbet ('Lollie') Yeats.

PATRICK RAFROIDI was a student at the first Yeats Summer School in 1960 and has come back as a lecturer in 1969 and 1975. He is the author of *Irish Literature in English: The Romantic Period* as well as a number of other books on Ireland, and the editor of *Etudes Irlandaises*. He was chairman of the International Association for the Study of Anglo-Irish Literature from 1976 to 1979 and is currently President of the University of Lille in Northern France. He will be a visiting Fellow at the Humanities Research Centre, Australian National University, Canberra, in 1980–81.

ANN SADDLEMYER was born in Canada, educated in Canada and England, and is currently Professor of English and Drama at the University of Toronto. She is the author of books and articles on Synge, Yeats, Lady Gregory and contemporary drama. Her most recent project has been the establishment of a new journal, *Theatre History in Canada*. She has held the Berg Chair at New York University. She has been involved for many years in the International Association for the Study of Anglo-Irish Literature, having served as one of its chairmen. She has lectured not only at the Yeats Summer School in Sligo, but in the United States and France.

HELEN VENDLER holds the degree of Ph.D. from Harvard University and has taught at Cornell, Haverford, Swarthmore, Smith, and Boston University. She is the author of books on Yeats, Stevens, and Herbert; her collected essays on modern American poetry, *Part of Nature, Part of Us*, appeared in 1980 from Harvard University Press. She is the Poetry Reviewer for *The New Yorker* and is engaged at present on a study of the odes of Keats.

257

SPEAKERS AT SLIGO 1960-1980

Professor Hazard Adams
Professor Jean Alexander
Professor Russell K. Alspach
Professor Barry Argyle
Mr Bruce Arnold
Professor C. L. Barber
Professor Eugene Benson
Professor Bernard Benstock
Professor Edmund Blunden
Rev. M. Bodkin, S. J.
Miss Eavan Boland
Professor Brian Boydell
Professor Muriel Bradbrook
Professor Curtis Bradford
Professor Birgit Bramsbäck
Professor Cleanth Brooks
Professor Vincent Buckley
Professor S. B. Bushrui
Professor Francis Byrne
Professor James F. Carens
Dr B. N. Chaturvedi
Erskine Childers, President of
   Ireland 1973-4
Professor David R. Clark
Dr Austin Clarke
Dr Anne Clissman
Dr Padraic Colum
Professor Lester Conner
Dr Dominick Daly O.S.A.
Dr Cecil Day-Lewis
Dame Ninette de Valois
Dr Cecil Day-Lewis
Dr Seamus Deane
Professor Donald Davie
Professor Myles Dillon
Professor Denis Donoghue
Dr Oliver Edwards

Professor Maurice Elliott
Professor Richard Ellmann
Mr Gabriel Fallon
Professor Richard Finneran
Mr Christopher Fitz-Simon
Professor Thomas Flanagan
Professor James Flannery
Professor Ian Fletcher
Professor R. A. Foakes
Professor G. S. Fraser
Professor Rene Frêchet
Dr Grattan Freyer
Professor Northrop Frye
Mrs Daphne Fullwood
Dr M. P. Gallagher
Dr Monk Gibbon
Professor A. M. Gibbs
Mr Oliver Gogarty S.C.
Professor David Greene
Sir Tyrone Guthrie
Mr Peter Hall
Professor R. P. C. Hanson
Professor Barbara Hardy
Dr Maurice Harmon
Professor G. M. Harper
Dr Barbara Hayley
Mr Seamus Heaney
Dr T. R. Henn
Professor Bernard Hickey
Mr Derek Hill
Professor Geoffrey Hill
Professor Daniel Hoffman
Professor John Holloway
Professor Graham Hough
Mr Ted Hughes
Miss Patricia Hutchins
Professor Samuel Hynes

Speakers at Sligo 1960–1980

Professor Hiro Ishibashi
Professor A. Norman Jeffares
Professor Richard M. Kain
Dr Colbert Kearney
Dr John Kelly
Professor Brendan Kennelly
Professor Frank Kermode
Mr Benedict Kiely
Professor Thomas Kinsella
Professor Johannes Kleinstück
Professor A. S. Knowland
Miss Mary Lavin
Professor Lawrence Lee
Mr Raymond Lister
Professor Richard Londraville
Mrs Edna Longley
Mr Michael Longley
Professor Seán Lucy
Dr F. S. L. Lyons
Mr Seán MacBride
Mr Louis MacNeice
Professor Oliver McDonagh
Professor Roger McHugh
Mr Derek Mahon
Mr Edward Malins
Professor Augustine Martin
Professor Graham Martin
Professor D. E. S. Maxwell
Professor Giorgio Melchiori
Professor Vivian Mercier
Professor J. Hillis Miller
Mr Liam Miller
Miss Ria Mooney
Mr John Montague
Mr M. P. Mortimer
Professor J. R. Mulryne
Professor William R. Murphy
Professor Shiro Naito
Professor Helen North
Professor Kevin Nowlan
Dr Margaret O'Brien

Professor Tomas O'Cathasaigh
Dr Frank O'Connor
Professor Robert O'Driscoll
Professor James Olney
Professor Diarmuid O'Muirithe
Professor Desmond Pacey
Professor Thomas Parkinson
Dr Jan Piggott
Professor William Pratt
Dr Hilary Pyle
Sister Bernetta Quinn, O.S.F.
Professor Patrick Rafroidi
Dr Kathleen Raine
Professor B. Rajan
Professor Lorna Reynolds
Miss Sheelagh Richards
Professor W. W. Robson
Professor Joseph Ronsley
Professor Marilyn Rose
Mr Brian Rothwell
Professor Ann Saddlemyer
Dr Wolfgang R. Sanger
Mr Michael Scott
Professor P. Shaw
Professor M. J. Sidnell
Mr James Simmons
Professor Robin Skelton
Mr Colin Smythe
Mr Robert Speaight
Professor Jon Stallworthy
Professor Walter Starkie
Mr Francis Stuart
Professor Ronald Tamplin
Professor Donald Torchiana
Professor John Unterecker
Professor Helen Vendler
Mr John Wain
Dr Richard Walsh
Dr Francis Warner
Professor Robert Penn Warren
Dr Timothy Webb

259

Dr James White
Mr Seán White
Professor F. A. C. Wilson

Professor Marion Witt
Professor Kathleen Worth
Mr Michael Butler Yeats

INDEX

261